Nina Subin

CHRISTA PARRAVANI is a writer and photographer. Her photographs have been exhibited internationally and are represented by the Foley Gallery in New York City. She has taught photography at Dartmouth College, Columbia University, and UMass-Amherst. She earned her MFA in visual art from Columbia University and her MFA in creative writing from Rutgers-Newark. She lives in Brooklyn with her husband, the writer Anthony Swofford (*Jarhead*), and their daughter.

Additional Praise for *Her*

"*Her* instantly became my reading obsession. . . . Parravani has the ability to make life, even at its worst, feel magic-tinged and vital and lived all the way down to the bone. . . . The final sentence, honest to god, made me cry."

—Heidi Julavits, *Bookforum*

"A searing account of photographer Christa Parravani's relationship with her identical twin sister, Cara."

—*O, The Oprah Magazine*

"This memoir is more than the tale of how Christa survives her loss; it's also a love story. The sisters' bond is every bit as profound as that between husband and wife or parent and child."

—*Real Simple*

"Christa Parravani's lyrical, no-nonsense *Her* ranks with the best American memoirs of the decade. This incandescent story of loving and losing one's twin is an uncompromising love poem to the joys and dangers of shared identity, and an unforgettable treatise on addiction, trauma, survival, and triumph."

—Jayne Anne Phillips, author of
Lark and Termite and *Machine Dreams*

"In this powerful memoir about the death of her identical twin and its impact on her own life, Christa Parravani explores what it means to be a woman of creative spirit as few writers have. I couldn't stop looking at the photograph on the cover, wondering what it would be like to be as close to another person as these sisters were to each other. An intense reading journey, an inspiring book."

—Julie Metz, author of the
New York Times bestselling *Perfection*

"The best memoirs should come with a warning label, the kind that makes you take a deep breath before you open the cover. *Her* announces its challenges immediately while also establishing the voice that will pull you through the darkness of loss, memory, and expiation. Suddenly bereft, twinless, distrusting the talent that has been her mainstay, and questioning what it means to be a survivor, Christa Parravani carries us with her into the excavation of what it means to keep living, a lost twin and a woman digging herself out of her sister's loss. That she comes out the other side is never predictable—merely miraculous."   —Dorothy Allison, author of
Bastard Out of Carolina

"Concise and captivating, Parravani's prose paints her phoenix-like transformation such that the reader feels the flames of her fire. A poignant, book-arcing metaphor illustrates Christa's battle to accept herself with a mirror image. Raw and unstoppable, *Her* illuminates the triumph of the human spirit—both individual and shared."   —*Booklist* (starred review)

"Parravani succeeds in 'writing Cara back to life' and saving her own life in the process. No punches are pulled here, and Parravani's matter-of-fact tone does nothing to shield readers from the enormity of her loss. . . . Imagine looking in a mirror and not seeing yourself. Imagine living the rest of your life with half of yourself missing. Imagine looking at your own corpse. You don't have to imagine: Parravani's story makes it all clear."
—*Library Journal* (starred review)

"Christa Parravani's new memoir, *Her,* is a glimpse into the most intimate chambers of the identical twin relationship. . . . *Her* is a tribute to the truly beloved, as well as a celebration of the push-and-pull between sisters."   —*The Oregonian*

"Moving . . . just the right balance of joyous, melancholic, and bitter. [We sometimes read memoirs hoping] for a small glimpse into the inside of someone else's reality in all its messy glory. With humility and an unbreakable love and respect for her other half, Christa Parravani allows us that in droves."

—*20somethingreads.com*

"Full of headlong energy, Christa Parravani's *Her* is reckless yet delicate, familiar yet otherworldly, precise yet with the soul of a fairy tale, and deeply moving in surprising ways."

—Nick Flynn, author of *Another Bullshit Night in Suck City* and *The Ticking Is the Bomb*

"Christa Parravani's exploration of her relationship to her troubled identical twin sister is deeply thoughtful, lyrical, even magical. As she struggles for identity amid her sister's suffering, Parravani's own strength and talents emerge. There is rarely much redemption in losing the people we love, but Parravani transforms her pain into true beauty on the page."

—Kerry Cohen, author of *Loose Girl: A Memoir of Promiscuity*

"Parravani delicately probes the fragile, intimate boundaries among love, identity, and loss." —*Kirkus Reviews*

"The courage it must have taken Christa Parravani to write the memoir *Her* took my breath away. Not only did she confront, headfirst and with clear eyes, the story of her identical twin's brutal rape and subsequent death spiral, but she had to, in essence, swallow her twin in order to summon the exquisite writer lying dormant within herself. The result is both a gripping tale of horror and redemption and a brilliant study of dichotomies, as only an identical twin adept at toggling

between brain hemispheres could convey: dark versus light, Thanatos versus Eros, good versus evil, love versus hate, and every shade of gray, red, and crazy in between. I unreservedly loved this book."   —Deborah Copaken Kogan,
author of *Shutterbabe* and *The Red Book*

"Out of a maelstrom of love, loss, and grief comes this beautiful clear-eyed memoir, one that reveals the power and peril of twinhood even as it explores ideas that affect us all: Why are we drawn to what may destroy us? What makes us hurt the ones we love? And when we experience tragedy, how do we keep grief from eating us alive? With a photographer's sharp eye and a gifted writer's penetrating insight, Parravani writes about being torn apart and then about piecing her life back together, brilliantly illuminating along the way what it means to be a sister, a daughter, a wife, an artist, and—ultimately, and triumphantly—herself."   —Julie Orringer,
author of *The Invisible Bridge*

A Memoir

Christa Parravani

Picador

Henry Holt and Company
New York

Author's Note

To write this book, I looked to my sister's journals and other writings not only to include some of them in this memoir but also to confirm my memories of the events of our childhood. I asked questions of patient family members, particularly my mother, who also kindly provided a box of personal letters and her own journals to help guide me. I also consulted many of the non-family who appear in the book and, finally, I relied on my own memory of these years. I changed the names of some people in the book to preserve their anonymity.

www.picadorusa.com
www.twitter.com/picadorusa • www.facebook.com/picadorusa
picadorbookroom.tumblr.com

Picador® is a U.S. registered trademark and is used by Henry Holt and Company under license from Pan Books Limited.

For book club information, please visit www.facebook.com/picadorbookclub or e-mail marketing@picadorusa.com.

Page 99 "Before the Meadows" by Cara Parravani © Christa Parravani

Designed by Meryl Sussman Levavi

The Library of Congress has cataloged the Henry Holt edition as follows:

Parravani, Christa.
    Her : a memoir / Christa Parravani.—1st ed.
        p. cm.
    ISBN 978-0-8050-9653-8 (hardcover)
    ISBN 978-0-8050-9654-5 (e-book)
    1. Parravani, Christa. 2. Parravani, Cara. 3. Sisters—United States—Biography.
4. Twins—United States—Biography. I. Title.
    CT275.P3846A3 2013
    306.875092—dc23
    [B]

                                                            2012029499

Picador ISBN 978-1-250-04439-6

Picador books may be purchased for educational, business, or promotional use. For information on bulk purchases, please contact Macmillan Corporate and Premium Sales Department at 1-800-221-7945, extension 5442, or write specialmarkets@macmillan.com.

First published in the United States by Henry Holt and Company

First Picador Edition: March 2014

10   9   8   7   6   5   4   3   2   1

for Cara Marie

Part I

Chapter 1

I used to be an identical twin. I was Cara Parravani's twin.

I forgot who I was after my sister died. I tried to remind myself with a trinity mantra. I whispered my mantra to the woman who stared back at me in my morning mirror: I'm twinless. I'm a photographer. I'm Christa.

I saw my sister when I tried to see myself.

We were twenty-eight when Cara overdosed: we had the dark hair we were born with; we had angular faces and we fancied red lipstick; we had knobby knees, slightly crooked eyeteeth, and fingernails bitten down until they bled. We had a touch of scoliosis: grade school nurses pulled us into their offices for yearly back checks. Cara had a steppage gait that caused her right foot to drag a little behind her left, an injury she sustained during a car accident in college. My stride is steady, but my posture is horrible; Cara stood straight as a pin—her shoulders were proud and strong and she held them back. I slouched. She said I went round like a little worried pill bug; I'd roll up into a ball tight as a fist. We both flinched at the smallest sounds: slamming doors, quick gestures, and laughter if the pitch was too high. We had looks and fears in common.

I gazed at myself in the mirror after she died and there she was. Her rusty brown eyes, frightened and curious as a doe's. In the mirror I'd smile at myself and see her grinning back. She was a beauty. And her square waist, narrow hips, and round breasts were now mine. I'd imagine all of my sister's regality and blemishes as part of my reflection: I saw Cara's weak chin, her cherry lips pricked into a bow, lipstick smudged at the corners of her mouth. I'd hold out my arms and turn them, exposing my bare forearms. I'd see each one tattooed with a flower from my wrist to my elbow. The stems of the flowers started at my pulse and grew up to the crook of my arm, blossomed. Cara had gotten these tattoos after many tough years, images that decorated and repelled. She had wanted to make sure she was rough enough around the edges, that she seemed impervious to danger, but the part of her that needed to be dainty and female selected flowers to mar her body. She designed a garden to conceal the evidence of her addiction. Her right forearm she marked with an iris. Its rich purple petals became the target for the puncture of heroin-filled needles. Her left arm she'd drawn up with a tulip. Tulips had been our grandmother Josephine's favorite flower, and the tattoo was meant to pay tribute. Near the end, Cara had run out of good veins. Her tulip's soft petals became blighted with track marks. Both of her flowers were drained of ink, which had been slowly replaced by scars.

My reflection was her and it wasn't her. I was myself but I was my sister. I was hallucinating Cara—this isn't a metaphor. I learned through reading articles on twin loss that this delusion—that one is looking upon their dead twin when really they are looking at themselves—is a common experience among identical twinless twins. It is impossible for surviving twins to differentiate their living body from their twin's; they become a breathing memorial for their lost half.

Cara's reflection became a warning. I would become her on the other side of our looking glass if I wasn't careful. It wasn't only her likeness I craved. For me, her self-destruction was contagious. I mimicked it to try to bring her back. To be nearer to her, I tore apart my life just as she'd shredded her own.

On my face I saw the thin scar our mother's carelessly long fingernail had made on the apple of my sister's cheek.

I remember the origins of all our scars.

We were three years old when Cara got scratched, on the way home from a petting zoo. The three of us—Mom, Cara, and I—rode unbuckled in the hard-shelled covered carriage of my uncle's pickup. Mom held us close as the truck bumped along. We were almost home when Uncle jammed the brakes to avoid an animal in the road. The truck stopped so short and fast that the three of us slid forward. I stayed under Mom's arm but Cara catapulted toward the metal hatchback door. Mom grabbed for her quickly and missed; Mom's fingernail sliced straight as a surgeon's scalpel into Cara's cheek.

The scar that remained was ordinary—it healed as harmless as a paper cut, but in a dotted line. It was difficult to see unless the light hit it in such a way that the scar would gleam, like a row of flat stones set out to dry in the sunshine after a downpour.

During the closest years of our lives, Cara liked to fasten bobby pins into my hair and admire the updos she invented. We administered weekly sisterly beautification, little animals that we were. We applied honey face masks, avocado hair glazes, and salt scrubs. We performed on each other the tedious process of individual split end removal with a pair of haircutting shears. She called me her "raven sister with the sexy beehive." I called her "my messy, unmatching flower goddess." Of course, there were other names, the cruel and loving ones we give our siblings. Cara took her nicknames for me with her when she died: pumpkinseed, digger, shave, and newt.

I am the sole historian left to record our lives. It's difficult to know if my memories are true without her. We mixed our memories up. Our lives were a jumble. I can remember being where I never was, in places I never saw: my sister's marital chamber on her wedding night, the filthy hotel rooms of her drug buys, sitting at her writing desk as she tapped away at her keyboard.

It wasn't uncommon for us to remember something that had happened to our twin. It can seem that I was the one who kissed Chad Taylor in the parking lot of our junior high school, his whale of a tongue bobbing back and forth in my mouth, his hands heavy as bricks on my hips.

But it was Cara who kissed him. She ran back home and spared no detail. I felt that kiss myself: my first kiss. My sister spun her tale until I knew it, too, until it was mine as much as it was hers. Nothing could happen to one without it happening to the other.

I could tell the story either way: me kissing Chad or Cara kissing him. Cara claimed what was mine, just as I took what was hers. We shared everything until there was nothing of our single selves left. It was my task in grieving her to unravel the tight, prickly braid of memory rope we'd woven—to unwind and unwind and unwind until I was able to take my strand and lay it out beside the length that was hers.

In October 2001, something terrible happened to my sister, something truly terrible, a capstone to some bad things in our lives that had gone before. That October, my sister was raped in the woods while she was out walking her dog. One of the consequences of the rape was that she was afraid to be alone. She needed me with her all the time. She asked if I would stay with her in Massachusetts, though she knew I had photography classes to attend in New York City. In my graduate studies my only assignment was to photograph, which made it relatively simple to accommodate Cara. I selected her as my subject.

I suggested she model for pictures, and in exchange I helped her cook and clean, and I kept her company. She'd feared going outside since the early autumn attack. She shut herself in. Mom bought Cara a treadmill that November, hoping to encourage her to stay active. Cara rolled the treadmill in front of her television set and walked loops like a hamster on a wheel. She quit the stationary machine by the new year: she was ready to brave the forest and followed me outdoors, where we took our photographs.

I spent all my free time with her, away from friends and away from my husband. I spent time with Cara from behind the camera and then in front of it with her.

Cara refused to dress, so I made adjustments for the pictures that allowed for this. We wore identical long black cloaks. Cara buttoned hers over her nightshirt and pants, painted red lipstick on her mouth, pinked her cheeks. I copied her makeup, became her duplicate. We looked like old-fashioned harlots wearing long blank faces, in our long black coats. It was the middle of a harsh winter. I had a vision: identicals in the snow. I used the doppelgänger in the literary Gothic sense: landscapes were to describe the psychological state of the characters of our novel. It was easier for me to think of us as characters than to grapple with the truth of our new reality. I wanted Poe's warring sisters, forever lost, women written with hysterical vapor. I wanted the fraction of history we owned.

We trekked over fields covered by feet of snow, so frozen on top that our feet didn't break through the crust. We drove together on Sunday afternoons and looked for bleak ruined landscapes, bickering.

"Have you noticed everyone in New England looks like a pilgrim?" Cara stared at a teenage girl making her way down an avenue, hauling a bag of schoolbooks. The girl stopped to rest against a building. She caught Cara's gaze, rolled her eyes, and pulled a pack of cigarettes from her knapsack, lighting one up and taking a shallow drag.

"Um, no," I answered.

"Well, just look at these people. They're all fat and red-faced and white and wearing big belts. It looks like the *Mayflower* just pulled up to port."

"I don't know what you're talking about." I looked through the windshield at the round-faced blonde in low-waisted blue jeans puffing on her cigarette and tried to imagine her in a bonnet.

In the summers we switched our black coats to white. I designed the white coats with precision.

Once, I set up a shot in a field of Queen Anne's lace. We dressed surrounded by flowers. Cara slipped both arms into her coat sleeves and fastened each of the buttons of the coat's toothy linen lapel up to her neck.

"Who the hell wears a coat in the summer?" Cara fussed with the hood, smiled. "I do, I guess." She pulled at the coat's skirt and swished it back and forth in the tall grass, like a girl admiring the costume she's given for playtime dress-up.

Cara stood at the back of the frame. I positioned her to my right, four paces behind, and crossed her hands gingerly over the middle of her waist. I pulled the hood of the coat up over her head, protecting my sweet twin from the horseflies buzzing around us. I looked down at my skirt and found a walking stick making its way to my hands, and flicked it off. A moth nested in my hair and frantically flapped its wings. Bees swarmed our skirts. Mosquitoes ravaged our legs. Light poured over our shoulders—we were backlit, sun blazing. I'd brought us to the hottest part of heaven.

I completed my photography project with Cara over five years, finishing in 2006. I called the pictures *Kindred*; we were even closer than kin.

Sometimes Cara didn't want to have her picture taken. She'd beg not to go out—there were always reasons: She'd had a nightmare and hadn't slept well. The zit blazing red on her chin was a crusty eyesore. She was waiting for an important phone call. It seemed to me that there was really ever only one reason: Cara was jealous that I still had the mind to work and she didn't. If she couldn't work, neither should I.

"The time we use to take your pictures, I could be writing." Cara would pace her living room as I packed the camera bag, my signal that I was ready to go. "Has it even crossed your mind that I work, too?" This argument happened nearly every time we planned to photograph. She'd wait to speak up until she was fully outfitted in her coat and lipstick.

"You haven't written a word in months," I'd argue back, dressed exactly as she was. We looked like Victorian misfits sounding off, spitfires. "You have nothing but free time and waste it trolling the Internet." This line of interrogation usually brought on tears for both of us.

"What do you even know about me anymore?" she asked.

She was right. I didn't recognize her. I felt like a woman stumbling through a pitch-black room looking for a hidden light switch. "I can't stay here with you unless you let me take your picture," I said, scaring her that I'd really leave. "I'll fail school."

It was true enough that I'd have to make other plans to work, but really I was falling in love with the pictures we made. The tension between us as we stood together in a meadow, the forest, or by the seaside was palpable. I was desperate to keep going, to keep shooting to see what we could make.

We eventually reached a compromise: Cara would write about each of the images, in whatever way she saw fit. I waited anxiously for each of her installments.

I contacted her therapist to ask whether taking part in the photography project was a good idea for Cara. Her therapist never answered my calls. I know it's against doctor-patient confidentiality for a doctor to discuss ongoing treatment without patient consent, but I tried nonetheless. Cara wouldn't agree to allow me to talk to Dr. Ferrini. She feared we'd compare notes and catch her overmedicating with antianxiety prescriptions. My culpability went beyond taking the pictures; I had a secret relationship with her doctor's answering machine. The phone would ring and the machine would pick up.

"Hello, you've reached Marjorie Ferrini. I'm unable to answer your call. If this is an emergency, please call emergency services. If not, leave a message and I will return your call promptly."

"Um, Dr. Ferrini?" I would say to the rolling tape. "This is Christa Parravani, Cara Parravani's sister. I'm calling because Cara is taking too many of the pills you've prescribed for her. She orders extra pills on the Internet." I left this message at least ten times over five years. There was never a reply.

After my sister died I saw her in my pictures as well as in my mirror. Was this a punishment for having used her as a model? I manipulated her for stacks of exposed film. I had gotten her to pose when she didn't want to. I'd asked until she cried and gave in. This was a shame I suffered after she died. Hadn't I killed her with my camera?

Wrinkles came early for Cara. By twenty-eight, she'd lived hard years. Crow's-feet and frown lines had begun to etch her skin, though not deeply enough for anyone other than her twin to notice. Her chain smoking, heroin slamming, X dropping, and poor diet aged her beyond me. The age lines starting on Cara's neck in the photographs began deepening on me in the mirror after she'd died. Her hair, which swirled on her shoulders in brassy Revlon-toned auburn waves, was now my own. I'd dye mine to match hers; when I grew tired of Cara's hair, I colored mine black again. Round and round went the cycle of bleach and darken. My hair dried to the texture of hay: chemical burned, brittle, broken. My stylist gave me a trim and demanded I stop.

I was the smaller of the identicals. One twin always has a rounder face. I was the one with the narrow face. We were called the *girls*. Mom called us her "ladies." Cara called me *her*. One twin goes and the other must follow. The big temptation after my sister died was to overdose or shoot myself. I got ready to die. I starved. I lied, and I swallowed pills. I wet my marital bed. I cut my arms with a knife. I divorced. I refused sleep out of fear of dreaming of Cara. I allowed any man who wanted me to fuck my body of bones so I wouldn't have to be by myself. I lived alone in a house I filled with my sister's furniture. I crashed cars, and I quit my job. I checked myself into mental hospitals. I scared our mother. I turned myself into Cara. I wanted to chase my sister into the afterlife. I saved myself at the brink of our two worlds. I cheated my own death. What one twin gets, the other must have. I declined my piece of our whole. I became a woman who owns half a story: I lived.

I spent years in the shroud of her white tattered scarf from Nepal; I wore her wedding rings and her favorite dresses. I slept in them until they tore. So be it. I love her, like I love no one else. I am in love with Cara. If I couldn't die with her, I could write my sister back to life. I learned another language: posthumous twin talk. I began to communicate with my sister by writing. When I write, I feel my sister come as close as I'll allow.

Cara had begun her own memoir. No one can finish it. I can take pieces, like she took pieces of me. I searched the files on her computer and found poems, recollections of our youth, and the short prose pieces she wrote to accompany my photographs. With my findings, I've patched together our tale.

Once upon a time we were one snake, with one head, one body and two sharp teeth. Once you cut a snake in half it grows another head. Once it grows another head, it heals, becomes two snakes. Once upon a time there was only one of us. When your body is a mirror, there is no word for individual. Is there one word for two snakes? Twin. Snakes shed their skin. Once I was tough. I had all of our sharp teeth and all of the scales.

I am Cara. What I am makes me us. Us makes me her. Christa is me. Us, me, her, we. I am, without her, half of her.

I am breathing another girl's breath. It's the reality of never being alone, even in death, I imagine, that will never end. I will always be her body, breath, blood, legs, voice. Christa will walk for me. I will speak for her.

We wore the same outfits as little girls but in different colors. My dresses were blue, with ballooned shoulders and bows. Sister wore pink and was smaller than I. Women, we are the same size. Still, if I were to draw a picture of us, I would be great big, and holding her like a baby.

Her face is prettier than mine. We look exactly alike.

"I have always wanted a twin." People say that. People want someone just like them, who thinks like they think and who will understand them even when they don't understand themselves. People think having a twin means never being lonely.

Nothing is lonelier than being separated.

"We are lucky," we answer back. But we are not. We are worried. "Cut yourself in half," we tell people. "See how that feels and you will stop wanting a twin."

People ask questions. "Do you know what the other is think-ing? Do you have ESP? Do you dream the same dreams when you sleep?" I answer yes. I say, "I think what she thinks." It's easier than telling the truth. Now we are conflicting languages, snake-spit Babel. Sister explains me with her camera. I tell on her with my words, and I also tell on myself.

Once upon a time there was a story with no present, no past, no future. The story was written in our same blood.

Cara's dying meant there was a strong chance I would soon join her. I researched our situation and read somewhere that 50 percent of twins follow their identical twin into death within two years. That statistic did not discriminate among cancer, suicide, or accident. The second twin goes by illness or the intol-erable pain of loneliness. Flip a coin: those were my chances of survival.

Certainly we'd talked about what we'd do if one of us died before the other. The answer was always suicide and our plans were the plots of girls who never suspected they'd really lose the other. We'd schemed since grade school about how we'd seal our pact: in the case of illness we'd hold a bedside vigil and ingest a dose of cyanide. In the case of an accident, the injured twin was not allowed to die until she stumbled to a pay phone and called the other. The unharmed twin would take her life by whatever means she possessed: Drano, phone cord, knife, swan dive from a cliff.

Chapter 2

I have a story, a tale I've never told. It was 2005 and Cara was looking for a new apartment again; her life still unraveling after the rape. She and her husband, Kahlil, had divorced. The weekend of the daylight saving time change, Cara and I had a slumber party at Jedediah's and my place and reset the clocks together. We turned the hands back and retired to bed, pleased at gaining our temporary hour, the sorely needed extra time for sleep and coffee and lingering over the Sunday real estate classifieds. I didn't mind the change in season—there'd be early sunsets, holiday feasts, and tree trimming. Snow would soon float quietly down from the sky until it stuck, frozen on the brown grass, building a fortress of white over the naked forsythia at the edge of the driveway.

New England winters are bitter—by 4:30 p.m. the light is nearly gone. Almost as soon as the sun comes up, it seems to blink down again. I had a secret plan to fight off the winter blahs that year, bottles and bottles filled with little yellow round friends, painkillers and downers prescribed to ease my aching back. I had primed myself for the coming blizzards. I had pain relief and I had my twin. We had a winter full of plans. Soon we'd trudge into the snow to take pictures. Soon we'd hold our post-Thanksgiving night family complaint session and our ritual Christmas gift exchange.

I'd been in trouble for a while with crippling pain. The doctor had said too many hours a day in the darkroom, standing on a concrete floor, hunched over developing trays had put my back out. I was going to need to start taking better care. Practical shoes and more calcium were in order. I'd needed to see a chiropractor, go to physical therapy, and, for God's sake, stand up straight. To get me through the worst of the pain he gave me a prescription for Soma, a non-narcotic muscle relaxant, and a script for Valium, a benzodiazepine that also helped soothe the muscles but should only be taken at bedtime, and never mixed with Soma.

Cara was staying the weekend while Jedediah was away on business. I never liked to be alone for very long, a consequence of being a twin, and I was glad to have Cara nearby. She didn't like to be alone, either. We spent that weekend watching stand-up comedy on television and drinking margaritas from salt-rimmed glasses until we were tipsy. We switched to giant cups of water with ice when we got too drunk—pulpy wedges of lime bobbing up against our lips as we sipped. We ate steaks grilled the right way: charred fast and hot so the outside was seared. The insides stayed cool and red and the centers bled when the knife cut. Twin weekends, the rare weekends we spent alone, were occasion for food and drink.

The music we listened to in college—Tracy Chapman, Indigo Girls, Violent Femmes—played festively throughout those weekends. We were like kids without parents, but we were wives without husbands. Cara liked to hold one of my cats, a slick gray Siamese, and dance through the house with him, bouncing him on her hip to the music, like a baby. The cat stuck his little pink tongue through his teeth in delirious joy, his head tipping back as he whirled with her.

Sunday rolled in faster than we would have liked during our daylight saving time fest—the extra hour wasn't enough. The woods around the house had gone dark and still. Jedediah was due home the next morning.

Cara and I sat together on the sofa. I hunched over my laptop, writing out lesson plans for the Monday morning photography seminar I taught at a local college. Cara was grading student essays for the Introduction to Writing course she TAed at UMass. Papers heaped on her lap, ink on her face, she tossed the essays one by one onto the floor as she finished. They lay in a mixed-up pile at her feet. The pages were marked with checks and commas, and long lines of notes ran down the margins.

"How the hell do you manage to keep all of those straight?" I bent down to tidy the papers, to give the pile some order.

"I don't. It's a song and a prayer at this point. They don't pay me enough to be organized."

"They never do, do they?"

"Nope. You think it's cold in here?"

"It's getting there." The woodstove had burned down to embers and I noticed the dog sleeping, my pampered Chihuahua, a fleck of cinnamon in a pile of white, burrowed up to her nose in a basket of warm linens I'd fetched from the dryer. "I'm going out for firewood," I told her.

"Want help?"

"No, no thanks."

"You sure? I know your back has been sore." Cara rubbed her hands together to warm them and tried to lay them on my shoulders. "I could rub your flip-flop muscle," she teased. This was her name for the tense, tight area between our big and second toes.

"I don't want your help," I said, surprised by my tone. We'd had a nice weekend, and I was sorry to spoil it. I tried to be kind, to turn the other cheek, but no matter how I tried to mask it, resentment returned.

Accepting help from Cara was a deal with the devil. She used my weakness as leverage against me. Her arsenal was well stocked—I'd recently confided in her that I was restless in my young marriage, feared it was unraveling, and had doubts I should remain. When she felt afraid that I might abandon her because of her drug use, she'd remind me that she knew my secret. She was willing to tell Jedediah and explode my marriage if I left her. My fall would be her pleasure, not because she didn't love me, but because she did—she wanted me for herself, down in the same muck she'd been flailing in. Nobody wants to be alone in misery. Cara experienced no shame in admitting that need. Not only did she not want to suffer alone, she demanded co-suffering from all who dared love her.

I knew she was back on drugs. It had taken years, but I'd learned the signs—no-shows for dinner, broken relationships, a lengthy paper trail she thought she'd hidden.

I'd been reading her e-mail for months, looking for receipts from Canadian and Mexican pharmacies. I was tipped off to look for them when I opened her glove box and stacks of half-empty unmarked foil-packaged pills tumbled out. A hand-written invoice for "Medicines," signed with a smiley face and wedged beneath an unpaid parking ticket, sat just below her stockpile. I did what I had to do. I logged in to her e-mail and guessed her password; it wasn't difficult. Hers was the exact same as mine: our beloved first pet's name, a cat.

I tried to intercept deliveries before she was able to get them. The pills were colorless and had a tooth to them—they weren't smooth but rough, and as round and large as pennies. Each delivery consisted of 120 pills packaged in punch sheets wrapped in thick brown paper. Some weeks she bought Vicodin and others Valium. No matter the drug, they looked the same, like rat poison molded into horse pills. She'd been spending hundreds of dollars weekly on them and, even though I seized half of what she ordered, she didn't allow the missing packages to deter her from ordering more.

Pills made her slower, sluggish. It sounds strange but her hair fell flat when she used; her hair had been limp for months. I knew I'd probably not even scratched the surface of what Cara was able to procure, but I continued looking. I convinced myself that there was no hiding her problem from me. That was true, but soon enough I'd learn that my discovery would never be enough to save Cara. Her life was in her own small hands.

I could see she was high as soon as she walked into a room. I looked for her flaws at first glance, just as she looked for mine. I relished them. Twins love, but they bicker and fight and judge. Twins are wicked and harsh, as hard on their twins as they are on themselves. Harder. All of the things a twin hates about herself are obvious in her twin. For twins, self-loathing means it's sibling hunting season.

Twins: it's always tit for tat.

We were constantly keeping score and upholding double standards.

That daylight saving weekend, our last alone, I wasn't giving Cara the satisfaction of accepting her help.

I walked to the medicine cabinet and took a dose of Soma, two pills, and walked out into the cold to get some logs and kindling.

I attempted to carry an armful of wood from a neatly stacked pile of seasoned oak. Cara watched from a window like she was rubbernecking a car wreck. She looked on as I dropped piece after piece of wood. I picked up each one, only to watch it tumble to the ground again. I struggled foulmouthed, a stubborn Quasimodo in a dress—I was furious at my sister for being such a lout. I did need her help. I thought of what I'd said, *I don't want your help*, and shouldered the weight of the wood.

I managed to hulk an arm full of it up the stairs and dropped each log in the big empty copper bucket beside the hearth. "This should warm your bones," I teased, trying to lighten the mood, a passive apology for snapping at her. The pills were starting to kick in a little bit. The pain wasn't lifting but my mood was.

I brushed off the bark and dirt from my dress and went into the bathroom, opening a bottle of Soma, swallowing two more. A half hour passed and still there was pain. I took two more. I worked away at my computer, and another half hour passed. The spasm in my back crashed down on my tailbone. I opened the medicine chest and retrieved two more pills, chasing them down with two tablets of Valium. An hour passed and I repeated the same dose.

I sat down at the kitchen table to resume my course work and lost consciousness.

I came to in my sister's embrace, and was surprised to see Jedediah standing in the kitchen off to the side. He'd come home early from his trip to find his wife strung out, cradled in her sister's arms. "It's not as bad as it looks," I slurred. We were like two kids caught snooping through a porn stash. It was exactly how it looked.

"What did you give my wife?" Jedediah walked over and pulled me from Cara's grip.

"Nothing, I swear." Cara picked up my purse, flipping through my wallet for an insurance card. "We need to get her to the ER, don't you think?," she said. She was defiant and deferential, taking claim of me but also allowing for the possibility that this scene didn't bode well for more weekend parties, just the two of us. She stood with her hands on her hips, bent down, and tilted her head to the side, baby-talking me. "Tell him. Tell him I didn't give you anything."

I didn't have the strength to answer her.

Jedediah is tall and thin; he stands six feet and weighs no more than 155 pounds. My husband was skinny and some might even say frail. He managed strength to pick me up, though, and carried me to our car, sitting me upright in the front passenger's seat. Cara chased close behind and got into the backseat.

"Don't you dare die on me," she begged.

"Just stop it. Would you?" Jedediah pushed the gas down hard, skidding out of the gravel driveway, rocks popping and then shooting out beneath the tires. "I can't stand your moroseness." We rolled in place for a few seconds, having lost traction on dirt and pebble, so Jedediah gunned it and the wheels screeched out loud as he hit blacktop.

Cara ignored him and leaned in over the headrest, whispering in my ear, "I'll kill you if you die, and then your husband will kill me." She reached around from behind my seat and straightened out the twisted shoulder strap and lap belt that Jedediah had hurriedly snapped into place. "What use are we if we're both dead?"

Cara wiped the sweat from my forehead. Jedediah rolled down the windows, and I craned my neck out, vomiting. "Do you want me to call anyone, let them know there has been an emergency?" Cara asked, slipping her hand beneath the collar of my shirt, stroking the bare skin of my back. "You might not be out for a long time."

My head hung limp from my neck and swayed as the car

moved. She'd caught me off guard. There was only one person I'd wanted to talk to for the last several months and I'd been doing it in secret. "Call D," I blurted. The pills had impaired my judgment and I immediately regretted mentioning D. We'd met over the summer and even though he was twenty years older, in my husband's mind he posed a threat to our marriage, to my fidelity. Jedediah shifted gears hard.

Cara said, "No problem, love. I'll let him know that you've gotten yourself into a bind."

The hospital was only a mile from the house. Jedediah had figured I'd be in the ER sooner, having my stomach pumped, if he took me himself. An ambulance would have taken too long.

Cara phoned the hospital from the car and told them to wait for us at the door with a wheelchair—she said there had been an emergency, an overdose, a suicide attempt. She told the nurse on call that I'd need a psychiatrist to approve an overnight stay, and then a transfer to a behavioral facility. My twin was a pro, she'd done this before, only, before, she had always been the one barfing out the window while I frantically drove, or stood by as doctors worked to bring her back to life.

The nurses were by the ER door as requested, with a chair. They wheeled me into a hospital room, where a doctor waited with a puke pail and a dose of activated charcoal in liquid form. I drank the many ounces of the thick, gray, chalky drink. Its dose absorbed the poison of my many pills.

The doctor asked me what I'd taken and I told him.

I explained exactly what I'd done, how I'd been impatient to get rid of pain and maybe a bit too celebratory from my sister's visit. I explained the back spasms and recent job stress, the frustration I'd felt with my husband for retreating so fully into a book he was working on. It was all run-of-the-mill, I assured the doctor; and it was. He nodded and scribbled some notes on a writing pad. He asked me several times if I'd wanted to harm myself on purpose or had any plans to die.

I told him I didn't, though I knew I lusted to numb my troubles, which seemed dangerous enough. I told the doctor I'd been reckless but didn't want to kill myself. That desire would come within the year, but that was far away, waiting for me in my new life, in the next winter. I pleaded with the doctor. It was an accident. I was a married professor, responsible. I needed the doctor to believe I hadn't turned into my sister.

The doctor warned that I might want to consider my behavior, clicked a pen on his clipboard. He told me that sometimes an accidental overdose is not such an accident. He closed my chart and walked into the hall. I could hear him talking to my sister just outside the door.

"You're not going to admit her?" Cara asked.

"She's free to go home as soon as her stomach settles."

"This is ridiculous," Cara whined. "An overdose should require at least a consultation with a psychiatrist. I know protocol."

The doctor was testy. "Your sister is fine. I think she's learned a good lesson here. Just get her home and have her husband put her to bed."

"I can't fucking believe this. If that were me, I'd be checked into the Happy Valley funny farm by now."

She was right. I was always getting away with things she wouldn't have.

"Well, good thing she's not you." I wondered if he'd been an admitting physician for one of Cara's ER overdose admits. "I've got to get back to rounds."

Cara tried another avenue with the doctor. "She's been stealing my pills on the side, Klonopin. I've counted and she's taken more than half the bottle this month. Thanks to her, I'm out. If you're not going to admit her, can you at least write me a script to replace them?"

The doctor turned from her, and his footsteps grew faint as he made his way to another emergency.

Cara *was* right. I did occasionally sneak into her handbag and take a generous helping of her sedative. My sister lost herself to a rape and drugs. I lost myself first in the fight to save her—my battle began before she'd taken her last dose of heroin. I was at war with her to live and then, quietly, with myself because I was powerless. I thought my occasional need to surrender to a pill was justified. But that need was also a warning: I was closer to being Cara than I knew. While she was alive I was vibrant, responsible, steadfast, and holding her up. I was her opposite. In the wake of Cara's death I became her. The events of our lives unfolded before me. There was no stopping them.

Once I was smaller than Cara. Once I cried more than she. Once she had to take care of me and tie my shoes and wipe my nose, and hug me on the bus all the way to school. Once we were on a bus full of kids and I kissed her on the mouth. Our classmates laughed and called us "Lezzies." I didn't know what that was, but I knew I didn't want to be one. Once Cara punched me and broke my nose. Once, she removed a shard of a red glass marble from my foot with a pair of tweezers. No, that wasn't it. Once, I had a red shard in my foot and I learned to walk with it.

The first time I laughed after she died I was driving in a beat-up Jeep with one of Cara's ex-boyfriends. I'd always frowned on her dating him; he was her former student as well as her boy-friend. It was her way to mix business with pleasure, and it was never a surprise when it ended badly, as it did with Ethan. He'd befriended me out of worry for me and curiosity and, most of all, I suspect, out of longing to be near to Cara again. I wasn't such a bad second choice. It was easy to rehearse with me what he wished he'd said to her. I nodded as he told me he'd loved my sister, that she was an angel in bed, the best sexual teacher as well as the best professor he'd ever had. He shifted gears and turned up the radio, smiled over at me as my hair whipped my face. Ethan was trying hard to fall in love with me. Winning my devotion was the only way to resurrect Cara. In our tryst, Ethan and I both tried to cheat death.

We drove the back roads from Northampton to Amherst, windows rolled down, the hum of the road between us. I held my arm out of the open passenger's side window and let it bob in the fast wind, ignoring the bugs that zoomed past and zapped hard against my palm. We passed a cemetery and Ethan turned down the radio and pointed out my sister's favorite tombstone. It read: DEADY. He looked at me and waited for my reaction, thinking he'd told me something funny about Cara that I wouldn't have known. He was right. I had no idea she'd loved it. Ethan couldn't have known that I, too, had long admired Deady, that I often pulled my own car over and showed the tombstone to friends and had a good laugh at the Deady family's expense. I'd even gone and photographed the waist-high marble grave marker and left behind a bouquet of flowers in thanks. I looked at Ethan, opened my mouth, and then the laugh came. The sound was as familiar as my own name, but it caused the hair on my arms to stand on end. My laugh was Cara's exactly. Its emergence from my body was as disorienting as being addressed by a stranger, only to discover it's not you they're talking to.

After Cara died, I saw in my reflection, too, the face and body of her corpse: sallow green and chalky, bloodless and rouged.

When I'd first glimpsed her like this, I'd jumped back. I gave this new look of mine a name. I called it Dead Face. I used the term often: When I wanted Jedediah to come and comfort me, I'd call to him through the house, "Hey! Could you come here? Honey? Just for a second? I need a hug. I have Dead Face." Once I invited a girlfriend over for dinner in and then out for a movie. We primped before the show. I glossed and lined my lips, saw that I looked a bit pale. "Could you pass the blush?" I asked. "I need a bit more. I have Dead Face." The name was perfectly acceptable, funny even. It became usual.

Chapter 3

We started from good intentions. Mom was big with us before she conceived. We swam in her mind. She asked God for a girl and called her girl Cara Marie. Mom held a single, imagined girl in her belly. Dr. Rosen told her she would have a baby boy. The sonogram said so. Mom knew better. Only a few months before we began, she'd lost her own mother to a brain hemorrhage. She wanted a girl to take her mother's place and she thought God couldn't be so unkind as to give her a son. Dr. Rosen said her baby settled like a boy. He knew it was an old wives' tale that babies settled, he said, but he'd seen enough women and babies to know there was some truth to it. Boys ride high and girls hang low. Mom thought her baby kicked like a girl. She never picked a boy's name or bought a single blue blanket.

She asked God for a loud girl, a girl as tough as two boys, a girl who could yell and fight her daddy. The girl would, after all, need to fight her daddy if she had any chance of surviving in his house. Mom knew she was asking God for something selfish. She could barely manage her own safety in her husband's house. Home wasn't a place fit for a baby, certainly not a girl.

Our dad didn't want Mom getting pregnant. They'd been fighting about it ever since her mother died. He didn't want babies slowing him down. He'd just gotten a raise at GE's main plant in Schenectady. The money was finally good. Mom was disappointed; she was a twenty-two-year-old orphan who needed a family. She was on the pill when she missed her monthly bleed. All the tests were negative, but the tests were wrong, she thought, so she only pretended to take the fresh pack of tablets on her nightstand. She put one on her tongue each night and faked a swallow, then spit it into the wastebasket. She took vitamins instead of birth control; her girl had to be strong.

Mom looked at the ceiling, tried to forget Dad on top of her. Sweat rolled from his armpits and dropped onto her face. Her baby made her sick. Mom thought of caramel apples rolled in sea salt to keep her nausea at bay. Dad took her tender breasts into his hands and squeezed. Mom imagined his pounding hips were a flower whose petals she could pull off: she's sex; she's not sex. She's sex; she's not sex. She's sex, but she's also a mother. She's not sex, and she's more than Dad's rag-doll wife. We, sister and I, grew together in secret.

Dad wanted a boy, if he had to have anything, and he bought baseball caps and blue bibs in support of their mistake baby.

Mom made an appointment to learn our sex. She prayed in Dr. Rosen's waiting room, asked God to make her baby girl cunning, a fooler. Her girl would have to be swift and keep one step ahead of her daddy.

The doctor's steel table was layered with a length of paper. Mom put her feet in the exam table stirrups. She shivered. It was winter, just after Christmas, and the blanket to keep her warm during her exam was thin and covered only her waist and knees. Dr. Rosen looked at Mom and nodded; he pointed at the black-and-white image of the baby on his screen, a single baby. He showed her where the penis was. Mom got dressed and made the sign of the cross.

Mom grew rounder and rounder.

She stood in front of her mirror and looked. She was so big, she filled doorways. Her ankles were swollen and the straps of her bras dug into her shoulders. Her nipples were hard, and dark. A thick brown line extended from her belly button down, halving her. My girl has eight more weeks to grow, our mother thought. She thought the mirror lied. She was too big for the months that had passed. We made fists, knocked on Mom like we were opening a door. Mom answered, "Hello, girl-baby. I'll never stop loving you, not from hello on."

Dad cracks an egg on the asphalt sidewalk while he's at work. The egg cooks solid in five minutes. His coworkers watch. The dirty, concrete contaminated egg breathes heat. The men take off their hats, stare in disbelief. If the heat can make this egg alive, it can do anything.

Mom woke up wet today. Time for baby to come out. She thinks the water is sweat. She wakes all this week sweating; can't turn down the heat as it rises with her breathing. She curls into a ball, hugs Baby, who is waiting, wanting to meet her.

Dad doesn't care; he wants breakfast. Mom cooks in a hurry. She hunches over his sausage pan and cracks an egg. She counts the minutes as Baby shifts and turns. Her legs shake. Oldest Aunt walks through the door.

Oldest Aunt is the coach for Mom and Baby. She brings Mom to Lamaze classes, rubs her back, and rubs the baby in Mom's belly. Oldest Aunt sings to Baby when Dad isn't home. She stays quiet after he comes home. Dad doesn't want any part of it.

"At least it's a boy." He eats his eggs.

Boy baby. His boy baby is making Mom hunch over the sink full of his dishes. She directs her soft, guttural muttering into the sink. Her words dissolve in the soapy water. Dad continues breakfast, watches Mom's baby belly. He chews and smiles.

Dad goes to work.

Oldest Aunt brings Mom to the hospital, puts her in the back-seat because her belly is too big for the front. They can't drive fast because the brakes are going bad. Mom is calm, closes her eyes when a contraction comes on. She sees her girl baby's face smiling, remembers throwing all her pennies into the park fountain, and watching the water ripple.

It seems Baby is not in birth position.

Oldest Aunt holds Mom's hand. Breathe. Breathe.

Mirror Mom and her naked mirror baby-body are prostrate, waiting. Her knees fold out. She is breathing hard; she pushes. It's like metal bands crushing down, Baby sinking down, crushing her. We wrestle to see who can get out first. Mom thinks in lita-nies. Pennies in the fountain, pennies in the fountain, make a water wish. Push.

Doctor numbs Mom and takes out his knife, pulls Baby out.

I'm first. I'm screaming for air.

Mom is not finished; she's still contracting. There's another foot.

You're a girl, too. We cry identical hellos.

Dad is watching a baseball game in the waiting room. He doesn't want to watch us get born. Grandpa didn't watch him. Men don't watch babies come. Dad cheers when the bat hits the ball. Soon, he thinks, he'll be proud. He's a man who can make a boy.

"Hello," we say. "You didn't want us." Dad has two hands. We've got four to beat him back.

My right arm was twisted behind Cara's back. Her legs wrapped around my legs; we were tangled up. There was no telling where one baby ended and the other began. Our room wasn't ready: no crib, no changing table, not a single diaper or pacifier. It was so hot Mom slept with a bowl of ice and a washcloth at her bedside. She dipped it into the bowl and wrung it out, dragging the cloth in long strokes across her breasts and brow. Her water broke a month early; she bore us in the middle of a July heat wave.

Mom pushed for hours but baby wouldn't show her crown. Dr. Rosen put one monitor inside of Mom and another on her belly, two monitors for one baby. He listened to the drum of our hearts. They played against each other, and the beats were doubled, pounding out of time. There would be no more laboring. Mom's baby boy had a too-fast beating heart. He'd have to be sectioned out. A nurse wheeled Mom out into the hall and then prepared her surgery room. Mom went in alone. Her girl would see Mom's face first and this calmed her.

Dr. Rosen put a mask on Mom until she was painlessly awake. Dr. Rosen cut her belly button to pubic bone, pried her open, and looked inside.

"Oh my God," he said as he saw the baby in Mom's womb. He saw a mass of doubled arms and legs, a single body, and two faces.

"What is it?" Mom asked, worried, trying her best to peek around the big blue surgery curtain that draped her middle and obstructed her view.

Dr. Rosen stayed quiet. He reached inside of Mom and pulled Cara out, finding me beneath. "There's two of them!" he yelled out to the nurses in relief. "Two beautiful girls."

The nurses washed us clean and wrapped us in soft pink blankets. We whimpered and then we yowled.

"Please, someone tell me he's kidding," Mom said through her anesthesia. "I don't believe it. Someone tell me he's lying."

"Look at your babies," Dr. Rosen said and picked us up and brought us over to Mom. Our short loud cries sounded out insistently like worried horns or honking geese.

Mom looked at us and cried. "I don't know whose babies

these are," she said. "They're not mine." But she kissed each of us on the forehead. We were twice the girl she'd wished for.

Dr. Rosen helped us over the IV drips and plastic tubes into Mom's arms. "Careful," he said as we settled ourselves toward her waiting breasts, nuzzling in. We stopped crying as she pulled us near, looking up for the first time at her adoring face. She'd pulled her hair away from it into a bun. She beamed with simple pure love, sweat, exhaustion, and fear. "They look exactly like you," he said. "You might not need them but they will need you."

"But I do need them," Mom said, carefully holding our small and breakable bodies in the crooks of her arms. "I always will." Mom ran her fingers over Cara's naked shoulder. "She's so small, she'd fit right into the palm of my hand."

We slept in our mother's arms until she needed rest of her own.

A cheering section waited in the hallway outside the viewing glass of the nursery: Dad, aunts, uncles, Grandma, Grandpa.

The nurses wheeled us in and our new family of admirers greeted us with applause, pressed their hands and faces against the glass to look.

Grandma Josephine squeezed Grandpa's shoulder. "Look, Freddy," she said. "She had one for each of us."

Dad turned away from the sight of his baby girls and slowly banged his head against the white cement hospital wall, both a joke and a worry. "What will we do with them?" he said to himself, wondering how he'd ever pay for two. "I guess there's always Doublemint Gum commercials."

"They'll need a daddy. All girls need their daddy," Grandpa said.

Dad walked to a chair and put his head in his hands. "Girls, two girls." He shook his head. "Can we send one back?"

When it was time, Dr. Rosen called Dad into the nursery to meet us.

He sat down next to our father and held us, our tiny heads wresting against his chest.

"Congratulations," he said. "Baby B weighs three pounds fifteen ounces. Baby A is four pounds nine ounces." He held us out for Dad to hold. "You've got tiny peanuts here now, but before you know it, they'll be strong girls. Soon you can take them home." Dr. Rosen shushed our crying and stood up to hand us off.

Dad shooed us away. "I don't know how to hold babies." He got up to leave, but turned on his way, wagging his finger at our mother as if he'd caught on to this joke she'd played on him. We were her responsibility, the three of us, this much she understood. All of us against one man who needed to own each of us, but didn't want any of us.

Mom and Dad brought us home to 24 Steers Avenue, a modest two-story white Victorian on a quiet street. Mom's beloved calico cat slept on the front porch beneath a rocking chair when we arrived, one of us in each of our parents' arms. An impressive weeping willow tree grew in the front yard, framing the house with soft yellow leaves. We played hide-and-seek beneath its ground-sweeping branches. We carved our names into its trunk with the sharp rocks we gathered from Mom's bed of lilies.

Dad let us eat ice cream whenever we wanted and allowed us to make drawings on the wall with washable markers. He took us to baseball games and bought us adult-size team hats that flopped over our eyes. He told us we knew our stuff. He showed us how to play pitch and catch and hide-and-seek. He ordered us monogrammed T-shirts in blue and red. Dad taught us how to spit in a steady straight line, like all the boys in preschool could; he said all the power was in our cheeks, we just had to blow it fast. I hocked a loogie and imagined it shooting out like Dad spat his angry words.

He gave us his love of music. He played records on his hissing, skipping 45. We held hands and danced through the kitchen and living room to the Rolling Stones, the Beatles, and Frank Sinatra. Cara and I shook and shimmied through the gauzy cigarette-smoked high afternoon light; it beamed across the room and lit us like singing stars in a cabaret.

But Dad's moods changed as quickly as traffic lights. Once when we weren't yet three years old, he shoved both of us twins into his car quick, after a fistfight with a strange man in a mall parking lot; he'd sworn at the man, for what I wasn't certain, and flashed him the middle finger, what he called "the great big bird." A scuffle ensued. We drove away after. Dad's face was full of thrill. He gripped the steering wheel so hard, his chewed-up knuckles turned white. He gunned the gas to the floor. He drove fast and erratically down the narrow avenue. I peed my pants in the backseat. Cara held my hand and stroked my hair. She said we'd be safe in our bedroom. We'd make ourselves as snug as bugs in a rug. I worried over soiling Dad's blessed blue vinyl interior and put my head in my sister's lap. She shielded my eyes and watched for us both as our car nearly careened into a ditch. She shushed me and whispered in my ear, telling me everything would be okay when we got home.

The man in the parking lot wasn't Dad's only victim. Dad blackened Mom's eye. He pushed her down the stairs and left her battered and weeping on the basement's concrete floor. He hit her in the jaw with the butt of his gun, kicked her shins with his heavy black work boots. He stole her photographs of her mother and held them hostage.

Mom and Dad fight.
  We are on the porch at Steers Avenue watching Dad through the window. Mom is talking. Mom is silent. Dad hits her. Dad is

not hitting Mom. We watch ladybugs crawl on the screen. I count their spots; Sister covers her ears and watches colors. The porch is white. The ladybugs are red. I am wearing a blue sweatshirt. Sister is wearing red all over. Everything is black and white.

We go to Grandma's house after the police come. Mom comes with us. Dad goes away. Grandma shakes her head. Grandpa taps his foot. Grandma tries to say something. Dad is her son. Grandpa keeps his lips pressed together. "How did we raise this man to be such a boy?" he asks Grandma. She looks down at his tapping foot. He is disappointed that the police have come. His son is not supposed to get caught. His wife is not supposed to call. Real men make their women quiet—that's what Grandpa's tapping foot says.

We stay with Grandma at her house. Mom tells Grandma she doesn't want us to think our life is normal. Mom kisses us good-bye. She's started looking for a new place for us to live.

She did finally leave him, with little except her life, her girls. She packed us up while Dad was at work. Grandma Josephine came over and helped Mom pack. She gave Mom fifty dollars and told her never to go back to her son.

Dad had broken our mother. And he'd terrorized us so deeply that we later refused him entry into our adult lives, as if closing the door on him kept him from peering into the windows. His abuse raised the bar on what was tolerable. There was nothing we weren't prepared to take from a man and nothing we didn't dish out in return.

When Mom left Dad, we moved to a squat redbrick apartment building on Barton Avenue in Schenectady. It was Section 8 housing, but Cara and I were rich because we had our own swing set, which previous tenants had left behind, and a boysenberry tree grew by the fence in our backyard. We shared the tree's ripe bounty with our neighbors in the summers. Mom made pies. She painted the hallway between her bedroom and ours a homey, dark cornflower blue and our room a grassy sage.

Victim and Monster was a game we played there: One of us would turn out the light and we'd run to our separate beds and get under the covers. One of us would stand up from bed and make a hideously scary face, stalking slowly over to the bedside of the other. When it was my turn to be the victim, I waited patiently for Cara to arrive. I curled my hands up over my blanket, clenched my fists, and giggled. The goal of the game was to make the scariest face you could and hold it until you got to your sister's bed. You were to hold your monster face and touch your sister, nose to nose. The twin who broke out in laughter or fright first would lose the game. We'd play a few rounds and laugh and laugh. A night's play always ended the same way: we'd sleep in the same bed, our backs pressed together.

"Hey?" I'd whisper to Cara from my side of the bedroom. "You there?"

"Yeah?" she'd answer, hushed. "Don't wake Mom up. She'll kill us."

"What are you doing?" I'd ask.

"Trying to go to sleep."

"I'm scared."

"What do you want me to do about it?"

"I don't know." The covers muffled my voice. "Can I sleep with you?"

"Fine," Cara groaned. "Just for tonight though, okay?"

It was never just for the night. Every night the dark frightened me. Every night, we played our game and then slept back to back.

Chapter 4

I warned Cara against moving to Holyoke.

Most graduate students in her program lived in the nearby college towns of Amherst and Northampton, sleepy villages filled with coffee shops and boutiques and craft galleries, where you found handblown glass vases in bright colors and brand-new lamps made to look antique. Both towns had several novelty stores that sold bumper stickers: THANK GODDESS, WE CAN DO IT!, FIGHT LIKE A GIRL.

"Why would you move to that nasty town?" I asked her. "Spend a few hundred dollars more and live in Amherst, where it's actually safe to go outside."

"You're always so paranoid," she said. "You know I'm not good at making friends. I'd rather live in a big apartment. And I don't need to hang out at cafés with catty grad students."

"Those bitchy students will be your peers," I insisted.

I tried in vain in the fall of 2001 to move Cara to Northampton, even setting up appointments for her to look at pretty rentals in remodeled Victorians (appointments she never showed up for). Maybe I was projecting my needs onto her. These little towns *did* look good to me. I had only a year left in my photography graduate program and had begun to hope that I might leave New York City for a quiet life as a college professor, near Cara.

Once a thriving mill and factory town, Holyoke was, by then, a skeleton of its former self. The impressive brick buildings that must have housed flourishing locally owned businesses were boarded up and tagged with profane graffiti. Bodegas, restaurants, and gas stations were built with security in mind: employees worked behind bulletproof glass panels that ran from serving counter to ceiling; a slot drawer pushed open for the exchange of money was the only point of contact between customer and clerk. I went to Holyoke to visit Cara during the first weekend of October. I saw the benefits of her living choice as soon as she opened her door: the rent *was* cheap and her place *was* expansive. Four hundred and fifty dollars a month bought Cara and Kahlil twelve hundred square feet of shiny hardwood flooring, high ceilings with intricate molding, a dining room with a china cabinet built into the wall, a front porch, and a back porch.

Cara whisked me back to the sitting porch at the rear of the building. "Isn't this great!" she beamed, pulling me down next to her on a softly pillowed wicker sofa set, her new backyard in perfect view; the porch faced an unpaved lot, where a couple of beat-up cars, caked in dirt and covered in leaves, sat parked alongside an industrial-size Dumpster; they looked as if they hadn't been driven in years.

A pair of girls—sisters, I presumed—played in the lot. Silky black ponytails hung down their backs, tickling the waistbands of their faded dungarees. They rode Big Wheels, pedaling back and forth through clouds of dust that rose up beneath the little bikes. Rocks crackled against the plastic wheels. Cara and I sat together on the wicker love seat, watching them play through the haze of the porch screen.

"They're funny girls," she said. "They're out here night and day." Her arm hung limply over the armrest. "Come to think of it, I've never seen their mom." She circled her wrist like a much older, arthritic woman would, as if relieving an ache. The smoke of her cigarette swirled into my face.

"I wish you'd quit those." I pulled the cigarette from between her fingers, taking a drag. "You like that?" I asked, thinking the only way to demonstrate my worry over her habit was to pick it up myself and show her how terrible it looked.

"You've got asthma, stupid." She grabbed the cigarette and snuffed it out. "What's okay for me isn't good for you."

"I know what's good for you, lady."

"Oh yeah?"

"A picture—that's what good for you." I brought my hands up to my face as if I were holding a camera and started clicking away.

"You know what I think? I think you know what's good for *you*."

I took a photograph of the two of us in Cara's bathtub that afternoon. A tiny crank window above the tub let in enough light to reveal the iridescent color base of the turquoise paint on the walls. The antique claw-foot tub was freshly cleaned; the shower curtain hanging around it clung to the wall, wet from the last bath. The tub was anchored into the floor and was deep enough to sink into. It was the kind of tub I longed to soak in. The tub in my apartment was shallow and fiberglass, with caulk peeling up under the faucet. I never felt comfortable bathing there—it always seemed there was something floating in the tub with me: grime, scum, and, occasionally, a millipede.

Cara's neighborhood wasn't fantastic but she had made a fine home there, a home where I could seek refuge from the hustle of Manhattan. I imagined days filled with me taking photographs and Cara writing. I filled up the tub with warm water and felt at peace with her choices for the first time.

It was time for our picture bath.

Cara set out an array of fruity soaps and soothing salts for our soak. I brought a handful of flower petals into the bath. I hoped they'd help Cara feel pampered and relax her for a better shot.

She sat behind me in the tub and shampooed my hair, twisting it up into a unicorn horn on the top of my head. I laughed, loud and throaty, and went under, holding my breath. Air bubbled out of my nose. Women aren't allowed to be childish, except for the camera, I thought. Then I got ready for the business of picture making. I said, "Let's get this show on the road." I picked up the cable release and set it beside the tub. Cara was a gifted model: comfortable enough that she gave me what I needed: a gesture contrived just for the camera that conveyed who she was. This was masterwork on her part. "Do what you want," is all I had to tell her. I got ready to pull the trigger. Cara wrapped my hair tight around her palm and yanked back hard.

"I'm ready." Cara wiggled her shoulders up out of the water, exposing her nakedness. She looked at the camera, confessing. "Go." Her eyeliner was ruined. It ran in black streams over her cheeks.

We'd run out of hot water by the time I finished taking our picture. The water went cold, but Cara still enjoyed her soak. I got up to warm our bath with water I'd kettle-boiled on the stove. Cara waited. Her left hand dangled over the porcelain rim of the tub. Her engagement ring caught the light, caused a lens flare.

We have four different kinds of fruit soaps, and milk bath, Epsom salts, pomegranate seed shampoo, apricot scrub, brushes, cloths,

pillows. Sister washes my feet, rubbing at the arches in small cir-
cles with soaped fingers, asking every so often, "Is this okay?"

I sigh. "Yes," floats from my mouth. I put my head back on the
wall of the bath, letting Sister bathe me.

For October, the sun was warm. Light shone down through
crimson leaves as I sat and read in their shade. I wasn't home in
the city where I should have been; I was at my mother's house
in Albany. I felt safe there, far from the downtown streets of
Manhattan, which I'd fled after September 11. I was embar-
rassed to have left my husband and taken time off from grad
school, but I was afraid to go home. To live in a constant state
of worry for my basic safety? I'd done that enough in my life. I
was fortunate that Jedediah was patient. Home could wait.
Jedediah worked Monday through Friday and my plan was to
drive back to the city on Saturday morning and go together to
the farmers' market we so loved to shop. We liked to buy
autumn apples there, careful to pass over the bruised ones in
the barrel. I haggled with the vendor as Jedediah stood by.

We'd come home from the market at sunset and brew a pot
of coffee. I'd open the paper bag filled with fruit and pluck out
one apple at a time, arranging them so the shiniest rolled to the
front of the metal hanging basket.

The sun was warm for October. The girl had just been to see her
therapist and returned weepy and wanting a walk. She was tired
of talking, tired of long, drawn-out conversations about why
her father never really loved her. Talk was getting her nowhere.
Bygones, she thought. I'm a grown woman now.

She was wearing red pants and a black shirt. She walked her
dog on a red leash. Red looked good. The warm wind warned of
autumn. It was warmer than it should have been. There is always
a sign. She didn't need a sweater but she had one. She wore a

sweater of her sister's that she'd borrowed. It was three o'clock. Nobody was expecting her. Her husband wouldn't be home for another hour.

She walked in the park with her dog. She didn't see the man on the park bench, the man who held on to a bottle of liquor he'd covered with a paper bag, the man who wore sunglasses and a hat. She chose the same path every day, one of two—the steeper choice. Her path sloped straight down toward the river and the railroad tracks. The dog moved forward eagerly, faster than the girl could hold her back; the girl wrapped the leash around her wrist, yanked back hard. "Heel," she said, knowing the dog had no use for commands. I'll tire her, the girl thought. She let her dog go off leash, so the dog could run.

It was fair for them both: she and her dog, to walk off the day, to walk off the face of the earth if they wanted to. They descended down into the woods, onto the path darkened by trees, branches, and orange leaves. The leaves had not yet fallen. A hard rain had not stripped them from their branches. She reached the end of the path and turned left, looking behind her at the right path. She picked up a stick and threw it. Her dog ran, caught it, and brought it back. Again she did this, for the satisfaction. She had taught her dog to fetch and return.

"We're good girls," she said to the dog. She threw the stick farther and her dog ran fast after it. She looked down for another stick, then she looked up and saw a man approaching. He had a bigger stick in hand, a thick branch that filled his fist. She smiled hello.

"Come with me," he said, slurring his speech. He was tall and she couldn't see his eyes. Her line of sight was even with his mouth; his teeth and tongue were tobacco stained.

"No, I don't think I'll do that, sir." He couldn't be serious, she thought. Her second thought: I must be polite. Girls are always polite: don't chew with your mouth open; cross your legs; keep two

feet on the floor. Don't talk to strangers. She had broken every rule there was.

She called for her dog to come. She had what she'd adopted from the pound: a dog with some tricks and no training. The dog understood little; she was young and hadn't learned to mind her master.

The man grabbed her arm tight and kicked her at the back of the knee, brought her to the ground and then yanked her back up. She felt her shoulder pop and give. "You're coming with me," he said.

One of her tennis shoes fell off as her feet hung, dragging through the brambles. He pulled her farther into the woods and she watched as her shoe was left behind. They stopped. She could see her shoe from the path as he lay her down. She tried to recall every stray shoe she'd seen strewn on a road, pointing in one direction on a sidewalk, hanging by its laces on a telephone wire, stranded in a ditch. She'd always wondered how and why those shoes had been left without mates. So this was why. She'd imagined strangers walking with one shoe on, but she was dragged, pulled, pushed. She wondered who might find her shoe.

She screamed, she kicked and bit and fought. Wet leaves soaked through her T-shirt. Her elbows were skinned and bleeding, dirty with mud. A branch overhead swayed in the autumn breeze, creaky as a door with a rusty hinge. And all the time she thought: How could this be happening, when so many people died last month in those towers? I'm only one person; if I die here it won't mean anything.

She stopped thinking when he began to hit her.

His fists were a hammer. Her cries were lost to the trees, to the roaring traffic on a nearby street. He covered her mouth and put his hands around her neck. It was rush hour. Nobody would hear her. His blows. It became a dream: slow, terrifying, unending motion. She was the body.

"Don't make me hit you more," he said. She couldn't hear him. She'd lost consciousness. He dragged her farther into the brush.

She tasted blood when she came to and felt him between her thighs, fumbling to pull down her red pants, the pants she'd felt so pretty wearing. "Please don't," she managed quietly.

"You never done this before?"

She reached for her left hand. "Here, take my wedding rings." She thought of her husband, past lovers.

"You think I want to rob you?" The man pushed her rings back onto her finger with such force, her knuckles jammed.

"Please don't kill me," she whispered.

"You think I want to kill you?" The man looked at her as if she were a child who didn't understand a game. "Be good to me." He stroked the side of her face, tender as a lover. "Don't make me hit you again. That's what I ask." His breath was heavy on her neck. He found his way inside her and thrust hard. A sharp pain shot between her hips. He ground his teeth against hers, kissed her face where he'd hit her. He came fast. "I'm sorry, chica. I don't know why I do these things."

She wept and looked into his eyes, meeting his gaze—his eyes were almond shaped and mahogany brown. The pupils themselves were dilated, wide as dimes. Pleasure had brought him farther inside himself: he was both far away and pinning her down. His long black lashes were curly and thick.

"Don't look at my face," he said coldly. He took off the black sweater she wore, her sister's sweater, and put it over her face. She hadn't thought of Sister until just then, and then—it occurred to her: her death would be greater for her living sister than for her. She struggled beneath him. He took the sweater sleeves and tied them behind her head. She couldn't see or breathe. "Can you see me now, bitch?" He was playing with her.

"I can't see you."

He pushed the soft cotton of the sweater into her mouth, gagging her. She breathed through her nose, smelled her sister's sweet perfume. She hadn't yet washed the sweater.

He pulled her up. "Come with me."

And where was her biting dog but still looking for a stick?

"I can't walk. I can't see." Her legs were stiff. He took pity and removed her blindfold.

"Carry me," she said. "You're stronger than me. You're so big."

He dragged her farther down the path, her feet sliding on the ground. She lost her remaining shoe and struggled to keep her pants up. She thought of her body, where he would put it. Who would find her?

He brought her off the path and propped her against a tree. He took and took her. It was late. The sun was setting. She looked up at it—pillows of clouds streaked with bright pinks and oranges.

"You think you can look at my face?" he asked, hitting her.

"I can't see your face."

He took his boxer shorts off and put them over her head. He pulled a length of rope from his pocket and tied it loosely around her neck. "You'll never see me," he said. "I'm nothing."

"But you're everything to me now." She could see his outline through the thin blue-checked cotton of the shorts.

"You're better than my wife," he said. "You're beautiful." He undid the noosed shorts and she tipped her head back in release. "Let me see your body," he said. "Take those off your face. Take off your clothes." She undressed fully for him. The ground was cold. He bit her shoulder and grabbed a fist full of her hair at the nape of her neck, forcing her head to the ground. He had her pinned by the hair, neck arched as far as it could go, chin pointing toward the sky. "I'm sorry I hit you," he said, "but you made me do it."

"I won't make you do it again."

"Will you marry me?"

"I'll think about it," she told him, as if she were actually thinking it over. She'd learned how to skillfully lie over the years, a quality she wasn't proud of. Her knees trembled and her teeth chattered.

He entered her again. "Do you love me?"

Love would make it better, easier. Love is sometimes wrong, she thought, but it is love and love does not maim or kill or hurt. "I'm so cold," she said.

He put her sister's sweater over her tenderly. Time stopped. She was in his hands, he was in her body. She looked up at the trees, their leaves, leaping yellows and reds dancing down to the forest floor. This, she thought, this is what I will take with me if I am taken from here.

"I'll never tell anyone about this if you let me go," she said. "It's getting dark and I think it's about time we both get home."

"How do I know that? Why should I believe you'd keep your big mouth shut?" He took his fingers and pried her mouth open, pushing a few fingers inside. He pressed her tongue until she gagged.

The girl cried, begged. "You have to know it because I'm telling you." She thought of all of the crime shows she'd seen, how police got confessions by playing nice. "I couldn't send you to jail—I don't believe in jail. It's racist and classist."

"Don't let me find you if you're lying, girl." The man pulled up his trousers. "Close your eyes and count to ten. I'll be gone when you're finished."

She counted until she couldn't hear his feet and dressed quickly. She sprinted up the hill, grabbing on to branches to make it to the top. The park was at the top of the hill where hours before she and her dog had played. She called for the dog. This time, she came, dragging her leash. She'd been afraid for the dog the whole time—the dog was confused and could have darted out into traffic. She began to run toward her apartment and crossed the street. A man *campaigning for reelection for the Holyoke town board saw her and moved away in horror.*

"I'm afraid of dogs," he yelled. "Get that thing away from me." He saw a girl with torn red pants and no shoes, her hair wild and wet with blood, her eyes blackened, but the aspiring politician was a coward before all else: he saw her pit bull before he noticed her need.

"She's friendly, please." She told him how to reach her husband. For the first time of many she said the words: "I was raped." The girl fell at his feet. Her dog licked the blood from her face in long slow strokes. The politician called the police and then he called her husband.

The last thing she remembers is her husband running toward her, leaning forward to hold her. "Get the fuck off," she yelled, and then more softly, "I'm evidence." Nothing was ever the same again; she was someone else entirely.

"I was raped," she repeated to her husband, in the same tone someone might say they had pasta for dinner the night before. It was like that, matter of fact, half-faced. She spoke the truth as though it was someone else's.

This is what she learned: There is one road of control, and two choices: take control and kill the body, or live and struggle; ramble in conversations, stop mid-sentence, hide in bathroom stalls and cry. Fear to leave your living room; watch The Accused, *watch* Sybil *and pick a personality. Cut your hair and dye it; waste yourself. Look at the floor, cross your legs, learn to carry flashlights and Mace. Read about yourself in the newspaper. Watch yourself disappear.*

Asked what life was like after her attack, she told everyone she remembered two things. The first was something she said in a phone call she made to an older friend.

"Now," she told her friend, "I know what it feels like to be a woman."

The second thing she remembers occurred the day after. It was five in the morning and the sun was coming up. She sat smoking a cigarette on her rear porch, watching a dump truck empty the receptacles in the back of the building through her one good eye. The other was swollen shut, bruised, bloodshot. She'd been chewing on the good side of her lip, the side not punched into submission, thinking, I've never been so old. She was twenty-four.

She put out her cigarette and called school. She told the receptionist she wouldn't be coming in because she'd been raped. She asked the receptionist if she'd need a doctor's note to confirm. She didn't wait for an answer; she hung up.

Before the rape everything was the same. It was autumn and some of the leaves were still green. She had just started graduate school. She had a sister and a mother. She weighed 125 pounds. Her hair was longish and dark. She walked her dog alone every day after class. She loved the woods and climbed its trees. She sang too loudly to the car radio. She liked to eat strawberry squares and she wanted to be a writer.

Chapter 5

We played airplane with Mike. He was strong enough that when he swung us around he could hold one of us in each of his hands; our four arms and legs glided through the air. Our two screams of glee shot out down the hallway.

Mom started dating Mike soon after we moved from Dad's house. She fell in love with him quickly and fully. Mike was a marine; he'd just finished boot camp. He was a bodybuilder in his spare time and liked to make health shakes in our kitchen: wheat germ, peanut butter, and vitamin powder. He stood over six feet tall and muscles bulged in his arms. His hair was shaved into a Mohawk; he flexed his arms in our hallway mirror, then pulled the hawk into tufts that stood straight up.

Mike let us wrestle in the house and gave us candy. Dad didn't come to bother Mom when Mike was over, so Mike stayed often. But he played less with us the longer their courtship continued, and he grew stern.

At a dinner of cube steak and shelled peas, I flung a spoon of food at Mike. I watched the peas roll down his face and smiled in pride of my aim. "Gotcha!" I said.

"Children should be seen and not heard," Mike said and picked up my plate. He placed the remainder of my dinner in the living room. "You'll eat here until you learn to eat like an adult."

We weren't allowed to talk at dinner unless asked a question, and we weren't allowed to speak a word on car rides. Our voices distracted Mike from driving. If we made a peep at dinner or on a drive, he'd shake his finger and say, "Children shouldn't speak unless spoken to."

On one of the rare mornings when Mike wasn't home, as we ate our breakfast, Mom asked Cara and me, "So what do you think of him?"

"He's pretty okay," Cara said.

My eyes said, I hate everything. Mike included.

We listen to the "Stray Cat Strut" with Dad on his weekends. We eat chocolate for breakfast and watch Dad play with his food. He spits out mashed potatoes, making a worm on his plate. He takes two peas and makes eyes for the potato worm. We laugh. The worm is watching us. Dad tells us how fun it is to be with him.

Dad dials Mom on the telephone

"Tell her how much you love me," he says.

"Mom, I love Dad." I am wearing his white undershirt.

"Tell her how much better it is here."

"Mom—"

"Tell her."

"Mom, it's good here. See you on Sunday." I hang up fast.

Mom says Dad will take us away from her. Dad says he will put cement shoes on Mom and throw her in the lake. Dad says if we say a word, he'll burn us all while we sleep.

Until we were five, we were at Dad's every other weekend; he liked it when we played games outdoors, so it looked from the outside like he was a perfect father. He cared what the neighbors thought even though he said they couldn't be trusted. Look at the ground, he'd say. Don't look the lady across the street in the eyes; she might think you want something.

When he and Mom divorced, he kept all of our video games and everything else that was fun. The joysticks for our game console sat on his floor. The wires got tangled. I liked to play the game where I got to be a frog and jump across the highway, on the tops of car roofs. One wrong move and you'd get splatted; game over. All of our toys, storybooks, and most of our clothes were at Dad's house. He'd kept Mom's baby pictures and her entire wardrobe; he'd taken her clothes from her closet and tossed them into a big heap in the basement, next to the washer and dryer. Some of her things he left out on the curb in the rain, for the garbage collectors to pick up.

We drove to Mom's with the radio turned up loud. Dad flipped the station off when we pulled into Mom's driveway. "Tell me what I want to hear, girls," Dad said. "Remember what I told you about your mother."

Every weekend we said the same thing before we got out of the car and went inside with our mother. "Mom is a witch. Mom should die. Mom is an evil bitch."

Dad had a swimming pool. He taught us how to swim by pushing us into his pool, one after the other. He said we'd have to learn how to swim for our upcoming vacation to Florida. The pool was a big, above-the-ground model that Dad put up at the side of his yard. He carried us, a twin on each of his hips, up the stairs of the wooden deck, to the poolside. We stood together and looked down at the deep water.

"Close your eyes, girls," he said, putting one of each of our hands in each of his. He pulled them up from our sides and asked us to cover our eyes. "Don't peek."

He pushed us in.

The air whooshed through our hair and we landed.

We were on our way to Florida.

Dad likes to comb our hair. Our hair is long and brown, hangs to our waists. He starts out softly with a brush, then works his way through until his fingers tickle the tops of our heads.

"Stop it," I say. Sister is crying. "She doesn't like that. You're hurting our heads."

"You sound just like your mother," he says, as mean as the meanest kids on the playground. "You look like her, too, with all that hair."

Dad has an idea.

"Did you know there is a place where it's summer all year?" he asks. "Don't tell your Mom. It's a secret." I know we will keep his secret. It isn't a lie if it's really summer all year someplace.

"It's hot there," Dad says. "You'll need to get your hair cut to stay cool."

Dad takes us to his barber. I like to watch the barber's pole, the spinning red and white. Christa and I sit in the chairs. Our eyes spin around with the pole. Men sit and get their haircuts. All of the shop's seats are full. The men sitting next to us talk about boxing and the new Rocky *movie.*

"It's just not realistic. But he's some actor," one man says. The rest nod, put their hands in their laps. They lose more hair.

The barber gets close to my face and talks loud. "Are you next, pretty girl?" Dad pushes me forward.

"I never saw Rocky." *That's all I could say.*

"Such pretty, pretty hair" the barber says. When he's done cutting, there's none left.

Sister is next. The barber cuts her hair shorter than he cuts mine. Sister cries harder with each snip of his scissors.

"You look like Dorothy Hamill," Dad says. "Don't cry, sweetie. She's a real sex pot."

We don't know Dorothy Hamill but we know Dorothy and her yellow brick road. We know her braids.

Dad buys us balloons shaped like Mickey Mouse heads.

"Don't tell you mother about the place where it's summer all of the time."

"Okay."

"Say it."

We said what we were supposed to.

But instead of dropping us off and driving away, like he usually did, Dad walked us to Mom's front porch. Mom answered the door and Dad stood back. He hid.

Mom was quiet for a minute, then her eyes grew huge. "Oh my God, my girls." Mom covered her mouth with one of her hands. "Ladies?" She scooped us up and slammed the door. We heard Dad laughing on the other side. Our balloons flew away.

She ran her fingers through our short hair. "It will grow back, honey. I promise," she said to neither of us. Mom paced the kitchen. I remember having the feeling that this wasn't like the time Cara cut the hair on my Barbie doll. Mom told her then that she'd have to apologize and save up her allowance and buy me a new doll. "Barbie's hair is permanent," Mom said. "It never changes."

"We look like Dorothy Hamill, Mom," Cara said.

Dad said he has a surprise. I tried to tell Mom. "We are going to a place where it is never winter."

I'm not sure what Mom would have done had she not married our father; I've asked her many times and she always says the same thing. "I love you girls, and once you were born I stopped wanting for myself."

"You couldn't have given up on yourself by twenty-three," I tell her, certain.

But she might have.

It seems to me that the difficult thing in life is to find what stirs you and move toward it. Mom put us first but also put us in the way of whatever moved her and, so, avoided the anxiety of the unknown, the fear of failure, the pain of opening up her heart and feeling her losses. Her selflessness was also her selfishness. But Mom told us that we were smart, funny, beautiful. "Capable young women," she called us, pushing us onward and out, fighting her desire to keep us home, though there was no question that should hard times come, home was the place to return to.

We are in the car to Florida: the drive to the summer place is long. We keep asking, "Are we there yet?" Dad says we are as close to there as we'll ever be.

We sing to the radio and drink orange juice.

When we get to the place where it is always summer, the sign says, WELCOME TO FLORIDA.

It's hot. I wonder how far away from home we are.

Dad says we can't call Mom and that we are the luckiest girls alive because tomorrow we are going to see Mickey Mouse. "That's right, girlies, Mr. Mouse himself."

"I miss Mom," I say.

Dad ignores me like he does when I repeat a bad word.

We check into a hotel and Sister and I get to share a bed. We fall right to sleep. Dad watches us and smokes a cigarette. He keeps the phone off the hook in the hotel room.

Disney World is better than on television. We eat cotton candy and ride Space Mountain. We go to the Hall of Presidents.

We watch fireworks and eat dinner in Cinderella's castle. We stop thinking about Mom.

One day Dad packs our bags and says we can't go back to see Mickey. He mumbled something about the police and Mom. I remember Mom. I feel sorry that I forgot her.

We drive home.

WELCOME TO NEW YORK, a sign says. It's warm here, too. It was June when we left and now it's July.

There is a truck in Mom's driveway and men are putting our things in it. Mom kisses us and hugs us hard. Mike comes out of the house. He has a fresh crew cut.

"Honey." Mom is looking at both of us. "We got married. Mike is your dad now. We are moving far away."

We look at our old dad in his car and wave at him. We are too young to know we won't see him again.

While we were away in Florida Mom had married Mike, in a small ceremony in her sister's backyard. In the photographs, Mom wears a white spaghetti strap sundress with tiny pink and purple flowers. She was tanned and tiny, had a modest bouquet; Mike smashed wedding cake in her face; she smashed it in his.

"My mom had a way with men," I liked to say, years later, raising a single eyebrow. "She ran as fast as she could toward the most obvious jackass in the room and then she married him in a hurry."

In place of a honeymoon beach vacation, Mom wrapped our dishes up in newspaper, gave our cat Randy to a new home, loaded the U-Haul cargo trailer, and prepared for a new life at Camp Lejeune. She waited for our father to bring us back from our trip, and when he did she packed us into the car, our belongings in tow; we sped down the highway, the furniture and dishes and toys bouncing about. She took us out of state and away from Dad. She sat in the front passenger seat with her feet up against the dashboard. What life would her girls lead if she didn't take them away?

Dad had thought we were moving in with our aunt to save money. He came for his scheduled visit with us the following week, our sixth birthday. When I was in my twenties and briefly in touch with him, he told me about this day, the worst of his life. He'd planned our celebration by buying us each our own ice cream cake and a cluster of festive helium balloons. He'd covered his dining room table with gifts wrapped in shiny pink paper, topped with bows. For weeks he'd left the gifts and party favors just as he'd arranged them, unable to bring himself to clean up after the party that was never to be and the relationship with us he'd never have.

But in the car to North Carolina Mom was doing something I hadn't seen in years; she was smiling.

Chapter 6

Mom said the trip to Camp Lejeune would take sixteen hours. We stayed quiet in the backseat. Mike stared out the windshield at the road and said we were making good time.

The route was all road and stars, turn signals and crickets. Before long the toll collectors' accents changed. Southern summers are too hot for travel in a compact car. The leather interior clung to our thighs. I tried to stretch my legs. Mike turned to the backseat. "You're getting too close to me," he scolded. My knee poked him through the seat, that's how far he'd pushed it back.

I tried to stay far away and small. When we stopped for breaks, we switched sides. Cara got the seat behind Mike. Being stuck behind him was like going to jail, but not for long. Mom said he had the bladder of a five-year-old and she was right. We'd learn to hold it: there was never enough time to make it to the bathroom and back if I wanted the seat behind Mom. The rule was to alternate, but neither of us was beyond stealing for legroom.

"We are a military family," Mike said like he was telling a bedtime story. "What that means is we don't talk much about ourselves. Everything we do is for the whole family. We are not individuals anymore. We are a four-part machine and I want it well oiled."

Our birthday was soon. I thought six might be a lucky number. I thought of Grandpa singing, "When I was seventeen, it was a very good year," and whistling the tune. Maybe for him seventeen was a good year. There was a war he told us that he fought in. It must have happened to him after seventeen. He said he had a very good year when we were born, but he didn't sing about it.

"Do you think we will both get very good years?" I asked Cara quietly.

"I don't know what you are talking about," she said.

"You know, Grandpa and his song about being seventeen and having a very good year?"

"It's just a song." Cara stared out the window like she was looking for someone.

"But it could be true, couldn't it?" My mind started to race. "And what if we have to share one good year like we share a birthday cake?"

"You miss home?" she finally said to the window, but she wouldn't look at me. "I do," she said without letting me answer. "But don't tell."

Mike said we would have to move a lot for the Corps. "That means you will have to leave behind your schools and all the friends you meet just like we marines leave our families."

Mom looked upset. "Enough, honey," she whispered. "They have been through enough today."

She looked over her shoulder at us in the backseat. "Girls," her voice dropped very low. "One thing you need to know is that wherever we are living is an extra special secret. Don't tell Grandpa. You will be able to see him sometimes but you can never tell him where your home is. Grandma can know and everyone else in the family can know, but not Grandpa, okay?"

"Isn't that lying?" I tried to pull my leg off the seat but the vinyl held on like a Band-Aid.

"What about Dad?" Cara asked.

"He's the reason Grandpa can't know. He'll tell your dad. I can't risk having him take you away," Mom told us.

"If Dad can't know where we live, how will he be able to take us out for ice cream?"

"You have a new dad now," Mom said, "and we all live together. As for lying, well, sometimes you have to do it. Period. That doesn't make it right. It just makes it the way it is."

Cara started crying right off.

"I know, honey, it's going to be hard, but Mommy knows you can do this for her because you love her so much." Mom reached into the backseat and put her fingers through Cara's hair until she stopped. "And Mommy loves you. That's why she is asking you to do this for her, okay?"

From the moment we'd taken off with the U-Haul that morning, I knew how different things were going to be.

"I don't think this is going to be a very good year," I said to Cara.

"Yeah," she answered.

"You should be sleeping, ladies," Mom said.

How could we sleep with Mike's music on? He sang "Leader of the Pack" and honked the horn when the motorcycle crashed at the end. He played his tape over and over.

Cara rested her head on my shoulder and eventually slept; I pressed my cheek against the window glass until I started to dream. The words to the music drifted inside me. I dreamed of Grandma Josephine. I dreamed of her big pink bed.

Both of our grandmothers were Josephines: Josephine Vivian and Josephine Marie. I often wished Josephine were my own name. With it I would have possessed the sass and determination and grace it implied. *Life would be easier as a Josephine,* I wrote in my high school diary. Cara and I both liked the name Josephine should either of us ever have a daughter.

Grandma Josephine Vivian was Irish, round, and red-headed. Cara and I spent lucky hours of our childhood in her kitchen eating bland chicken and potatoes. Grandma loved us with ferocity, anticipating our every need and our every breath. She did this in the place of her son, whom she never forgave for not doing it himself.

We played games of pool with her and Grandpa in their basement rec room, dancing around the table to Top Forty radio, scratching cue balls. She bought us pretty matching dresses in pink and blue. Our first trip to the ocean was with her. We went to Maine to a tiny rented cabin on the lower eastern tip of the state. There are photographs from the trip. Grandma is holding each of us in the waves. Cara hangs in a turquoise bathing suit with ruffles from one of Grandma's proud arms, smashing the waves with her chest, all smiles, sticky saltwater hair caught in her mouth. I'm propelling from Grandma's other arm, up to my waist in water. I'm more timid than Cara, and Grandma swishes me through the tide, my tiny feet kicking up sand.

Josephine Marie was my mother's mother: Italian, olive skinned, and stout. She dutifully did her job as a home chef after she was widowed, caring for her five children without help or complaint. She died when my mother was only twenty-one, a year before we were born. To us, Josephine Marie was only another face of the past on the wall of pictures that hung in my mother's living room. Straight regal chin, knitted white sweater, wire specs that slid to the end of her nose; she smiled for the camera like a Mona Lisa. What did she know and take with her besides her recipes?

Cara and I fought over the name Josephine like kids fight for the last piece of candy.

We fought over the name long after we were kids.

"When I have a daughter I'll name her Josephine," Cara told me matter-of-factly as we sat at her kitchen table sealing invitations to her wedding.

"I love that name, too," I said, licking a gluey flap. "I'd always thought I would name my daughter Josephine."

"I guess you were wrong," she said and straightened the messy pile of cards before her.

"What if you only have sons?"

"Then I have sons," she smiled tensely. "But you still can't have the name."

"Why?"

"I would find that too upsetting," she said as if that made a bit of sense.

"You do realize how ridiculous you sound?"

"I guess so," she said, retreating. "I just can't imagine it any other way."

At last, we decided the eldest should have first dibs. Cara had first right. She said that if I had a girl child before her, I'd better not take the name.

"The world doesn't stop for you," I heard Mike say once. But it does in a way; it stops. Your old world stops for you when you aren't there.

Did Grandma put her plastic curlers in her hair that morning? Or, was the dog next door still barking.

"We are almost there," Mom said when she saw that we were both awake. Her eyes were tired. Only Mike knew where we were headed. He'd picked our trailer out months before. He said it had a swimming pool and there were lots of other kids to play with. I saw Mike tickle Mom's knee under the dash and I kicked Sister. "Gross," I mouthed.

"Stop it!" she yelled and pulled away.

"*Do you want a crack?*" Mike raised his voice. *His neck got big when he ate and when he yelled. A thick line lumped up and down when he bit down to chew things up. I thought: he wants to chew us up. A crack sounded like a new kind of candy bar to me, like a Whatchamacallit. Sister's eyes got wide. I saw mine get wide in hers. Her face was my mirror.*

We didn't know what a crack was. But soon we'd know, not because we got them, because we never did, but because a crack was so often offered.

"*Honey, really,*" Mom said quickly.

"*Sorry,*" he said to both of us.

"*I don't hit my children,*" she said. "*I will be damned if anyone else will.*" Mom stared at Mike across the car. I guessed Mom knew what a crack was. "*Honey, I was just saying,*" Mom apologized.

"*Let's not talk,*" Mike interrupted, and the rest of the drive was quiet.

The South is full of swaying pine trees and buzzing cicadas. To my ears it sounded like a jungle of fast-ticking clocks and TV static. Every house in the Pines was actually a parked trailer, metal siding covering the wheels beneath. This was temporary housing until Mike earned a house on base. Our trailer was mostly dirty white with dark brown trim at the roof and a little bit of orange on the sides. It was striped like a racecar and doublewide. There were cinder blocks stacked up as front steps.

We all waited on the top step as Mike tried to unlock the door. The knob stuck, so he karate kicked it open. It was dark inside even though it was sunny outside. I noticed the windows rolled out with a crank instead of up with a push. When Mom turned the lights on, big black bugs ran for the corners to hide. "There are bugs the size of my hand crawling up the walls," Mom screamed.

Mike made a phone call. "We want them gone now," he said.

He really meant us, I thought. I looked outside. I didn't want to be a pest. I'd heard about homes for girls with no parents or parents who didn't want them. I'd seen *Annie*. I'm not going to one of those places, I thought. I'm no redheaded stepchild.

Our mother left our father, and then our stepfather's career uprooted us. When we were children, Cara and I moved constantly. We were girls who felt on the outside of things, on the edge of each community. Was it too painful to integrate only to leave again? Whatever the reason, we never fit in. Identical twins have a difficult time adapting even in normal situations— they are curiosities to their peers; they are freaks.

"Does it hurt Cara if I do this to you?" a kid at school asked once, pulling my hair.

"Fuck you," I said back.

It was because it was partly true that I answered that way; not because the hair pulling was painful, but because our bodies were each other's property. When she suffered, I suffered.

"Does it hurt you if I do this?" I hit him, and split the skin of his lip.

My sister, my twin, we fought like alley cats and then walked down the street together, wherever it was we were living, holding hands. We tangled each other's hair, bloodied each other's noses, bit and scratched each other. We knew who we were: We were best friends. We were enemies. We were all we had.

MARCH 3, 1989

Dear Diary,

Today my stepdad tried to kill a spider with a can of my hairspray. I was sitting on the toilet and it was behind me on the wall,

all hairy and disgusting. It was the most humongous thing I have ever seen. It made me scream, loud, loud, loud, and we didn't have any toilet paper, either. So my stepdad walked into the bathroom, all asking what was going on. I just had time to pull up my pants and drip dry before he saw the spider and screamed like a girl!

MARCH 5, 1989

Dear Diary,

Today was the best day ever!!! Me and my sister and Misty took a cab to a bar. We did it while Mom was out. My stepdad was at work and the neighbors were at bible school. We wore black sweat suits out of the house and did our hair in the car, teased it with our fingers. Finger test! Hair has to be as high as the middle finger on Misty's hand. She is the biggest of the three of us, fat, with a witch's nose. I hate Misty. She wears all black all the time and dresses like a fat ho bag. At least my sister and I are skinny. We look good with our hair and in our clothes. Anyway, don't tell, okay? God, if anyone reads this I am dead meat, but who else am I going to tell? Anyway, we went to this bar to meet this band and we changed into our miniskirts and band T-shirts in the cab. I actually saw the cabdriver look at us in his mirror!! How gross is that? I mean we are only twelve. Anyway, so we went to meet this band and I flashed the drummer on a dare. He took my picture and hugged me. . . .

JULY 1, 1989

Dear Diary,

Tomorrow my sister and I are going to fly to New York for the summer to visit Grandma. Grandpa used to say flying is dangerous and that you have to be careful not to die. He used to say he would

*never get on an airplane and didn't. I wonder what he would say
now? I hate flying, too, but I pretend not to be scared. Grandma
needs us to visit now that Grandpa isn't here anymore. But my sister
and I made a pact that if we do die on the plane, everyone will know
that we love heavy metal. We are going to wear our Mötley Crüe
T-shirts on the airplane in case it crashes so when they find our bodies, everyone will know we were fans and maybe the band will write
a song about the girls who loved them so much they would die with
band T-shirts on. . . .*

R.I.P.,
ME

AUGUST 7, 1989

Dear Diary,

  *Life sucks. I am so grounded. Mom found you while I was gone
and read about the bar. My sister and I put black lines with a
Sharpie on white T-shirts and wrote* INMATE *on them. We are like
prisoners so we figured we should dress like them. Mom says we are
going to be grounded for at least a month. I feel like dying. She is
such a bitch.*

AUGUST 20, 1989

Dear Diary,

  *Mom and my stepdad have been yelling at each other a lot
because he says she is never at home. My stepdad is a jerk. I hate
him. He is always pinching Mom's butt and calling my sister and
me fat. He should be nice to Mom. She does everything for him but
wipe his ass and for all I know she does that, too. Mom went back to
college this month to get her degree. She said she is tired of waiting
tables. I don't think I'll ever go to college. I don't think you need a
degree to be a rock star. Mom looks tired all the time.*

AUGUST 28, 1989

Dear Diary,

School started yesterday. One of my teacher's names is Bunny. What kind of name is that? One of her legs is shorter than the other and she likes to pull herself up on two desks and swing back and forth in the aisle. She wears weird shoes. She is pretty okay but the rest of my teachers are idiots. By the way, I am still grounded. I took off my prison shirt for school and wore my Warrant shirt instead. I don't want the whole world to know I am an inmate. One day I'll get out of here.

SEPTEMBER 12, 1989

Dear Diary,

My sister and I saw my mom kissing one of her teachers at the beach so we spit in his shoes and took a walk in the other direction. I am never going to tell Mom that I saw that. I think she feels guilty, though, because she gave us extra money to buy French fries and ice cream at the pier. We usually aren't allowed to eat crap.

MAY 1, 1990

Dear Diary,

Mom says our stepdad is leaving home for a little while and that we are moving back to New York, after she finishes college. She says the three of us can live with Grandma until she can save up enough money to buy a house. Mom didn't say if our stepdad is going to live with Grandma, too. I hope not. I say don't let the door hit him on the ass on the way out. He is not my real dad anyway. Mom has been crying a lot, especially to really bad love songs on the radio. We are not grounded anymore. Mom says she doesn't have time right now to keep us out of trouble. If you ask me, no man is worth crying *over, especially not a big Marine who walks out on his wife and kids and screams like a girl over something as small as a spider.*

Mike left our family on a North Carolina high summer afternoon. He wanted no more of the Marines, either, and didn't reenlist; his plan was to move back to upstate New York to be nearer to family. He packed his clothes and his extensive collection of cassette tapes and paperback mystery novels into a car top carrier attached to his tan Nissan Sentra and pulled away. Cara and I did a dance in the driveway as his car crested a right toward the highway and out of our neighborhood. Mom wept on the living room sofa in a room full of boxes. He'd wanted nothing in the divorce but out.

"Good riddance to your Ben-Gay-smelling bathrobe and beer burps," Cara yelled at his fading taillights.

Chapter 7

We only pretended to be each other once.

We were in seventh grade and had just moved back to Albany. We invited our boyfriends over for the evening to watch television. The room was lit by the glow of low-wattage lightbulbs and the ambient gleam of a game show. The boys ignored us and dipped their hands into the large plastic bowl of popcorn between them. Cara and I got up and went into the kitchen.

"These guys are lame," she said. "Let's teach them a lesson." Cara pulled her shirt over her head and passed it to me. I did the same. We wore matching jeans and brown oxfords.

"Let me fix your hair," I whispered, my heart beating hard in my chest. "Can we really do this?" I asked, a flutter of remorse caught in my throat.

"Give me one reason we shouldn't."

"It's wrong," I said and pulled the band from my own hair and tied hers into a tight ponytail on top of her head.

"Don't be so serious," Cara scolded. "It's all in good fun." She fluffed my bangs with her fingers and smoothed my fly-aways. She patted my cheek and pulled me toward the living room. We walked in together, coy, our hands in our pockets.

I sat down next to Cara's boyfriend and waited. A quiz show began at the top of the hour. We all shouted answers. Her boyfriend yawned and stretched, placing his arm over my shoulder. Cara looked at me, hot with jealousy. "I'm so sorry," I mouthed to her, hoping her boyfriend could spot a decoy.

But then my boyfriend put his hand on Cara's leg, above the knee. She picked it up and moved it to the inside of her thigh. I glared at her and she smirked back at me. I tipped my head against Cara's boyfriend's forehead and kissed him with my tongue. I hoped Mom wouldn't catch us.

Cara stood up and grabbed my hand, pulled me up off the sofa, and twisted my fingers back against my wrist until I cried out in pain. Our boyfriends looked worried. "You're dumped," she said to her boyfriend, "for kissing my sister." Cara undid her hair from the style I'd made for her and shook her long locks over her shoulders, dramatically exposing her true identity.

Our boyfriends sat stunned. The blinking blue screen of the television flickered on their faces.

"Whatever," one of our boyfriends said to the other. He got up to leave. "They're the same chick anyway."

Identical twins are not exactly alike. They begin in the womb, at conception, with a single egg and sperm. Twins are made after the egg is fertilized and splits. Similarity is a result of how long the egg takes to divide. The longer it takes for the egg to split, the more alike a set of twins will look. We must have split early. My feet and nose were larger than Cara's. As adults she usually outweighed me by fifteen pounds. Identical twins share the same DNA but do not have identical DNA. The egg splits into two halves to form identical twins, but the DNA does not divide equally between the two cells. We were like an apple sliced in half: two halves of the same fruit, one with more seeds, one with fewer.

We constantly teased each other for our differences. She called me "Big Foot" and "Horn Nose." I called her "Piggy."

Cara bought me a present the summer before I was married: two pairs of shoes. Converse All Stars: one pair black, one pair red. She'd picked them up for me because they were priced to move, at a 60 percent discount. Cara, like all the women in our family, couldn't pass up a sale. She bought the shoes in a women's size 9; I wore a size 8. Cara wore a size 7. She'd razzed me throughout our childhood about my "Bozo" feet, my "flippers." In her loving gift, she revealed her opinion of my feet— they were huge. My feet were the one feature I possessed that made me less dainty than she. Cara cherished them. She was more than happy to dress my boat feet; the shoes were her thank-you for my being imperfect.

Cara couldn't resist the shoes. She stole the black pair from my closet even though they were two sizes too large. She was raped in those shoes, and in a sweater of mine she stole; the shoes were lost in the forest, sliding off her feet as she was dragged. The police kept them as evidence. She should have laced them tighter.

As children, I picked on Cara for her weight even though we were both undersized for our age. I remember sliding next to her on the floor one night when we were ten years old, preparing to watch a movie after dinner. Mom had spread out a blanket for us; she'd set out two bowls of ice cream: one for each of us. We lay down hip to hip, our small bodies too close; I wanted more room. I thought of the low-fat bacon commercial that played constantly on TV, and repeated the slogan. "Slide over, bacon. Make room for something leaner." I pinched at the tiniest roll of fat on Cara's upper arm. She looked at me and blinked sadly, moving over slowly, like a cow resigned to a prod. She scooched several inches to the right and stayed there. Years of dieting spoke for her from then on. She wasn't alone in this: I had the bump in my nose filed and the bones on the bridge straightened while we were in high school. I gave the surgeon Cara's senior portrait to show how I wanted it.

Starting in sixth grade, Cara was the prettier one. Yes, we were twins: we looked alike, but Cara had the kind of attractive sass that helped her pull off her imperfections.

I was bony, big-nosed, bucktoothed, and pimply. I had legs long enough that the boys called me frog, and my bulging, dark-circled, terrified eyes confirmed that the boys were right.

Cara's nose was the perfect ski jump; her slender wrists were ringed with friendship bracelets. She'd filled her bra at eleven, stolen her first kiss at twelve, and in sixth grade she was voted Queen of the Dance—an honor akin to prom queen for the prepubescent nominees. On the sixth-grade dance floor my sister had the right moves and the attention of all of the boys. I stood on the sidelines, manning the punch bowl and handing out ballots for the sixth-grade presidential election, my name in bold letters at the top of the list of candidates.

When Cara won her crown, I helped her pin it into her hair. The gymnasium had been transformed into a disco, complete with a glittery turning ball. I was careful to set the tiara straight on her head and arrange it just so. I wrapped my arms around her shoulders. "I'm proud of you," I yelled over the booming music.

"What?" she mouthed and pointed to a blasting speaker. "I can't hear you."

I pushed her out onto the dance floor to meet her king.

She was always ahead of me: born, lived, died.

Chapter 8

One weekend when I was in high school, I woke at noon to find my mother—who stands no taller than five feet two inches and weighs no more than 105 pounds—in the backyard wielding a chain saw, slaying a tree. Her long black hair fell away from her slender face at the nape of her neck and curled in a shiny S all the way to her waist. She blasted through the tree's bark, a hacksaw dangling from her belt. Wood chips flew at her arms and face, fell at her feet, or were caught in the web of her mane. "Timber!" she shouted to the neighborhood. The tree snapped loudly against the earth. Tools and machinery were scattered around the lawn. Her smile was wide enough to be visible beneath her paper face mask.

Mom spent years learning how to build furniture and refinish floors and coffee tables. The grass was hers to mow. She cleared the snow-covered driveway with a push plow. Earning a living could be easily done: she took two jobs. Cara and I pitched in, but Mom took on the brunt of the housework. And she endeavored to be upbeat, as if to say, "Look how easy it is. It's okay that your father is no good and your stepfather left us."

When Mike left, Mom had yet to finish her degree program in laboratory technology at Coastal Carolina Community College, so for that summer we rented a modest house just off the base. She traded in her long hours as a waitress at the Officers' Club at Camp Lejeune for longer hours hunched over science equipment: pipettes, syringes, circular petri dishes with shiny bloodred bottoms. She brought her schoolwork home. Petri dishes sat stacked like candies in our refrigerator beside the butter and milk. She'd swab our sore throats and incubate the bacteria, in steamy showers and on top of warm radiators.

It didn't take her long to find a position in Albany after graduation, and her new degree brought a better life for us.

Mom tried to be both mother and father. We celebrated our mother on Father's Day. We dutifully gave her drills and screws, barbeque grills and tanks of fuel—and overlooked the enormous pain of our father's absence. If we expressed to Mom the sadness of our loss, she was hurt. She took our sorrow as slight.

Cara and I both had teachers in high school who took notice of our abilities in English and the arts and tried their best to foster the feeling that anything was possible. It didn't matter to them that we'd grown up in a single-parent home without enough money to buy books. It was clear we both loved reading. It had been that way since we lived in North Carolina and Mom made sure we went to the bookmobile every week. The bookmobile was Camp Lejeune's traveling library, a cross between an ice cream truck, an RV, and an armored vehicle, full of musty books with dog-eared pages. It came to Tarawa Terrace, our neighborhood on the base, once a week, curbside at 3 p.m. on the dot. Like everything marine, it was never late or absent. Books were not to be overdue, or a demerit for the marine, our stepfather, would be issued. But we read promptly out of love as much as out of fear. Cara and I raced to finish, so we could discuss our discoveries before having to slide the book into the abyss of the return bin, which was located directly beside the van's fuel door.

Cara wrote as avidly as she read. She won a state-sponsored contest in second grade with a short story about a girl who abandons her family to move into a hot air balloon. The girl floats above her small town for weeks and subsists on a stolen picnic basket filled with pies and cakes. Eventually the weather turns from fair to lightning and the girl falls ill with motion sickness, vomiting on the roofs of her neighbors' houses. After Cara's win, Mom set her hopes on Cara becoming a writer. Mom thought maybe I'd be an actress.

Ronald Milligan was the teacher who changed the course of my life. An ex-hippie with long white hair receding at the crown who taught in blue jeans and T-shirts, he was rumored to smoke weed and attend anarchist meetings; he was never afraid to swear in class or frown at football players. He'd ridden his bicycle across the country and back twice, raised a daughter who was a war reporter for CNN, and married and loved another English teacher at our school, Mrs. Legge, whose graying blond hair hung nearly to her knees. She was stern and big-eyed, his perfect opposite.

Ron Milligan was the hero I'd been waiting for.

He insisted that his students call him Ron. He taught me about Wounded Knee and Emma Goldman, kept me reading Steinbeck and Faulkner and attended to my class journal as if it were the greatest literature he'd read. I wrote three times as many pages as were required and turned them in every two weeks for comment. I went from writing about symbols and plot to exploring my relationship with my father and my seemingly bottomless fears.

When college application time rolled around, Ron helped me prepare the list of choices for the meeting with Mrs. Fairbank, the guidance counselor.

My mother went along with me and Cara to our meeting with Mrs. Fairbank, who welcomed us in and pulled out the list of colleges she had compiled, reading out the names of the more selective state schools that she had calculated were in our budget.

I had other ideas.

"By my calculations," I told her, "we can afford Smith or Vassar or Bard." I pulled the list from my purse. I showed her that all of these schools offered aid for less-well-off students. Ron had even helped prepare pie charts. "Given that we'll both attend at the same time, we'll certainly be given scholarships. It will cost less than state school."

Mom looked at my figures and ran her tongue over her teeth. She always does this while she considers something important. "I was thinking more along the lines of community college," Mom said, "Like I did. It makes good sense."

I gasped dramatically, as only a teenager not getting her way can. "We're not like you," I said. I looked over at Cara and she nodded in agreement.

"We need you to get the most bang for your buck," Mom said matter-of-factly.

"Bang for your buck?" I repeated, certain that other Bard College parents would never refer to financing their children's education that way. I imagined Mom sporting jeans and tennis shoes while trying to mingle with parents who wore tweed blazers with leather elbow patches. I knew we were in for a long battle. I also knew that once we toured the campus and received award letters Mom would be swayed, and I was right. By the time we'd begun preparing to go off to school, Mom had studied our course catalogues and picked out all of the classes that she would have enrolled in had she had our opportunity at eighteen.

Ron was the first person I called when we were accepted to Bard through the early decision process.

I was to study poetry and Cara fiction. Unlike my friends'

parents, Mom had no worries about our major. We were the first in our family to attend a four-year college. A degree is a degree and therefore, my mother reasoned, good. She assured us that if we followed our passions we'd be fine.

Ron pulled me aside on our final day of class. He told me that someday not too far from then, he expected to come into a bookstore and find the first volumes of my sister's and my memoirs sitting side by side on the front sales table. I promised that someday he would find that.

We decorated our first-year college dorm room like our mother's house.

"The rug is a soft place to rest your studious feet," Mom said as she removed the price tag and hoisted it into our small moving truck. It fell with a thud beside the Tupperware under-bed storage units. "You can never have too many shoes," she said, "so I found you an extra place to put some." She liked to playfully nettle us about our teenage vanities. "Big hair. Big star," she'd say. And it felt like her way of letting me know that no matter how high I teased and sprayed my hair, I was still her girl.

Before we left for college she took on the task of building for us trinket boxes, shelving, and, in her most clever feat, what she refers to as "Atta girls." These are pencil holders cut from blocks as high and thick as bricks, from identical pieces of sunny blond pine, and finished in a slick shiny glaze: Mom cut and sanded the wood herself, shellacked it with polyurethane, drilled five holes in the tops, and completed them with a handmade carving with her Dremel. She engraved each with our name and a tender joke: Writer's Block. As we set up our room at Bard, Mom filled each Writer's Block with pens and set it on the appropriate desk.

Mom has Cara's now. It sits beside her computer alongside several pictures of Cara. In one, Cara stands in a piazza in Venice, laughing, her arms out at her sides like a child playing airplane, pigeons flying away from her open hands full of bird feed. I still have my Writer's Block. It sits on top of Cara's desk, which I inherited and where I work. I fill it not with pens but with fresh daises, lavender, and the dried rose I took from an arrangement at my sister's funeral.

Cara and I played Tracy Chapman while we unpacked at Bard, singing along. We arranged the room so our beds were against each outer wall, our desks pushed against the footboards. Cara interspersed her newly bought books for freshman seminar with the picture books our mother had read to us as children: *Snow White* beside the *Tao Te Ching*, *Cinderella* beside *The Odyssey*. I had made certain that our wall posters were framed and Cara tapped each picture-hanging nail into the wall delicately so as not to disturb the neighbors. I festooned the curtain rods and doorway with strings of white Christmas lights. We hung light pink drapes on the windows, covered the stiff gray industrial carpeting with an oval rainbow hand-knotted rug that looked as if it should furnish a senior living apartment. We'd brought vases for freshly cut flowers and enough plates and utensils to stock a full kitchen. We'd packed an air-popper and a mini refrigerator. We filled the fridge with condiments and the tiny clear glass vials that contained my inhalant medicines for asthma.

Pleased, I stretched out in bed and cranked up the air-conditioning unit that was installed only inches from my pillow.

Our resident assistant stood in our doorway to greet us. We had set up our room in three hours, a record, she informed us. We were sweating and exhausted. The air conditioner blasting, we lay on our twin beds in the room, a small room, no more than ten feet wide. Identical pastel quilts that felt like cardboard topped our beds and hung stiffly over matching white dust ruffles.

"Wow! You guys really know how to make a home." The RA looked around at our suburban-style dorm, bewildered.

"Thanks," we chimed back; we were pleased with ourselves. Home was only an hour away, but Cara and Mom and I knew it was much farther.

Chapter 9

Cara married at twenty-two, which seemed foolishly young.

She had known what marriage meant for us as twins. She'd wanted to marry, but needed to include me. She bought me a tiny engagement ring as a gift, a token for fulfilling the duties as her maid of honor. She slipped it onto the ring finger of my left hand and told me that I was also a wife in her marriage. When I married, I did the same for her, and bought her the tiniest diamond cluster ring for being my matron of honor. We both wore our rings every day until she died. The undertaker gave me Cara's cluster ring after her wake. I pulled my wedding rings off and put both hers and mine on, one next to the other. The set didn't match, but it was ours. I wore my engagement diamond and my wedding band on the wrong hand from then on.

There was no reason for me to marry young also except because Cara had. And that's exactly what I did. I made a plea to Jedediah that we should marry even though he thought we should wait. We'd save money living together, I'd argued, appealing to his practical side. Jedediah and I were married in August of 2001; I was twenty-four.

But then we were rarely alone.

Cara often stalked us.

On the fourth day of our honeymoon in Cape Cod, just as we finished up brunch at our bed-and-breakfast, Cara called. Jedediah and I had stowed our cell phones in a drawer of a vanity in our suite. The world was to be shut out; the world meaning my sister. But Cara rang for me at the reception desk, and the innkeepers brought me to the phone.

I knew who it was before I even said hello. There was not another friend or family member who would dare call.

"Hi, Cara. What's up?" I asked, short and measured.

"How'd you know it was me?" She giggled, innocent as a girl.

"Lucky guess." I laughed back. "Who else would care enough to interrupt my honeymoon?"

"Good point! I miss you."

"It's only been a few days."

"You're married now." Cara's voice cracked at "married." "It's different. I feel like you don't need me anymore."

"Jesus, Cara. You've been married for over a year. Stop it."

I'd done my best even though it broke my heart to pair Cara off with Kahlil; they loved each other then. At their ceremony the summer before, I'd read a passage from the Bible on love and sharing, and had broken down in tears as I read, having to stop when I got to a line about parting from birth family into a new married one.

On the phone Cara sniffled. "It's not the same. Kahlil knows you're the most important person in my life. Jedediah doesn't care. Now you're far away on your honeymoon and I'm stuck all by myself at home."

"Please don't start this now," I said. Cara had bullied Jedediah all through our wedding weekend, beginning on the night of our rehearsal dinner. She'd gotten falling-down drunk at a Catskill mountain lodge where Jedediah's family hosted the meal, cornering him as he made his way to the bathroom. She pushed him up against a wall outside of the men's room, standing on her tiptoes so the two were face-to-face. Cara told Jedediah that he'd better understand that marrying me meant marrying her, too. He was also to know that I would never love him as much as I loved her. These were the rules for marrying a twin, and she thought he should know. Her hair was crazy, windblown. She was unsteady on her feet, and Jedediah kindly held her up. She'd just come in from a smoke on the porch, her silky blouse had been pulled back over one shoulder when she'd taken off her coat, and she'd not adjusted it back into place. She'd had enough vodka, and not a care left for her tidiness. My husband-to-be didn't comment on her rules for his marriage. He put his arm around her and walked her back to the table where a tall vanilla cake waited for the bride and groom. I held on to the cool handle of the cake knife and motioned for Jedediah to come over. He had placed his hand over mine and we had pushed the knife down through the layers of cake and kissed. Cara had poured herself a tall glass of water and a taller glass of wine.

"How's the lover's nest?" Cara teased. Our Cape Cod honeymoon was about to end.

"It's cozy," I sighed. A beach bag packed with towels and sunscreen sat at my feet. Jedediah had excused himself from our brunch table and stood near the reception counter, waiting to hear what Cara had in store. He'd propped the perfectly collapsed and tightly snapped beach umbrella on the railing to the stairs that led up to the second floor, to our room. He carried a paperback copy of *Invisible Cities* and a crisp black Moleskine notebook. "We've had a good time. Lots of fish and chips, and we still have four more days of what looks to be good weather," I said.

"I see." My report wasn't what Cara had hoped for. Her own honeymoon had been a disaster. They'd taken a cruise and were lodged in a windowless cabin. The food was lousy, and they'd both gotten serious cases of scabies. I could hear the usual compare and despair in her silence. "I'm lonely."

"Where's Kahlil?"

"Who knows? Busy, I guess."

"How about you write, or go visit Mom?"

"I want to see the ocean."

I looked over at Jedediah. "She wants to come," I mouthed. "What do I do?"

Jedediah looked up from *Invisible Cities*, alarmed. "Hang up," he whispered. "Hang up now, before she won't take no for an answer."

Cara piped in. "I've already bought a bus ticket. I get in at eight o'clock tonight."

"What about our privacy?" I begged.

"Don't worry. I booked a room down the street. You'll barely know I'm there."

Cara hung up before I could protest anymore.

She arrived on that evening's bus as promised. I picked her up from the station and Jedediah waited at the bed-and-breakfast. She descended the bus stairs with an overstuffed backpack and a bouquet of my favorite flowers. "For the bride," she said and smelled the bunch of purple hydrangea and red roses. How could I tell my husband that I wanted her with us? It was difficult to appreciate the ocean without my twin; to see the world apart from her was to be there only by half.

In the end, Cara kept her promise to Jedediah: his marriage to me was all she'd said it would be. She called whenever she liked. She showed up whenever she liked. She still had me, like he never could.

Chapter 10

I try to understand the truths and see how *what-if*s and *if-only*s have altered my memories. I remember in plain terms what I could have done and didn't, what I did and fumbled. I see my sister's life through the veil of my failure to save her.

It's as simple as this memory: the day after my sister's attack, I refused to get her a glass of water. The pain medicines caused her thirst; her nose was broken so she breathed through her mouth; she'd wept herself dry. I had been with her through the night—she'd allowed no other inside her room. I sat beside her and held her up as she struggled to swallow, put a soft pillow at the small of her back. The next morning I heard her call my name and pretended not to hear. I couldn't bring myself to see her battered face in the daylight. What would have happened to Cara had I answered her call? Not just that one, all that I missed?

The moment my sister fell under her rapist's hand, he un-twinned us: the bodies were the same but Cara became lost in hers. My body became a vessel of guilt, reminded us both of the past: the free, easy, joyful giving of sex, ripe exposed youth, and the naive belly that still tickles at touch.

It's not like this old, boring question: When something happens to your twin, can you feel it?

It's more like this: you've eaten something spoiled and it's made its way into every part of you, itching the skin, and you can't get at it. Or it's like a withered phantom limb you can't see, but you can feel every inch. It's your broken bedridden twin, sobbing as you attempt to comb the knots from her hair. You try but you can't reach the tangles: her neck, it's been twisted too hard. She can't turn her head. She hates you for reminding her of what she was. You fear her for showing you what you could become.

The events of October 18 are a patchwork. I went inside from the backyard when the sun went down and decided to color my hair. I heard the phone ring from the kitchen and ran for it, thinking it was Cara calling me to tell me how her story had been critiqued in class. But it was several hours too early for that call. She shouldn't have been home yet.

My hair was still goopy and wet and weighty with coloring, slicked up and twisted into a knot. I lifted the receiver to my ear and then pulled it back; I left a murky ring of L'Oreal Midnight circled on the earpiece.

"Christa?" Kahlil asked for me, said my name as if he were apologizing.

"Heya Tall Glass of Water." I liked to nickname him. He usually had one to toss back at me. Not this time.

"I've got some terrible news," Kahlil said. "Cara was attacked."

"Attacked?"

"Yes."

"What do you mean?"

"She was raped." He said the word as if he didn't understand what it meant—and he didn't. It would take two years and the dissolution of his marriage before he understood.

I fell back as if I'd taken a blow. "Was she out with the dog?" I hated that doofy dog. I'd told my sister again and again not to walk the dog in the woods; she never listened.

"Yes."

"By herself?"

"Yes."

"Where were you?" The question landed like a bomb.

"I was home playing video games." But not like my husband, I thought. Kahlil didn't just play games; he escaped into them, abandoning common sense and all responsibility as he played. The man was a boy.

I sped toward Holyoke to get to Cara. Before I left I called my mother, who was still at work on an evening shift. Then I tried to reach Jedediah, who was home playing his own game. The phone was busy. I wouldn't reach him for hours. I sped west to east on the thruway; I remember that. Memory plays tricks, and when I try to recall that evening I see Jedediah beside me in the car. I can't remember how and if he held my hand, what was said or wasn't, how he consoled me. What I see is my young husband looking out the passenger's side window tapping his finger lightly against the glass, humming softly to the radio. In my memory of Cara's rape I've put him in the place I needed him at that moment, beside me.

In my memory we drove together through the night without talking. I nervously flicked through the stations to find music that could both soothe my nerves and help keep us awake. In reality, I rolled down both windows all the way, a shock of cold air stinging the side of my face, helping me focus on driving and not the violent thing I was about to see.

Mom called after eight o'clock. I was nearly halfway to Cara. She told me she was making good time. She didn't know what to expect, she said. She'd called Kahlil to try to understand what had happened. He'd said that Cara had been raped, which confused her. It's not possible, Mom said again and again. Could we check with the police that a mistake hadn't been made? Maybe Cara had only been beat up a little? There must have been a misunderstanding? Cara had probably just been involved in a scuffle and hurt a bit, a pride-bruising black eye, a snatched purse?

I followed the glowing white median and watched the mileposts pass. I was alone; Jedediah wasn't with me. Cara had been raped; this was the new reality.

I arrived at the hospital before nine. I pushed through the carousel doors into the crowded emergency room and saw her right away; the curtain to her room had been left open. She was sitting in bed, still dressed, talking to the police. Kahlil stood to the side. Cara cried upon sight of me. I barely recognized her. Where was my face in her broken one? Her jaw was bumpy and distorted by purple and gold welts. Swelling had nearly shut both her eyes. Her front teeth were jagged, chipped; I didn't know then how many were missing.

I thought about all of the years we'd been competing to be the prettier twin.

"She's refusing to undress for the nurses," Kahlil said. "She says she doesn't want to take her clothes off."

The hospital waiting room was crowded with patients. Cara had been there for hours and was yet to be seen by the attending physician. Nurses dressed the deepest wounds on her face with strips of gauze and gently tried to convince her to undergo an exam.

"You've got to cooperate with the doctors so we can get you home." I put my hand on her shoulder and she flinched.

"I don't want to go home." Cara looked up accusingly at Kahlil. "What if that guy is there?"

I didn't have an answer for this. She was right. I thought of climbing the three flights of stairs to her apartment door, wondering if the rapist would be waiting in the hall. Then it occurred to me: except for the bruises, he would certainly think I was Cara.

"We'll escort you home," one of the police said, his hat in his lap.

Cara agreed to undress for her doctors. She removed her tattered red pants, the black cardigan she'd taken from my closet, a pair of yellow ankle socks stitched with racing horses, and her bloodied, dirty, white rainbow-adorned panties and placed each into an evidence bag. She stepped into a blue hospital gown. She was administered a rape kit. Afterward, the detectives and a rape advocate were called back in.

When we arrived home Cara insisted I wash her clean. I closed the door on us to the clicking sound of the loose doorknob.

I brought my sister to the tub for a bath and helped her undress. I filled the tub with water hot enough to soothe, tepid enough not to scald. The nurses sent Cara home wearing scrubs and a white T-shirt. She turned her back to me and pulled off her shirt. I saw the mirrored marks: crescent-shaped gouges her assailant made with his teeth: more than a dozen deep bites. Cara turned to face me, asked me to undo the string on her pants. Her fingers and knuckles were bruised from fighting. Her pants fell around her ankles and she stepped out of them, into the tub. She settled in and reached for my hand, pulling me fully clothed into the tub with her.

I splashed water on my face and rested my wet forehead at the base of her neck. There were too many bites to clean. I poured peroxide, watched her wounds fizz white. I cleaned her with a soft cloth and lavender wash.

I bathed my sister, just as she'd asked.

"I floated outside of my body," Cara told me in the tub.

I imagined my sister's airborne soul, the back of the rapist's round head, Cara pushing him away at the chest: 250 pounds thundering down against her, snapping back her wrists like flower stems. I see the hulk of him pinning Cara against the soggy autumn earth, turning her over, pushing her onto her knees, and taking what she'll never have again: amazement at the sight of the world.

"I watched myself die," Cara said. "I would have been happy to go, to leave—but then I saw our grandmother. She said I needed to stay put, to live."

"You didn't die," I reminded her.

"That's easy for you to say."

"Did you think of me?"

"No," she said into the water.

Fuck her, I thought. If I'd been dying in the woods, she'd have been the one I thought about.

Cara sat up, rigid in the bath, her knees bent. I tried to recline to avoid touching her. My legs rubbed against the sides of her thighs. She was cradled between my legs and stared past the faucet, beyond the tile, through the wall.

I cried every day when we were children. I used to try to count the days that I didn't cry when I was a kid. I was seven and had a calendar full of failed days when I cried and shouldn't have. Nothing and everything brought tears. I had every reason to weep as a child, yet I couldn't as an adult, in this tragedy; I couldn't find tears when I needed them.

I got out of the tub and wrapped myself in a towel. I went in search of a cotton nightgown in Cara's bureau, picking up the softest, whitest one she had. I left her alone to dress.

Chapter 11

I want my sweater back. I want my black cashmere cardigan returned. It has flat black buttons and it's fitted at the wrists. The sweater was neither too big nor too small. A good cardigan is hard to find. It was sexy over a wiggle dress, or homey with jeans and a belt. It was an every-dayer, a hip-accentuating waist-whittler. Cara and I both wanted my sweater. We stole it back and forth. The sweater traveled from city to city, closet to closet.

I bought the sweater on sale and wore it more often than I should have. The first time Cara spied the cardigan, I was wearing it to fight off an early autumn chill.

"I like that." Cara looked at the sweater, not in appreciation, but in need. She flipped the tag up at the neck. "Cashmere?"

"It was on sale."

"Fits perfectly." Cara examined the sweater's lapel. "I've looked forever but haven't found a sweater I don't feel like a square body in. We have thick waists."

"Speak for yourself. I'm not thick-waisted. I'm short-waisted." I curled my fingers around a belt loop in Cara's jeans and tugged, teasing her. "And, don't you dare talk about my twin that way. " I shook her back and forth, shimmying her hips, and kissed her cheek.

"Can I wear it tomorrow?" Cara asked.

"Nope. You think I trust you to give it back?" I took the sweater off that evening, folded it up, and hid it at the bottom of my suitcase, beneath boxes of film and a well-worn copy of Van Gogh's letters. I unpacked the suitcase at home in Manhattan, no sweater to be found. Cara left a decoy in its place: a faded black cotton cardigan, frayed at the cuffs. A loose button dangled from the collar; fabric pilled beneath the neck; the right side stretched out at the shoulder; a side pocket was coming unstitched, flapping down where the thread had given way, and inside the pocket there was a smoked-down and stubbed-out cigarette. Her ribbed sweater, size medium, was my sweater's sorry replacement. It wasn't meant to fool, but left to teach a lesson: twins should have identical things. I was too selfish to share and had broken code—the sweater Cara left was punishment.

Cara was in the habit of taking my things, not just sweaters; lipstick, belts, dresses, and books were also ripe for lifting. The tradition kept up after the rape, right up until she died. Stealing didn't only go one way. I felt free to help myself to anything that was hers as well. I took from her often. But Cara's need for identical possessions went beyond sisterly borrowing. She deployed straight-out mimicry. She hoped that if we possessed the same things, we'd have exact lives. I wasn't similarly motivated. Her life never looked good enough to me to try to make it for myself.

Jedediah and I were gifted a full set of dinnerware for eight for our wedding. We were given every kitchen item on our registry. We stacked the tiki green salad plates rimmed in earthy brown on top of the dinner plates. Deep soup bowls painted in matching hues and finished in shining glazes were pantry neighbors to the plates, and to a taupe sugar and creamer set embossed with flowers. The ceramic edges of the plates, mugs, and bowls chipped over the years, each half moon's chalky exposure revealing the brittle insides of the dishware. As time went on and our marriage progressed, I was more and more careless: too many clumsy slips of the hand, and setting after setting crashed, enamel pecking off in the sink.

After Kahlil left, Cara came over and opened our cabinets, inspecting our dinnerware. She said she'd donated the plates they'd gotten as wedding gifts to Goodwill. Now she wanted to see for herself what a happy couple ate their meals on. She promptly bought an identical service for twelve for her new household of one. She purchased our same bath towels and television hutch, too, and the exact clothes hangers covered in silky pink satin that I used for dresses. She found our coffee table on clearance. She stole one of Jedediah's books and wrote her name on the title page, shelving it on a hardwood bookcase identical to one of ours, in her house.

I inherited my house in duplicate when she died. I added her service for twelve to my service for eight. I had service for twenty, and a husband who was ready to walk out and take nothing. After our divorce, I kept all of the relics of our happy home and all of Cara's hopeful duplicates.

My family kept watch over Cara after the attack: Mom cooked and nervously cleaned. Jedediah organized cabinets. Friends came and brought flowers, more food. Cara's professors sent letters and called. I don't remember how Kahlil helped, though I'm certain he did. I stocked Cara's pantry with food she didn't eat.

Her rapist was still on the loose as I browsed Cara's neighborhood grocery. I tied a patterned blue scarf around my hair and wore huge white sunglasses. My heart beat in my throat as I stacked my shopping cart with boxes of Cheerios and pouches of Hi-C. He was still out there. He might see me in the grocery; we knew he shopped there. The police mentioned at the hospital that it was likely the man who'd raped Cara had bought his alcohol at the liquor counter inside that grocery store. It was the only shop for miles, and the rapist told Cara he didn't have a car.

I had fantasies as I shopped that he'd see me, and I'd recognize him from Cara's police sketch. I'd call 911 and a SWAT team would take him down. They'd shoot him dead. I was naive, horror struck, only twenty-four; I couldn't have known him from a drawing, but he certainly would have recognized me. He wouldn't know he'd done what aging or a haircut or a disguise couldn't do to twins. He'd un-samed us. When he defiled my Cara, he separated us.

I secretly hoped he'd take me, too, not really, of course; but deep down, I'd lost Cara. I wished he'd discover me in a grocery isle and drag me to the path where he'd raped her. I felt her pulling far from me in the days following her rape. Attacked, I'd be the same as Cara again—we'd both be as dirty as she said she felt. It was the only way I'd be able to know what she meant when she told me we couldn't be twins anymore: I was "still clean." It could happen to me, too, I reasoned, on my dangerous shopping trip.

It was dangerous; I was right. He shopped while I shopped. This time the police were watching. They caught him on camera in the liquor aisle. I was told later, after they'd arrested him, he'd been observed on surveillance tapes the afternoon I was there. All men looked the same to me as I shopped: menacing, ready to strike out and steal me into the woods.

I wheeled my cart over to the autumn vegetables and picked out the roundest, brightest orange pumpkin I could find and put it with the rest of my bounty. Mid-October is the time for jack-o'-lanterns, hayrides, reaping. The leaves had just peaked.

The grocery aisles were filled with cider doughnuts, gourds, and sugary candies for trick-or-treating. The bakery counter was lined with stalks of Indian corn. White plastic tarps with holes cut for eyes hung from displays for soon-to-be ghosts. Ghoul masks were stacked on shelves, one on top of the other, beside bins of plastic fangs and tubes of fake blood. The masks rattled as I pushed my cart by.

I turned the corner in the canned goods aisle and plucked green beans from the shelf. Canned green beans had become a comfort, a reminder of our days in North Carolina, when they were served on our school lunch trays. I imagined that I saw Cara's rapist turn the corner and head up the cereal aisle. I ran with my cart past shelves of ketchup and mayonnaise and followed the invisible man into aisle 6. I didn't find him among the Cheerios and went looking for him at the butcher's block.

There was only one male customer there. He ordered pork chops and ground chuck, tossing both into his cart where his infant sat mouthing a teething ring.

I bought a steak and a pack of chicken legs, placing them at the front of my cart, next to a bag of organic premixed salad and a box of raspberry pastry, and headed to the checkout. It was time to go home. I hadn't found my man.

All of the food I bought spoiled. Cara liked these things, thanked me, but she wasn't eating. Her life had been cataclysmically altered. Why would she eat? One of her eyes was blackened; she'd lost hearing in one ear—the rapist had smashed the side of her head again and again with his blows. Cara said first she heard a sharp ringing as his fist fell down against her, then a hiss. Eventually she couldn't hear a sound. She refused to change from her nightgown. It was stained with antibiotic ointment that had escaped the bandages that covered the rapist's bites on her back.

Cara woke crying in the middle of the night; I heard her from the living room where I slept. I jerked awake, startled. There was a moment, before I recognized her weeping, when I felt at peace. I slept in a darkened room on a portable mattress, surrounded by Cara's belongings: a cracked pope snow globe from Rome; all its water had run out. When she tipped it, the sand inside fell dryly on Saint John Paul's head; a leather-bound diary from Venice; a feather duster; a jar of coins; a bunch of plastic grapes. I rested in her soft peach sheets, and *then* I heard her sobbing. I'd been dreaming of the two of us floating together on a raft of twigs, like the one the children craft in *The Night of the Hunter*. Cara steered with a reed in the back and I drank water from the side of our boat. I woke thirsty and cold, my blanket on the floor beside a spilled glass of water. I got up and rummaged through Cara's medicine cabinet, through painkillers prescribed by her physician at the emergency room. I shook one more than Cara's prescribed dose into my hand and poured her a glass of water—I knew what it would take; one wasn't enough. I brought the pills to her. She swallowed the medicine and fell back to sleep. My sister had been stolen and my sweater was missing.

The police, a male and female pair of detectives, came the Monday after the rape. They called that morning to say they'd gotten a lead and arrested a suspect—Edgardo Hernandez. They needed Cara to identify some of his belongings. If she made a proper identification, she'd go to the station downtown and pick the suspect out of a lineup. Cara would also need to identify her own belongings collected at the scene and sign off officially on the items they'd taken into custody at the hospital. Her clothes: pants, panties, socks, my sweater.

Mom let the detectives in. She offered them coffee, brownies, a sandwich. They carried my sweater in a clear, ziplock plastic bag. It was covered in bits of leaves and torn at the shoulders.

Cara looked at the evidence bags. "Sorry about your sweater."

"I'll find another," I said. "Don't worry."

I've yet to find that sweater's replacement. Nothing I've tried on or bought fits as well, or succeeds in replacing my memory of what happened to Cara.

We waited for Cara to identify Edgardo's things. The detectives had gone inside his apartment and had found the clothes she'd described: a turtleneck sweater, dark jeans, a pair of plaid patterned boxer shorts. He'd been arrested and detained.

She'd given an excellent account. Hernandez was discovered because of my sister's recollection of his garments. She'd told them he smelled of whiskey and wore a tan sweater. He'd pulled the collar up over his chin, to conceal his face. She'd gotten a good look at him, remembered the color and fit of his sloppy clothes. A twin is a perceptive observer. A twin learns how a person is made through watching, and then makes herself into a copy. Twins size people up. Observing keenly is a path to love and acceptance; for this, the twin keeps a sharp eye.

The female detective, Jennifer, wasn't what I'd expected. I'd expected someone less stylish and groomed. She looked tough in her smart black pants. She was petite with round, sorry blue eyes that peered out from under the long wave of hair that covered one. I could tell by the way she stood and from her tone that she probably cursed without apology and held her own among her male colleagues during drinks at the bar. Jennifer quickly became my hero. She was not a drunkard; she was kind, empathetic, soothing, motherly, and assuring. Jennifer was calculating. Her senses were amped like a hound's. She seemed to hear for miles and, like a hunting dog scenting prey, she already smelled her man. There was no question she'd get him.

I saw this clearly: Jennifer would kill the animal who'd

done this to Cara. She'd do it with her own hands if she had to; she'd do it with her pistol, without remorse or hesitation, not only for justice but for a paycheck. I wondered who it was that had hurt her; it was written on her face that someone had.

Jennifer's buttery blond hair grazed the handle of the gun she wore on her hip. Jennifer, tough and tender, looked down at the bags of Cara's clothing. Jennifer, Venus De Milo standing in her clamshell, understood nakedness, saw the shame and fear in the room. We were relieved to know she was on the case. She told us she'd make her visit short and to the point. There was no need to linger.

She didn't want a sandwich.

She laid the bagged items out on the coffee table and waited for her partner to reveal them one by one. I asked if I could have my sweater back.

"You'll never see that sweater after today. Evidence stays in a vault at the station." She looked at the sweater more closely. "This sweater looks expensive." She set the bag down.

I thought of a college friend who had a job in an evidence room at a London police precinct. He'd told me all about the things they stored there. I remembered a few of the odder items: a bloody guitar someone had used to bash in the head of a lover, an empty box of matches used for arson, a murderer's diary. There was a wheelchair they'd had for over a decade. An elderly man had used it to wheel himself off a cliff, a suicide who was depressed over Alzheimer's. The wheelchair had somehow survived the fall. It wasn't damaged in the least. The boys who worked in the evidence room liked to take it for rides around the building when the higher-ups weren't watching. My sweater would soon be a casualty of an evidence room. I imagined strangers touching it, even trying it on.

We sat on the sofa: Mom, Kahlil, Cara, Jennifer, me, and the male detective. I can't remember his name; he looked worried and hung his head, sad at himself for being a man in a world where men did these things. Cara sat in the middle and I sat on one side of her. Kahlil was on the other. The sofa was a green sectional and fit all of us easily. It was brand-new, but the fabric was ripped away at the corners, stuffing falling out. The cats had gotten to it, clawed it up. They'd torn into the sofa like they did every stick of furniture Cara ever owned.

Cara and Kahlil had purchased the sofa with money from their wedding. Cara had never owned one before. In college there had been a futon, and an ice-blue velour recliner she'd rescued from the street—but never a sofa, a *real* sofa. A sofa wasn't just a place to lounge; the purchase of a sofa meant she was finally an adult.

Mom was smoking and Cara was chain-smoking. The living room was thick with smoke that wafted up to the ceiling and twirled in the air. Jennifer coughed and cleared her throat. The male detective's eyes watered.

"This is embarrassing," Mom said. "Cara doesn't usually live like this." Mom patted Cara on the shoulder and Cara pulled away. "Right, honey?"

"It's fine," I said, suspecting they'd seen and smelled much worse.

"This is nothing." Jennifer handed my mother the tea saucer my sister had been using as an ashtray. She didn't miss a beat.

I opened a window to clear the room. Air relieved the room of the burden of smoke, like fresh water from a mountain diluting a toxic stream. I pulled the bronchial inhaler I used for asthma attacks from my pocket and took a puff.

The male detective opened the first bag and pulled out the jeans. They were faded from years of wear, caked with mud at the knees. One of the back pockets had been ripped clean off the pants. Specks of dried brown blood flecked the legs. He must have been standing over her as he punched her pretty face.

Cara flinched at the sight of the pants, leaned into Kahlil's arms and whimpered. She nodded, yes.

The detective pulled the turtleneck out next and held it up by the shoulders. The sweater hung limp and was large enough that it obscured his face. It was enormous, split at the seams. Edgardo must have worn it for years. It was filthy; the fabric had been exhausted by the task of containing him. The detective turned it around and stood up, holding the sweater to his side.

Cara moved to the edge of her sofa cushion and got a good look at the garment. She'd not yet changed from her pajamas. It had been four days and there was no convincing her to freshen up. She pulled a purple chenille throw blanket off the sofa arm and covered herself. She stood up and touched the body of the sweater. "Yes, that's the one. The neck of the sweater kept getting caught in my mouth. I remember the texture."

Our mother got up and went into the kitchen. She turned on the tap and water rushed loudly against the sink's basin. I could hear her sharp, short sobs beneath the drumming tenor of the water's tide. She opened the microwave and warmed her cooled cup of coffee, put away the untouched turkey sandwiches she'd made for the detectives. The fridge door banged shut. The microwave chimed. My mother walked slowly back to the living room, careful not to spill.

The detective placed the sweater back into the paper bag. "Thanks," he said. "We have just one more item, and we'll be able wrap things up." He pulled out a pair of boxer shorts patterned with electric blue and black checks. The elastic waist of the shorts was coming undone; the inside band poked out through holes in the fabric.

Cara cried out at the sight of the shorts. They were a stand-in for the man, as close as she would come to sharing a room with him before the trial, two years later. Her voice warbled at its highest pitch. The sound moved up and then down in register, over and over, until she lost her breath and quickly caught it again. She beat her hands on Kahlil's chest and screamed her throat raw. This time there were people to hear her.

Chapter 12

Albert ate too much
Barbara hit the booze
Carolina free-based crack
Duncan was depressed
Enid had an eating disorder
Floyd followed a Florida cult
Georgia gulped Geronimo
Harold slammed heroin
Inez bought Internet porn
Jared jacked a jeep
Kenny took Klonopin
Laura left her little ones
Mark snorted methamphetamine
Nancy nailed her neighbors
Otis smoked opium
Portia popped pills
Quincy needed Quaaludes
Rebecca repressed a rape
Stan sniffed glue
Trevor tripped on acid
Una underwent cosmetic surgery thirty times
Vera vacuumed on Vicodin

William wore nothing to work
Xavier took X
Yardley yearned for yellow jackets
Zach smoked Zambi

Getting to Cara was mostly a straight run out of New York City. Once the lights and smog and noise and the guilt of my weekday life, a life free of my sister and her rape, were behind me, I'd hit Interstate 91 and shoot through Connecticut, then Springfield and Holyoke to Northampton. Before long I was on her doorstep. It had been a year and a handful of months since October 18. I'd been making the trip back and forth for all of that time and had miraculously carved out a routine with Jedediah and work. I'd settled back into the city, my marriage, and graduate school. I worked every night in the darkroom printing color photographs of us until dawn. Cara limped along. She, too, was in a graduate program. I wasn't certain how she completed her course work. I had the feeling that her passing was an act of mercy on the part of her professors.

And her workshop peers' whisperings about her only increased her stress.

"I don't understand why they don't like me," she complained to me over the phone. "I try so hard."

"Maybe they think you're teacher's pet?" I consoled. She *was* her professor's favorite. Cara had been given the largest scholarship the university had.

"I've heard some people think I'm having sex with her, my teacher," Cara said proudly. "It's better to have people gossiping about me than ignoring me, I guess. That means I'm on their minds."

"Perhaps."

"Well, at least I know how to dress myself," Cara said. "So what if I get a little drunk."

She told me how the grad students showed up to her dinner parties empty-handed, wearing jeans and beat-up shoes. Cara answered the door in floor-length cocktail dresses and flowers from the supermarket pinned into her hair. Kahlil manned the kitchen while she hosted out front. Everyone ate happily and heartily and waited for Cara to drink enough so that she couldn't stand.

Cara had no inclination to spare those around her.

Her first appearance at school after the rape was at a reading for first-year fiction-writing students. Cara stood at the podium fat-lipped, arm in a sling, both eyes still blackened. She pulled out her pages and cleared her throat. "I'm Cara, for those of you I've not met," she said. "I'm glad to be alive." The crowd shuffled nervously in their seats. A few people glared at Kahlil, who sat rapt, watching his wife. Cara read a short story about an unhappy marriage and took a bow. Word was that Kahlil had roughed her up.

She and Kahlil had moved to Northampton immediately after the rape. They'd settled into a new apartment in a quiet suburban neighborhood, a pretty two-story white Victorian with a front porch and yard, a duplex. The street was named for a tree: cherry, oak, or maple, a tree that sounded solid and safe.

I made the drive weekly. I came to know each bend and curl in the road as well as I knew each of Cara's needle-pricked veins. The prices and calorie counts of rest stop fast-food menus turned as familiar as pantry items. Radio personalities became old friends: I listened to Delilah. She had a song for everyone, sometimes the same one for different people in vastly dissimilar tragedies. "Wind Beneath My Wings" for a breakup, death, favorite teacher, war hero? Sure. But what was the song for a just-raped, drug-addicted identical twin sister in a doomed marriage?

There were no songs for us, only silence interrupted by the popping sound of prescription drug bottles.

I focused on the condescending calm of Delilah's voice. On her breathy sigh of condolences and convincing. I knew better than to believe her. Conversion from the land of fire to the Lord's would never be my escape. But her voice soothed me.

Have you lost faith? Delilah purred into her radio microphone. *Have you lost hope?*

Faith? Mine was broken on a trail of glass and leaves.

Hope? I feared having any. To lose one more shred of naïveté—that would be saying good-bye to innocence completely. I wasn't prepared.

Cara's dishes, crusted with food, waited, piled high in the sink. Cara herself waited for me stoned on the couch. She never said more than "Hey" when I arrived, as if I'd journeyed no farther to visit her than from next door.

"This house is nearly condemnable," I'd say as I walked in the door. I never held my tongue. "This place should be boarded up, demolished!" I'd say.

Kahlil would sit at the kitchen table, crunching away at a bag of chips, reading the newspaper. The place wasn't breaking health codes, but no one should live that way, especially not a young lady who used to tidy up pridefully, who had liked to be the "wife" taking care of the roost.

After the rape, tracked-in mud and snow salt shellacked the tiled floors. Pebbles of kitty litter became coated in the mud and stuck to the bottoms of bare feet. Animals whined in hunger. Spoiled milk curdled by the gallon. Soiled laundry tumbled out of baskets and closets, hung from the kitchen table onto the floor, and pushed open the doors of the china cabinet, which Cara was using as a makeshift closet. The china, packed away in the basement, awaited better times. The house was full to the rafters with clothes.

Cara bought an endless array of outfits after her attack to help her feel dressed. She'd also pierced her nipples. She wore T-shirts without bras, her nipples blooming from beneath like rosebuds stabbed with spikes. Whenever she was feeling better, feeling more like living than dying, she'd take out the spikes and let the holes heal over. Whenever she retreated back to blackness, she'd have the piercing done again, through the scar tissue. This happened five or six times over the rest of her life. I gauged her mood by looking at her tits.

In the new Northampton apartment, there was not enough storage for her wardrobe. Her skirts, dresses, blouses, and pants lay everywhere; there was no surface free of them. The furniture was striped with stockings and socks. It wasn't possible to tell what was clean or dirty without a whiff test. Cara lay on top of all of it. The sofa she was once so happy to have bought held her odor and the impression of her body; her imprint had permanently reshaped its center. This could not be corrected even with a flipped cushion. She'd indented both sides. Where she propped her feet, the dust from her house slippers dirtied each arm. She'd tossed empty bottles of her antianxiety prescriptions onto the floor and kicked them under the sofa; they rattled and rolled when she got up or down. She had covered herself in blankets and with the gauze of sedation.

I asked the question then; I ask it now: Where was her husband?

He hid in a den crowded with his belongings—tins of half-eaten takeout stacked into a swaying tower; closets crammed with old sports equipment and barricaded shut by chairs loaded down with boxes. Kahlil stowed his collection of mixed cassette tapes from youth next to his CDs, in an open drawer, the tapes' insides twisted and pulled out in shiny tattered ribbons. A sizable collection of CDs—free of cases and scratched to silence—were shoved beneath the twin guest bed, which was naked of sheets and pillows. I slept instead on the sofa.

He'd tossed an ambitious collection of vintage 35mm cameras loaded with exposed film into a far corner of the room. Pictures of happier days would have to wait to be developed. They're still waiting—stored deep in my basement with the other things Kahlil left behind. I can't bear to take them to be processed, to witness again the days when Cara's life promised her everything.

Kahlil's room was also full of cookbooks, dog-eared syrup- and butter-splattered pages of his favorite recipes. The man could cook up a storm. He favored crepes and roasted meats. In the early months of their marriage, Cara had put on fifteen extra blissful pounds. They both saw the weight as proof of their love.

Folded-up love letters from their courtship were the only items in Kahlil's room that were well cared for. He kept them organized and sorted by date in a scrapbook. He placed it on the very top of a tall bookshelf, away from chaos and the active bladders of the cats. When their litter pans were full, the cats pittled on the piles of clothing he left on the floor. He wore the clothes anyway.

Kahlil stands six feet three inches tall, a disarmingly handsome man, a weathered model type with a strong chin, deep-set dark eyes, and springing warm brown curls. His arms were sleeved in tattoos. His favorite, the word *VIVA* in black block letters, covered his entire forearm. He got the tattoo right after he and Cara met, a reminder to live boldly.

Instead, he sat in his room, hunched over a child-size desk, playing video games or sometimes watching basketball.

He also spent more and more hours at work as a construction foreman, and more hours attending classes for a degree in architecture. He would come home from a long day and retreat to his hovel. The task of taking care of Cara was left to me and sometimes to my mother. I cleaned and cooked as if Kahlil were no more than another piece of clutter to be stepped over. Sometimes he'd watch a sitcom, sometimes porn. The porn infuriated Cara—a porn argument preceded her arrival at Westfield State, the first mental hospital, following a suicide attempt.

"You could've erased the history." Cara pushed the laptop at Kahlil over the breakfast table. "I didn't care before. But now I don't want that in my house. We've had enough sexual violence in our lives."

"Sorry, baby," was all he could say. I sat between them through this argument, wondering how Kahlil was managing in his newly sexless home, thinking, Just let the poor guy watch porn. There was no touching Cara now. It had only been six months since the rape. She wasn't ready. She'd barely been off the AZT.

Edgardo had refused an HIV test, a right he had as an accused inmate in Massachusetts. As a result, my sister was subjected to monthly testing and a harsh, preventative drug regimen that left her nauseated and exhausted. With each test and pill she felt at the mercy of her rapist again, haunted, convinced of her own contamination. The tests had all been negative but she quarantined her shaving razor and sanitized her toothbrush every night with boiling water. She did not want anyone she loved to come close to her imagined infection.

"If you'd take a shower once in a while maybe I could fuck you," she said to Kahlil that afternoon. "I just can't with the way you smell. You smell like *him*."

After the argument died down and I'd cleared the table, I went out. I don't remember where, but as I left, Cara was in her usual place, on the sofa with her laptop open, writing.

I came back to the apartment late in the afternoon to find

Kahlil at the kitchen table, head in hands. He'd found Cara lying unconscious in the front yard, naked except for a bathrobe. She'd pulled all of his clothing from his room, piled it on top of the snow, and sprawled on it. A stack of *Hustler* magazines lay scattered around the clothes, pages turning in the winter wind. Cara had binged on pills; Kahlil had taken Cara to a locked ward.

She went to many rehab centers and mental hospitals in the year following the rape. At first she'd seem better when she returned, pinker in the cheeks, rested, but the respite effect would soon fade and she'd return to her usual tricks. She'd disappear a couple of evenings a week and come home stoned, pockets full of her precious packets of white powder. I'm not sure how long after the rape it was when Cara began to use heroin. I think it began around the first Christmas. That was the first time I remember her with eyes like slits, heard her voice raspy and worn, watched her shoulders and face slump toward her dinner plate. Heroin caused her to squint, as if everything, even me, was in fine print.

She'd check into a hospital, desperate after a suicide attempt or after Kahlil or I had found her unconscious. Sometimes her suicidal hospital peers were close to homicidal. Sometimes local homeless shelters were filled to capacity, so hospitals beds went to rowdy homeless drunks and displaced vets, who roamed the wards alongside the agitated and the addicted. In these facilities there was no real hope of medical intervention, and although Cara was safe inside their walls, she'd petition to get out as soon as she checked in. And who could blame her?

I called her that first night at Westfield State.

"You okay?" I asked. I heard a high-pitched wailing in the background.

"What do you think?"

I wasn't sure what I thought. I heard a man's voice. It sounded like it was coming from an intercom. "We need a nurse, stat. We have a takedown," the voice said.

"A guy is walking the halls with his pants around his ankles. He banged his head against the walls all night. That's not a figure of speech." Cara tried to persuade me to aid her in her bid to escape. The hospital in Westfield had looked perfectly fine from the outside: two stories of regal brick covered in climbing ivy, manicured lawns, a small duck pond. I've learned that when it comes to hospitals, grounds are never a measure of what exists behind bolted doors. "They ask him to stop and within twenty minutes he's at it again. I have to get out of here."

"Can you find a quiet corner and sit and read? You just got there. You can't leave."

"Quiet? Do you have any idea where I am?"

"Kahlil and I filled out your admission paperwork."

"I'm in hell, that's where I am."

It was difficult to argue with her. She was right. She was in purgatory at best. I hung up and I hoped she'd stay put. She did, for three days.

The doctor at Westfield said Cara had post-traumatic stress disorder with borderline features. He said being border-line meant teetering: she could alternate between composure and the terror of being left. She might make frantic efforts to avoid being alone. This fear might be so strong that she'd want to die.

He spoke a new language, but I understood it. I'd seen all of these qualities in her. They made perfect sense: how else should she behave given her experience?

I visited Cara at Westfield two days after she'd checked in.

"I knew you'd make it," she said, as if considering every word. They'd put her on something to slow her down and take away her anxiety, but my anxiety spiked.

Someone had replaced my sister with a mental patient in a sweat suit.

A woman sat beside Cara at a short table, making drawings and macaroni collages. The woman's wrists were bandaged.

"My friend Regina helped me make this." Cara held up a drawing of us. I traced my finger over it. Cara'd sketched herself to be almost twice my size. "I'm not really as fat as I think I am. Am I?" Cara smiled brightly.

While she was at Westfield, Cara wrote me a letter.

Dear Sister,

Don't be mad.

I just wanted to sleep. That's why I didn't call. My husband drove me here. He had to leave. I get to wear pajamas all day. They give me medicine. I am contaminated. I don't like it.

Don't tell Mom.

There are other people here, too.

They watch me all the time. I wish they wouldn't stare so much. I want my perfume back. They took it away because it contains alcohol and has a sharp dispenser. I had to ask for my pen today. Tell them it isn't a threat. I've got clean clothes so I don't smell bad.

I have to light my cigarettes from a push-button box outside.

I know, I shouldn't smoke. I'll try to stop, promise. There is a gazebo. I can sit there until bedtime. I learned how to play chess. Now I can be more like a man. Will you learn, too? When I sleep, it's with three other girls.

How are you?

Don't worry. I didn't leave without thinking of you.

I'm glad you're not here, too. Don't be mad.
  Love,
  Me

I thought the doctor's diagnosis was the first step to mending her. I know now that a diagnosis is taken in like an orphaned dog. We brought it home, unsure how to care for it, to live with it. It raised its hackles, snarled, hid in the farthest corner of the room; but it was ours, her diagnosis. The diagnosis was timid and confused, and genetically wired to strike out.

Flashbacks woke her at night from a sound sleep of nightmares. A slur lingered in her speech—and doctors couldn't find a cause. "You don't have brain damage," I'd insist when she complained of feeling wobbly and seasick. Her ears rang. A high-pitched raspy chime sounded out in her head so there was never quiet. But I'd say, "Your head is fine."

I think I knew she'd never be fine.

She was dizzy and often lost her footing if she stood too quickly. There was always a new bruise to explain. When she fell, she'd often bump her head. She'd shoot up and blame the purple blotches on the insides of her arms on her undiagnosable clumsiness. There was no believing her.

I wouldn't allow my sister the reasonable pain she was in. I couldn't admit defeat. I denied her the space and time and outlet for which she needed to grieve. I was one of the insensitive people whose only power in a powerless situation is to deny it away, to ignore it, to hope the truth will fade.

I was able to sidestep reality until a snowy March day, a year and a half after the rape. It was a Thursday and I was unable to get Cara on the phone. I was planning to spend the week of my spring vacation with her, on a trip to the New England coast, even though it was still winter. I had looked into Salem and had found a bed-and-breakfast that was rumored to be haunted. It was just the thing to cheer both of us up: ghosts, ocean, and the House of Seven Gables. When I still couldn't reach her after hours of calling on that icy March afternoon, I sped through flurries and snow squalls, arriving in the early evening to find her asleep in her car in her driveway, an untouched envelope of McDonald's French fries scattered on her lap, her hair pulled back in high pigtails.

I knocked at her window to wake her and my rapping roused her. She brushed the French fries off of her lap and rolled her window down.

"I thought I'd take a nap."

"In the driveway? With your lunch on your lap?"

"If the mood strikes." She reached her hand out of the window and adjusted the car's driving mirror, looking at herself. "I feel like shit."

"No doubt about it." I noticed her pupils had constricted into pins, tiny black dots lost in the sea of foggy eyes.

Bags of groceries had spilled onto the floor of her backseat, beside bags of dirty laundry that had never made it to the Wash-n-Go.

The last straw was broken. I demanded she get serious help. The rehab center I found was expensive. I was under the impression, the deluded perspective of the desperate, that the more money we threw at the problem of Cara's addiction and despair, the more likely it was that she'd recover. With this logic I sent her to the kind of place where celebrities go for rest and regular families send their loved ones for fear of what will happen if they don't. Homes are mortgaged and jewels sold to pay for the treatment there. My mother chipped in by taking a home equity loan. Amazingly, money for Cara's stay came also from a state of Massachusetts fund for victims of violent crimes, a fund that wasn't regularly drawn upon. I don't remember who helped us secure payment. I do recall they were surprised that anyone was asking for help.

She had her last hurrah on the airplane to Sedona. She washed down her Klonopin with wine from the beverage cart. At the baggage terminal, overcome with drugs, she fell flat on her face onto the airport floor, chipping her front teeth and blackening one eye. This was how she arrived into the custody of her handler from The Meadows, like a has-been prizefighter gone down in the first round.

Chapter 13

Four weeks later, Kahlil, Mom, and I met Cara at The Meadows. We were hoping to find that she'd taken it upon herself to save her life.

She'd written us letters, told us she was happy and ready to make amends. She'd made friends with others like her and she'd finally seen her faults. We flew to meet her weary, after a year and a half of battle. We flew to meet her rested, after the luxury of weeks without her. We flew to meet her because we had to, because it was Family Week and we were family; the code of supporting treatment, even if it means leaving your life and spending many thousands of dollars, shouldn't be broken. And we flew to her because not meeting her would mean never rescuing her—so high are the stakes for the family of the newly rehabilitating.

First, the three of us dropped our suitcases off at our motel—a flat-roofed, white aluminum-sided motor inn with a stardust sign and failing lights: the *o* and the *d* were out in LODGE. My mother and I shared a room. I set the week's therapy itinerary in the top drawer, beside a King James Bible.

Mom turned on our room's air conditioner and pulled the crisp white covers down on her bed, stretching out on it, sounding a hearty yawn. She marveled at our luck, that we'd left cold New England for Arizona heat.

She slept, clenching her jaw, grinding her teeth. I read pamphlets on horseback riding and jewelry making and the Navajo. I listened to Mom snore. I went outside and called Jedediah from a pay phone and described the scene. I told him about the cactus, yellow flowers, fast-moving lizards, and flatland. I hung up and looked around for an ice and soda machine, scouted for others who might be Meadows patients' families but didn't see anyone. Later, we'd learn that most families stayed at the Hilton.

We drove through the desert to meet Cara. Mom counted the red rock monoliths. I'd read about them in a motel brochure. Once, Sedona was beneath the ocean. Over millions of years, the sea receded and layered sediment from volcanic activity formed mountains, weathered towers. Years and wind and water sculptured the sandstone into brilliant crimson buttes. Mom counted and gave them names as we drove: Coffeepot, Cathedral, Thunder Mountain, Rabbit Ears, Mother and Child, Twin Nuns.

Mom hadn't had a vacation in years. Kahlil couldn't hide his excitement over seeing his sober wife. He'd missed Cara.

We made it to The Meadows by three and signed in at the lobby and were searched for sharps (knives, needles, pens). A security guard showed us the way to Cara. We saw her for the first time in Sedona smoking in a gazebo among a group of patients, who were gathered like a losing baseball team in a dugout. They were hunched over, cigarettes dangling between their knees, kicking dirt. Cara sat next to a slender fashion designer who'd checked in for exhaustion. I recognized him right away from her description: hair waved over to the side with gel, smart tailored linen chinos, toffee spring oxfords with no socks. His shoes and pants were his uniform, his dignity. I wondered if he troubled to take his shoes off and pour them clear of sand. The horizon divided the landscape in half: sand and sky. There was no avoiding either.

"He's been making excellent progress," Cara had told me over the phone the week before my trip. "Just don't tell anyone he's here. It's a secret." He'd gone downhill after the failing of his latest collection.

"That's fine, but I don't think anyone we know would really care who you're in with."

"There's a guy here from TV, too, a comedian."

"Mmm hmm."

"He has taken a liking to me."

"Yeah?"

"An alcoholic all the way. He couldn't hack the pressure when his sitcom was canceled."

"Red nose?"

"Yeah."

"You know it."

"And you?" I wondered what on earth my sister had spun up to tell these men about herself. It didn't surprise me that she was getting on well with them. I'd learned over the years that some men like beauty with tragedy. A lovely woman with a dark rotten story is like sweetened chocolate with a hard caramel center that sticks in the teeth. For a certain kind of man, winning a blighted woman helps him stand taller. I hoped Cara had been careful.

There were others at The Meadows: a rotund man with square glasses and a head like a bowling ball, midwestern and middle class. His wife had put the money up for treatment after he'd holed himself up in a Vegas hotel with hooker after hooker and spent most of the family money. His regret went only as far as his having to endure the claustrophobia of his swanky incarceration. The other patients hated him. Sex addicts were the lowest breeds at The Meadows, sorrier than drug addicts and gamblers. Love addicts were the weirdest, Cara had said.

And there was Mitch, a depressive who had taken a liking to stimulants. He became Cara's true friend. She nicknamed them Team High and Low, the upper and downer duo. Mitch and Cara talked weekly up until the day she died. He never wanted her; he loved her like a sister. I called him the day she died. All he could think to say was "Shit." His answer to every detail I gave him was "Shit." Time, cause, place. It was all *shit*. He was right. I hope he's still alive now, living in California somewhere, riding his dirt bike and surfing.

At the gazebo Cara was new, gleaming, suntanned, and sober; she was wearing a necklace of cactus flowers. This was her final week of rehab. She was twenty-eight days clean. No small feat.

She left her tribe at first sight of us, her long white skirt swishing in the dusty yellow sand. She wrapped her arms around Kahlil and he pulled her up in embrace, lifting her feet six or more inches off the ground.

"You look like something sweet, baby." He buried his nose in her hair. "Honey and vanilla cream, that's it."

Cara was toned and with it. She'd lost her soft middle. As she swayed back and forth with her husband, her T-shirt peaked up, exposing her girlish belly. She'd not only lost drugs, she'd lost years.

Mom looked at her watch. "It's time to go in and meet the therapists."

"I've got meds first." Cara looked around at the group. "Hey, everyone, it's meds time."

The patients shuffled up and walked quickly back to the main building. Cara grabbed my hand and pulled me along. I waited in line with her. A nurse stood behind a door that closed at the bottom and swung open at the top. She shook three pills into Cara's palm and gave her a Dixie cup filled with water.

"Swallow," the nurse commanded politely.

Cara obliged and tossed the pills to the back of her mouth. She opened wide for the nurse and lifted her tongue.

The nurse nodded and moved on to the next patient.

"They need to see that I've not hidden the meds in my mouth."

Family Week was five days of intensive therapy. It began with a session where we were all given sketchpads, crayons, pencils, and markers and asked to draw an important memory from our childhoods.

Cara and I both made the same picture: a car driven by our father, our luggage piled high in his open trunk. My image was of the back of the car. The license plate read: FLORIDA. Cara's picture was a side view that showed us both sitting in the backseat, me looking small, crying, sitting directly behind our father. Cara is penciled into the car in faint lines, a smoky outline with her hands pressed onto the rolled-up windows, her mouth drawn in an O. In her picture she is screaming.

Kahlil drew himself at eight years old, kicking the winning goal in a soccer game.

Mom drew her family arranged around a fallen Christmas tree in their living room. Her mother stands with one hand on her hip, the other shielding her eyes. Her four siblings are scattered about in various poses of disbelief. Her father has bolts of lightning flying off of his head and dots for eyes. Mom drew sweeping lines beneath his arms to indicate movement. A broken bottle of liquor is smashed at his feet; a puddle of bourbon pools around his children. Drunk, he had knocked down their tree. Mom told the therapist he did this every year. Her brothers glued the ornaments back together and hoisted the tree back up. They all tried to imagine nothing had happened and got on with having Christmas morning.

The week went on like this, in group sessions, until Wednesday, three days into Family Week. We'd all cried and apologized and vowed to live more honest lives. Cara was going to be clean and take it one day at a time. We were being given the tools to help her accomplish this. It was to be a family effort.

Wednesday morning began like all the others, with decaf coffee and danishes in a conference room. The clock struck nine but as the other families made their ways into therapy suites, we were asked to report to the front office.

We were led into a windowless room and met by a woman who had a cardboard box filled with Cara's belongings at her feet. Cara's clothes were stacked and neatly folded; half-full bottles of shampoo and conditioner were ziplocked tight in baggies beside bars of packaged soaps. Her diary was there on the top of the stack to be seen, with lock and key. The box was topped with a construction-paper tiara glued with plastic jewels. Cara's name swept the front of it in a streak of silver glitter.

We all sat down.

"I'm afraid we're going to have to ask Cara to leave," the woman told us plainly.

"We've traveled all this way. There must be some kind of mistake," Mom said.

"Your daughter has violated the rules here. She's had sexual relations with another member of our community. As much as we'd like to, we can't overlook it." The woman folded her hands in her lap and pursed her lips as if she sucked a lemon.

"There must be some kind of mistake." Mom was confident. Being expelled by an uptight droid hardly seemed in good keeping with the spirit of Family Week.

"I'm afraid not." The woman gestured to Cara. "We'd all like you to explain, please. You know the first step. Acknowledgment."

"I did it." Cara's words were flat, matter of fact. She was entitled to her misdeed. There hadn't been a mistake—she'd met a younger man there, Charlie, a depressive. The accusations were right. The two had not only had sex, they'd fallen in love.

I looked over at Kahlil, who was picking at a cuticle and staring curiously at a reproduction of Monet's *Water Lilies* in a thick, gaudy, gold plastic frame. I was furious at Cara for screwing all of this up, for humiliating her husband in front of me and my mother and this counselor. Also, strangely, I felt the weirdest kind of relief. Her infidelity offered evidence that my sister was ready to be sexual. I considered this a good sign, an indication that The Meadows was doing its job: she'd allowed herself to be desired, and this seemed like a first movement beyond the trauma of her rape.

This is how Cara was caught: Another patient—a woman, a sex and love addict—had been watching Cara and Charlie when they snuck off. The woman had tried to strike a deal with Cara. She wouldn't tell on the two lovers if Cara did her the simple favor of allowing the woman to smell her fingers after sex. Cara had refused.

I thought of the money, the care that had been put into our last-ditch effort to help Cara get well. "What about the pervert who tried to get off on their fumes?" I was boiling, hating the sex addicts as much as anyone else there did. I'd been converted to the ways of The Meadows in just a few short days. "She's going home, too?"

"The other patient has been talked to and put in an intensive session for caving to her whims. She'll remain here. The young man will also be expelled."

"This is ludicrous." I pulled out a pamphlet for The Meadows from my pocket and scanned the patient rules.

There was nothing to indicate the sex addict should go.

"I can't go." Cara fell to her knees on the floor and wept. She begged the woman to reconsider. "I just want to get well," Cara sobbed. "I can't do that if I don't have the extra week here. Please."

But I could see she was sobbing crocodile tears. She wasn't sorry for the sex. She was sorry she'd been caught.

"Cara, please take your belongings." The woman got up and attempted to shake my mother's hand. Mom rejected the gesture.

"Cara, get off the floor. Kahlil, grab the box." Mom picked up her purse and slung it over her shoulder. "Let's go." She smiled wickedly at the woman. "We'll gladly take our exit." She grabbed Cara's hand and pulled her toward the door. "We've been kicked out of classier places."

We rode horses at a ranch after Cara's eviction from rehab, took a daybreak beginner's ride. Mom wasn't wasting a perfectly good vacation. Our guide took us through the desert with her trusty dog, a blue point mutt, a herder with matted gray fur and swift feet. He nipped at our horses' heels. We rode on through flatland and through dust kicked up from the horses' hooves, all of us silent except for the chatter of our guide. We passed over winding cliffs on narrow paths into a valley scattered with junked-out cars. We crossed over sun-beaten railroad tracks that had been forsaken long ago for highways. Mom says what she remembers of the ride is that the landscape was colorless except for the growth of an occasional pink flower. She says the desert is like an old hand-colored black-and-white photograph of a baby holding a rose.

We traveled through Arizona all that week. Our last trip was to the Grand Canyon.

Remember this time last year? We drove through Sedona on our way back from the Canyon. You kept asking, "How many people do you think fell in?" I stood as close to the edge as you would allow, near enough that I could see the distant green river at the bottom. There were awkward pauses in conversation—you didn't know what to do with the too clean me. Mom hit the brake and then the shift. It was a rental. I was red cliffs, towering.

In Sedona I learned to play Ping-Pong, and to touch the yellow flowers of Sonoran cacti without bleeding.

I walked the same path everyday with Mitch. Nothing but swearing from him. We wore name tags, hated them. We sifted desert sand though our fingers and counted roadrunners. We couldn't cross the red line without alarms going off.

Love was stupidly next door in a closet, in a bathroom, a patient's empty room. I left my wedding rings on a table. It started with a kiss. I gave Charlie my cloak as a hiding place and took his body as refuge. I wore his crown. It was makeshift, pink construction paper and paste. It read beautiful. We made plans to camp and make love near the Colorado without a tent. We got as far as Family Week and life and over.

Returning home I was the same battered girl without a throne.

On the plane ride home from Sedona, Cara asked Kahlil why he hadn't come to look for her during the rape. Had he not loved her enough to notice she'd left behind her wallet and purse? Why had he not known to search the path where they always walked the dog, before sunset? Why had he waited?

Kahlil said he stayed home in case the police called. He was worried if he'd gone looking for her, he'd not be home if she returned. He said he knew something must be wrong, but didn't know what to do.

Cara told me when they arrived home, she opened the front door on Kahlil's mess. Bags of garbage were heaped one on top of the other as high as the kitchen table. Every dish needed washing. Bed linens were stained with dirt and food and the cats had peed on them. A small turd floated in the dog's water dish. Maggots swarmed the sink. Empty pizza boxes littered the living room.

But now Cara was sober. She saw her home with clear eyes, and she promptly told Kahlil to leave. She hired a maid. Together they vacuumed Kahlil out of the house.

Chapter 14

Kahlil filled his pickup truck with his belongings. He'd said he would come back for the KitchenAid mixer, his sharp paring knives, and a few pieces of drafting equipment, but he never did. Cara told me he had driven away with his clothes flapping around in the back of the truck bed. She'd stood on the porch and watched him crest the hill toward the end of the street and wondered if he'd miss her; she hadn't planned for him not to. I'd never seen her so lonely as the months between their separation and Edgardo's trial.

Kahlil pulled up to the courthouse for the trial in his truck, the open cargo bed still filled to the top with his clothes. Even though he'd been gone since late spring and now it was September, he still had nothing but a tarp to protect his belongings from rain and thieves. He'd moved to a hippie commune and the bed of his truck doubled as a closet.

I met him in the parking lot and tried to hurry him in. Cara and my mother were already inside. The DA was prepping her. It was her day to testify. Kahlil was late. He, too, was supposed to be informed of protocol and given a run-through in questioning before he went on the stand that afternoon. He stepped out of the truck and kicked his work boots against the truck's front tire, dislodging chunks of mud and a few stray stones. I hadn't seen him since the trip to Sedona five months before. He greeted me the same way we'd last parted, with an untroubled embrace. He wore torn jeans and a moth-eaten wool sweater.

"We've got to go," I told him.

"I can't yet, not wearing this." He picked at his unraveling sweater sleeve. "Hang on." He reached into the truck's bed and pulled out a damp wrinkled suit jacket and a matching pair of pants. "I brought something civilized to change into," he said, and quickly undressed in the truck. He emerged in his suit. It reeked of cat urine and showed signs of mold under the armpits. "How do I look?" he asked, in earnest.

"Just like I always remembered," I said and put my arm around his hip.

We went through the court metal detectors and took an elevator to a third-floor waiting room where Cara and my mother sat with the DA. Court resumed an hour later.

Cara and Kahlil sat together for a while. He had something to tell her. Why he chose this day out of all days to do it, I'll never be certain. Before Cara went on the stand, Kahlil told her he'd met another woman, and now that woman was pregnant, expecting their baby.

There would never be a man she trusted, Cara said to the room, and got up to excuse herself to cry in the hall.

I thought of my husband's gentle embrace, the slope of his shoulders as he hugged me, his laugh for which I teased him. It sounded like a woodpecker nailing a tree, and it always answered my jokes. I was sad on Cara's behalf, thinking of my loving spouse. She'd just not found the right man. I was certain she'd find him if she kept her will and opened herself.

I saw Edgardo for the first time that day. He was as I'd pictured: tall, with a wide, round head, cropped black hair, broad shoulders, stocky legs and arms, scowling mouth. He turned to look at me sitting on a court bench and smiled, showing his teeth.

We sat in the courtroom with him for nearly a week. Evidence was presented, pictures of my sister's beaten body blown up big and pasted to flip charts. The DA pointed to the bites on Cara's neck and back with a yardstick—the bites matched the cast taken of Edgardo's teeth. Doctors testified that semen they'd collected from Cara was an exact match with Edgardo's DNA. Surveillance videos from the supermarket parking lot showed him leaving the liquor store and walking toward the park. It was clear, he was guilty. He was sentenced to life in prison, many lives, consecutively.

Start out with a white speck. A black speck came cuddled in a leather jacket. Kahlil's jacket had words written on it: We are all brothers under the skin and I for one am willing to skin humanity to prove it. The speck poked her nose from out of his coat. I could not hug my husband in his coat. I could not hug my husband because of his armor and his size. My arms couldn't reach around his shoulders. The black speck leapt out from his coat. White specks leapt kamikaze from the sky. The black speck was a dog and the white specks were snow. It wasn't going to stop, any of it: the growing dog, the failing marriage, the blizzard haunting the sky. The speck weighed two pounds before it grew to weigh seven pounds. The marriage grew from one year to three years and then it was gone.

Chapter 15

In April 2005, **Cara** and I stood shoulder to shoulder and looked out on the city of Burgos, Spain, watching the sunrise from the balcony of my flat. I was living in Burgos for a spring semester, teaching photography in a study abroad program. Four years had passed since the rape, three years since the trial, and we were leaving for Venice the following night by train. Cara had the idea that if we stayed up all night before our trip, we'd sleep soundly through the eight-hour-long train ride.

Our bellies were full of a wheel of rich sheep's milk cheese. Two bottles of wine from Bierzo that I'd been saving for a special occasion rolled around, empty, at our feet. We were drunk and laughing at our silliness; freely, lovingly, poking fun at each other. Early that afternoon, Cara had gone into a salon to have her hair cut. Her poor language skills and elaborate explanation of what she'd wanted had confused the stylist; Cara had left the salon with a pink-streaked asymmetrical bob. That same afternoon, at the cart in the center of the city where I'd daily ordered a cone filled with churritos, a French fry–like doughnut, I'd discovered I'd really been asking for pussy. The word for pussy was *coño*; the word for cone was *cono*. I'd switched them. That afternoon, as usual, one of the pair of women who operated the cart had stuffed my pastry, humming along to the plucky music that played over the cart's loudspeaker (part music box, part Muzak), then handed me my *cono*, smiling mockingly. The other woman had grinned, too, leaning back, hands in her apron pockets. I'd thanked them both. I'd picked out a fry; it had dissolved sugary and oily on my tongue, and I'd turned back for home, bumping into a woman who'd been standing behind me in line. The woman was mortified. Hands clasped over her mouth. "*Basta! Basta!*" she yelled at the vendors, wagging a finger at them; then in fluent English, she said to me, "Check the dictionary," scolding me in the way of a teacher.

On the balcony of my flat in the dawn, I stood twirling my twin's curly neon bob in my fingers, while she sweetly called me *cono*. All of Burgos seemed a less dim, gray place with Cara at my side. The warm golds, taupes, and reds of the buildings collided with the rising sun, and the streets came alive: the local baker pulled up the gates on her *panadería*, displaying a full case of crusty breads, cookies, and tarts; the cathedral tolled its 7 a.m. bell; the police made morning rounds, joking with one another; farm trucks moved their cargoes of sheep and pigs; children cried out, skipping down the streets toward school.

I'd spent most of my first few months in Spain in solitude, keeping occasional company with students and with the boys who ran the local Internet café. My vocabulary was limited and I kept it simple at the café—please and thank you and see you tomorrow. I'd pay them and they'd slip me a piece of paper with the number for a computer terminal. Sometimes one or the other of the boys would say thank you and call me *guapa*, which they called all of the girls.

I checked my e-mail as often as possible, looking for word from Jedediah. He figured his time alone would be the perfect opportunity to get a leg up on writing his novel, a noir about a detective who investigated crimes people committed while they slept. And I'd needed to take the job in Spain; the teaching experience and pay were both necessities for us. We were bringing in very little money; after Jedediah sold his book we'd begin thinking about starting a family, he said. By then we hoped I'd be able to secure a full-time teaching position in a city we both liked. The idea of my time in Spain had seemed reasonable, practically speaking, but emotionally I wasn't prepared to handle the time away. And Jedediah had not counted on a miserable wife, a furious and sexually frustrated wife, phoning constantly, weeping into the headset provided for phone conversations at the Internet café. The howling winter wind whipped my bare legs on the walk from my flat to the café.

"I'm exhausted," I cried into my headset one evening. "I'm not sleeping without help."

"Help?"

"Ambien," I told him.

"Don't we have enough on our hands with your sister?" Jedediah twisted the H knob of our kitchen sink, the one we'd bought at Ikea and installed just before my trip. I recognized the high-pitched squealing sound the faucet made as the hot water rushed into the pipes; as the rumble of water on metal faded, the pitch of my rage grew. Jedediah had visited for seven weeks, but that time had felt much shorter than it was. He regularly sent thoughtful messages and photographs via e-mail, but they only made my homesickness worse: our dog, Tillie, dreaming in front of a blazing fireplace; the geranium in bloom, reaching toward the window for a drink of muted winter light; the first sprouts of spring grass, poking through melting snow.

Unlike Jedediah, Cara had been making the effort to visit me monthly from Massachusetts; she had discovered that the *pharmacia* across the street from me in Burgos dispensed Klonopin without a prescription. She'd go to the *pharmacia* during the afternoons I taught and fill her cart with boxes of Klonopin. But Cara couldn't keep her pills a secret. One afternoon, while she napped, I opened her suitcase and found her diary; I picked its lock, read it as if it were my right. I needed to know what she'd been taking. She deserved that the door be closed on her affairs; I could never give her that. There were so many drugs.

Cara's penmanship, a bubbly cursive, looked harmless. She wrote in purple ink. The paper stock of her journal was imprinted with a sunflower field in full bloom, buzzing bees at the margin. On that cheery paper, she railed against Kahlil for divorcing her, not so much angry as bereft. There were suitors she mentioned with hope, but never more than a page went by before one name disappeared and was replaced by another. She'd sometimes write about her shame in turning back to heroin.

MARCH SOMETHING, SHITTY MASSACHUSETTS

Dear Diary,

I don't care to write anything that sounds beautiful. Relapse. I'm a drug addict: veins dead, bitter, drunk on powder. I'm the twin to be ashamed of. Sister would never do such things. How did I become that one person in every family who is sick and needs to be kept hidden?

The lovers that I have taken are sour replacements for my husband. My wedding rings are on my dresser. Pictures of my husband are in the bureau drawer. When I can't recognize myself, I remember that egg-frying antidrug commercial from the '80s:

Cara, this is your brain. This is your brain after rape. This is your lonely rape grief on drugs. This is the marriage you shoved your husband out of. I can't ask any questions. There are many, too many to ask—there are things that need doing: miss Christa, forget to dream, sew my skirt.

In her suitcase, next to her diary, I found five boxes of Klonopin stacked neatly one on top of the other, held together by a thin rubber band stretched to capacity. She'd wrapped the bundle—about a month's worth of pills—in a light green scarf printed with a tarot motif from the Crowley deck. She'd return to Spain when her supply ran low.

My husband didn't move with me to Spain because he had his head buried in a book. My sister visited me because she needed to bury herself in pills.

In the years since The Meadows, things had spiraled downward. Now that Cara lived alone, she'd disappear for days and tell elaborate lies about where she'd been. I'd been stood up for dinner more times than I could count, only to find her beat-up car parked in front of the dive motel where everyone went to score in Northampton. It became my duty, nearly weekly, to check on Cara in her apartment to make sure she hadn't offed herself by hanging herself from a chandelier or by finally coming across something sharp enough to slice instead of cut. I didn't have keys to her place, but I learned how to jump high enough to pull up onto her building's fire escape, climb the four flights of rickety metal all the way to her kitchen window, and slip inside from there. Of course, I'd never found her dead; I'd only found her with the TV turned up too loud, shopping eBay, speeding on Ritalin.

"You scared the shit out of me," she'd say, not at all afraid, just happy for the company.

But in Europe, I felt I should turn a blind eye to what Cara was doing. I'd spent too much of the last four months alone. I was willing to tolerate Cara and her irrational ideas in return for her company. It seemed better to humor her dramatic plans than to face another option: shut her out and spend the next months in near isolation, eating the solitary meals I bought at the *supermercado*.

Exhausted from having stayed up all night and day, but Venice-bound, Cara and I walked through Burgos in the late evening hours to catch the night train to Ibiza. I'd tried to be penny conscious when I booked our trip to Venice, and I had saved us one hundred and fifty dollars. But in exchange for our savings, we would endure a travel caper: trains to small-town airports to trains to bigger airports that flew planes to smaller towns. The trip would take us one full day.

At Burgos's Central Station, an hour early for our train, I pulled my luggage wheelie toward the ticket counter, avoiding eye contact with strangers. The homeless slept on benches. Mothers rocked fussy infants. Men checked wristwatches and newspaper stock pages. Vendors sold day-old *jamon* and *queso* sandwiches for half price. I heard the swift dry sweep of a janitor's broom against the station floor, and only half understood the announcements for train departures. I still only spoke common phrases and used them as frequently as I could: I don't know. How much? I need a phone card. I'm hungry, tired, thirsty, *lonely*.

We were almost at the ticket counter, when a man stepped into our path. His thinning black hair was pomaded and combed back to expose his broad shining forehead. I brushed past him, but Cara stopped and the two entered into conversation. He looked woozy; he wobbled from side to side, foot to foot. He was drunk or stoned—or both. He licked his lips nervously. The skin at the corners of his mouth was chalky and split. His lips were parched, cracked. He needed a drink of water and a rehabilitation center. He'd made it his mission to include us in his intoxication, skulking in to peddle his wares.

When we were younger, Cara had been unable to see the clearest signals of menace in a man. She had trusted instantly and universally. Her naïveté was charming. She filled out the Publishers Clearing House sweepstakes forms yearly for most of her life. She didn't hope she might win; she was certain she would. The first year she sent in the paperwork for the contest, she inflated a dozen pink balloons and strung them to our mailbox with silver ribbon. "It's for Ed McMahon," she said. "I want to make it easy for him to find us."

Cara fell in love with Venice the very first time she laid eyes on it. She was nineteen then; we were juniors at Bard. Her life and dreams for herself were all in front of her. In the photographs I'd seen of her then, in Venice's piazzas and gardens, she radiated promise. Venice is a city of magic—its narrow streets of stone are really alleys, and they are indulgent, romantic, and impossible—so like Cara.

But Edgardo Hernandez had beat the hope and wonder out of my sister, and in the Burgos station that early spring night, she was not just making chitchat with a forlorn traveler; she was on the hunt for what had become the great love interest of her twenties: heroin. Her affection for downers had alerted her to every hidden and obvious place to find them. She was far now from the girl who set out balloons for Ed McMahon. When she found her best chance at scoring drugs before our train trip in an unshowered stranger, she took it.

I walked toward the ticket counter, turning back to see if Cara was following behind. She wasn't. She was off in a dark corner, digging for euros in her change purse. She handed her cash over to the man. He counted it twice and tucked it quickly into his back pocket, nodding. He carried a backpack from which he produced a small baggie that he slid into her palm.

She shoved the baggie into her pocketbook and turned from him, her face bare of expression. Neither the dealer nor my sister was more than a blink to the other, a hallucination to be forgotten. "Sorry," Cara said. "He was lost. I helped him find his way."

We stood in line among the other passengers, near the loitering drug sellers and the handful of homeless. The new Europe milled around us: Moroccan women with baggage and babies at their feet. Tourists shortcutting through the Camino de Santiago, running to catch departing trains. Spring-break youth from everywhere, sleeping in packs on piles of luggage. Of course, by now, the sleeper car was sold out. I frowned at Cara but didn't mention her drug buy. We slumped toward the train.

We boarded and pushed our way down the aisle. Our car was filled to capacity, save the two seats we'd been able to reserve: a middle and window seat. The middle seat was next to a guy who'd fallen asleep counting his rosary. The clear carved beads glimmered from the station lights shining through the train's windows.

"I'm not sitting next to that guy. He's drooling." Cara moved away from her new cabinmate.

I shoved past her to the window seat and took it. "I think you've got something to distract you. You'll be drooling in no time." I pushed my carry-on under my seat. The train jolted and chugged forward. "Don't fuck with me," I went on. "I'm not keen on spending the night in a Spanish prison."

I looked out the window, pleased with my verbal jab. I refused to look at her, but I could feel her squirming next to me, trying to push her snoring cabinmate off her shoulder and onto his side of their shared seat.

She nudged me with her elbow. "Hey." She drew her hand up to her face and turned toward me, shielding her mouth from sight. "What's with those guys?" She nodded toward the trio of men across from us, who watched us bicker. I hadn't noticed them, but they were unmistakably the least desirable people with whom to share a night ride. They looked like the three stooges, except deranged and fresh from a bank heist.

Cara hid her overstuffed backpacks under our seats and tried to sleep. Our rail car held twelve strangers. A pair of lovers necked. The stooges talked quietly among themselves. A man gazed out the window and watched the dark fields zip past. A young woman with blond hair held her luggage on her lap and tried to doze, keeping one eye open. Cara and I sat together, fused, I placed my head on her shoulder. I closed my eyes and pretended to sleep. Cara pulled away. She took a dollar bill from her wallet and rolled it into a straw. She headed for the train lavatory.

Cara glided back to her seat, dreamy, drifting down the aisles of the train, palms skimming the headrests of the other night travelers. She walked one foot in front of the other, a line straight as an acrobat on a wire. She tipped back and forth with the sway of the train, reaching out to touch the shoulders of strangers for balance, occasionally gripping one too hard and issuing a breathless apology.

Beside me, she reached and uncrossed my arms. I'd possessively folded them across my chest to protect my broken heart and help me off to sleep.

"Remember when we were little and you'd cross your arms?"

"Yes." I did. I remembered. I was nearly thirty and still doing it. How could I forget?

"Grandma always knew you needed a hug when you'd do that. She said you'd go on hugging yourself unless one of us learned to do it for you."

"Remember how you'd cry when you didn't get exactly what you wanted? You're still doing that too."

"Oh Newt," she whispered. "I love you. I always have." Cara smiled and put my hands down in my lap, running her fingers against the ridge of my knuckles. "We're off to Venice. Let's be happy."

I closed my eyes and rested my head on my sister, nuzzling into her neck, nesting, ready to nod off. Cara laid her heavy head down on top of mine, her hair a soft veil falling into my eyes. We were twenty-seven years old. We'd been sleeping that way together since we were girls traveling in our mother's car. I forgave her. We fit perfect as puzzle pieces.

Our Burgos train brought us to a tiny town in eastern Spain, where we caught a flight with a bare-bones air carrier. In the early morning hours we flew a discount puddle jumper to Bologna, then caught another train to Venice. The sun was going down as we made our way to the city of water. Daylight had only a handful of hours.

I sat sideways as we neared Venice, staring blankly at a travel pamphlet and the discreet empty vomit bag tucked into the seat back in front of me. The pamphlet pictured families eating and shopping. None of them looked to have just bought drugs and none of them were twins. We were nowhere to be found in those brochures. Still, I was deep in imaginings of me and Cara and pizza and pasta. I saw us retiring to soft pillowy beds at the end of a day of touring church museums. She pressed her face up against her seat, indenting her cheek with the upholstery's zigzag pattern. She smiled sleepily and watched the world pass as our train whizzed by little towns. She saw the Italy she remembered from her travels in college, and she was eager to share this Italy with me. She pointed out goats and sheep and lines of fresh laundry that flapped in the breeze. She'd been waiting since we were nineteen years old to show me the country she loved. Finally, we were here.

We crossed the footbridge from Marco Polo station into the city, pulling our suitcases along, and for the first time it occurred to me that "city of canals" meant "no cars." We'd have to carry everything, no matter how far our accommodations.

"This way." Cara pointed down a winding street. "I remember."

"You've never even been to our hotel. You don't know the way."

"I do so. I remember the way to our piazza. It was just past a vendor who sold key chains."

I looked from one end of the street to the other, east to west. There were at least two dozen carts selling key chains. I stopped to ask for directions to our hotel at a cart that sold postcards and commedia dell'arte souvenirs. The man shrugged, pushing a mask with a full white face and teardrop into my hands. Its cheeks were painted bright green on the left, yellow on the right; both cheeks rimmed in gold. "You like?" The vendor seemed confident I would.

"No. No *gracias.*" I did like the mask, but I didn't want it.

"It's *grazie,*" Cara corrected. "This isn't Spain."

The mask in my hands was the crying Pierrot. I pulled the elastic string on its back, slipped it over my head, adjusted the fit to see and breathe. "Don't be ridiculous," I said from behind Pierrot, to Cara, changing the subject from language to directions. "We'd better ask someone else or we'll never find the hotel." My voice was muffled by the mouthless mask.

"What? I can't hear a word you're saying."

I flipped up the mask and showed myself, but Cara wasn't attempting to hear me; she was admiring herself in the shop's mirror. She wore a Zanni mask with eyes cut like a cat's. A plume of feathers covered her forehead. A long nose hooked down over her mouth. I lifted her disguise. "Let's go."

"You're no fun. You've never been fun." Cara frowned at me. "I've planned for this, of course, for your lack of funness. We'll have to have gelato first, then pasta. No one, not even *you*, can mope after gelato." Cara plucked a tiny chocolate bunny from a dish beside the cash register and tossed it in her mouth. "Tastes like Easter." She grabbed a second chocolate and placed it in my palm.

"If we ever find our way to the hotel," I said, "I'm sure I'll be plenty of fun."

An hour later, we found our tiny hotel, nestled in the center of a small piazza, next to a pasta restaurant with terrace dining. The bistro wasn't special, just a stop-off for tourists. We dined outdoors there, sharing a deliciously salty Bolognese. Our room had a view of a fountain in the center of the piazza where teenagers gathered to share wine and soda tonics after dark. At dusk men congregated outside a tavern directly downstairs from our room, hobbyists with guitars and drums. We danced with other girls who were staying in other run-down inns. Two doors down from our abode, the old bell of a gray, stone cathedral rang out every hour.

The hotel was run by a married couple. The innkeeper dressed well in brightly stitched handmade Italian suits sewn from tweed and twill. He combed his hair back in graying blond waves and wore small round wire specs. He was a dead ringer for Jeremy Irons playing Humbert Humbert, his well-practiced Italian charm—the accent, the dress, his harmless seduction— put on in hopes of more advance bookings.

We spent our days wandering the maze of streets and eating gelato and talking about our mother and father, Cara's divorce and recent romances. Over a plate of grilled sardines, she confided her regret over her infidelity and her fears of ever finding new love.

"Will I always be alone?" she asked, moving a bite of fish

around on her plate with her fork. "No one will ever love me. I'm damaged."

"Don't say such a thing," I said. "That's not fair."

"You don't understand." She set her cutlery down and pouted. "You're perfect."

I told my sister her affair was of no consequence, that she should not burden herself with remorse. I understood how she must have needed to feel the warmth of a new body, a lover who hadn't known her before she'd so nearly been snuffed out. "You've survived to live," I told her, drunk, not knowing what I meant. If only that had been true.

There were many pasta dinners, just as I'd imagined there would be, and shopping trips where we browsed trinkets that we'd never need. I have all of the things Cara bought then on my desk now: a Virgin Mary key chain, four Venetian masks— one with rabbit ears and a crying clown face, and a red leather diary embossed with a roaring lion—this Cara stole, sliding it into her handbag in a crowded shop as the store clerk helped a woman carry a ceramic Jesus to her waiting gondola. We also searched tirelessly for a birthday gift for Jedediah to help him ring in his twenty-eighth year. I would miss his birthday, and thought I should send Cara in my place to have dinner with him and present him with my gift.

I looked and looked but no gift said everything this one needed to: I love you, but I hate you for not being here. Thank you for allowing me to see the world, even if it's without you.

In a shop near our hostel, we found a toy maker who constructed three-dimensional puzzles. The puzzles were pre-painted brightly in blues, magentas, and golds. The toy maker had miniature puzzle gondolas, buildings and cats in windows backlit by moons. We liked the facsimile Venetian houses best for Jedediah and bought one of the few unpainted ones and a set of watercolors. I liked the bare sanded wood of the house we bought, and was happy that we could choose any color palette we wished to anoint our house for Jedediah. Cara and I spent our last night in Venice designing Jedediah's house.

The upstairs had arched windows that we painted dark gray to show that nobody was awake on the top floor. The light on the second floor, above the entrance, we painted yellow. The life of the house was there; our beaming yellow windows made it so. I imagined that's where living quarters would be: a hearth full of fire, vases of flowers on polished tables, sleeping dogs. We colored the front door red and the eaves, green; the roof, gray; the chimney, black to match its soot.

After the house dried, we disassembled it and put it in a long, flat, silver box that opened at the top. Taken apart, the house looked like a wooden children's puzzle, good decoration for a nursery. I wrote Jedediah a loving note on the back of a postcard I'd selected at the hotel gift shop; the card featured the commedia dell'arte character Pantalone. Cara and I both signed our birthday wishes.

I gave my husband a children's house puzzle for his birthday, and had it delivered in pieces to him by my sister, who insisted he assemble it in front of her. The card was stamped with the image of an ego-driven, needy philanderer and bachelor. I hadn't bothered to read the significance of the character. But Jed did. The broken-down fragile house and card worried him.

He wasn't always so perceptive, though. He gave me pages of his novel to read as soon as he'd written them. I waited eagerly for each new batch. The week before I left for Spain he had given me a new section. In it, his protagonist had been kidnapped by a set of identical male twins. The pair played cards in a bar and were known to be con artists, hit men. The twins knocked the detective unconscious and left him for dead, setting his body off floating on a barge filled with stolen alarm clocks. The detective woke heavy headed and confused from the twins' assault and realized the gravity of the situation: in order to survive his abduction, he'd have to kill the twins, an act that was out of character for the gentle, passive detective. In the rain, on the barge, he did just that—but the detective murdered only one twin. He did it in full view of the other, escaping both, leaving the forlorn surviving twin to rock his limp brother's body. Killing one was the same as killing both, worse. It was the detective's ultimate revenge. I read the pages and wept. Jedediah asked me if I liked them. I said I did. I said I liked them very much. Had he no idea how much we feared this? His plot was so like our life.

Chapter 16

A little more than a year after our trip to Venice, Cara came for a visit. It was the last time I ever saw her.

She'd just defended her MFA thesis. Her divorce had just been finalized. She'd recently moved in with our mother in Albany, to save money after classes ended. Her new degree gave occasion for her stay in the turn-of-the-century cottage where Jedediah and I lived in Massachusetts. Before she arrived, I put fresh sheets on her bed and made sure that the guest-room closet was empty of winter coats.

I liked that Jedediah and I owned the house, and I fussed over it. I wanted the home to be a haven for sleep and books and reading. I stoked fires in the hearth. I made dinners with lots of olive oil and salts. I decorated the porch with plants, and with candles that flooded in the rain; I emptied the pooled water out of the candleholders, and always set them back outside, but the wicks were soppy and wouldn't relight. The plants, by contrast, grew wild. Roots poked out from their plastic buckets and terra-cotta pots.

An excellent vacuumer and a dreadful dishwasher, I liked to drag the vacuum over the floors and watch the cat hair and dust disappear. The house had hardwood floors throughout, except for the guest bedroom, which had bead board. Cara stayed there when she visited. I painted that floor laurel green by hand. I made those walls cobalt blue and painted the trim a sunny fiesta yellow. I chose the colors by flipping open a book of Edward Hopper's paintings, stopping at an image titled *Chop Suey*. A pair of women sit in a café next to a window, an afternoon glow casting heavy, stark shadows. The women are in conversation, holding cups of tea, slouching in to listen. The woman with her back to the viewer has said something. Her friend in the flapper hat looks over the rim of her teacup, past her friend in the smart navy cloche.

I heard Cara's car pull up before I saw it. I hadn't seen her for weeks. I'd been waiting, pacing by the door. Her car had a belt loose in the air-conditioning unit and made a screeching, whirling, over-and-over noise that asked, did you miss me?

She pulled into the driveway and let herself into the house, heading straight for the guest room. She pulled a small red suitcase behind her, laptop bag hanging heavy over her shoulder, banging on her thigh. I'd followed her to the doorway and watched as she tossed her things carelessly onto the bed. Dirt from the suitcase's wheel made a straight, greasy line on top of the down comforter. She hadn't bothered with a hello and was already unzipping the front pocket of her bag.

"How'd your thesis defense go?" I asked.

She whipped around, surprised. "Oh, hi. You're here?"

"I live here, don't I? I was waiting for you."

"It went fine," she sighed. "I need a minute, do you mind?" She fished through her pockets.

"Can I bring you anything? Something to drink, a snack?" I noticed the flap of a plastic baggie emerging from her suitcase.

"Nope. I just have to pee. Do you mind?"

Cara slid her fingers into her suitcase and wrapped her hand around the baggie, holding it in a clenched fist. Fifteen, twenty minutes later, she emerged from the bathroom looking flushed and happy and went straight back to the bedroom. "Look what I brought!" She pulled a bottle of champagne from her shoulder bag and uncorked it. "Let's celebrate the end of thesis-writing hell!" She brought the opened bottle to her mouth and took a thirsty gulp, bubbly golden champagne running down her chin.

"It's noon, Cara."

"Yeah, but how many times do I get to be finished with the first draft of my book?" She batted her doe eyes at me and ran the back of her hand over her mouth, wiping it dry. She passed the bottle.

I took a tiny sip. "I want to head over to the gym before it gets too late. Want to come with?"

"You and your working out," she complained. "I'd rather stay home and relax."

"I won't be long," I promised.

"I see how it is," she sighed. "I get here and you're already leaving." She took another long drink. "Wait!" She jumped excitedly.

"What?" I bent down to tie my sneaker.

"I brought something else. Hang on." She shooed me out of the room and rustled through her bag. I heard her struggling with a zipper. She opened the door. "Ta-dah!" She wore the bridesmaid's dress she'd worn at my wedding.

She walked from the guest room into the living room and spun around. She tilted her head back and closed her eyes. The dress—black, floor length, and spaghetti strapped—brushed the floor and pulled up some dust that collected at the hem. The outer layer of the chiffon skirt was translucent, two pieces of fabric stitched together at the empire waist with a thin braid of matte black thread. She held her arms out straight, the left a little more weighed down than the right. Her half-empty bottle of champagne sloshed and fizzed as she twirled.

"This is the most beautiful dress I own." She lifted the skirt of the dress up to just below her knee and did a clumsy curtsy, admiring herself. "I think I'll sell it on eBay."

"Don't do that," I said. "You might have a chance to wear it again."

Cara sat down on the sofa, taking another swig. "I've got nowhere fancy enough to wear it." She sulked. "I bet you'd have a place to wear a fancy dress like this, in your fancy life, with your fancy friends." She picked up the skirt of the dress and dropped it. The fabric floated in waves onto her lap. "This is a dress for a princess, even if it's black."

I came home an hour later from the gym and found her in the same position on the sofa—except she'd finished her bottle of champagne and passed out. The empty bottle had rolled under the coffee table, spilling what little was left over the floor. I shook Cara awake and helped her up, guiding her to her feet. I walked her to bed and pulled the covers back, kissing my drunken sister's forehead, putting her down for the night.

It's always been the same house in my dream. I see that staircase. I see the cellar where we learned to shoot pool and dance old and talk dirty when we weren't supposed to know how. I see the bedroom with the two diagonal beds. We scared each other there with faces and deep voices until we were one, in one bed. I see the living room. The fuzzy, green carpet was like grass you could curl your toes in. This was our grandmother's house. The windowsills she filled with plants and knickknacks are bare in my dream. She loved her figurine of an Amish couple seated on a bench, sitting too intimately apart. And they were always like that, the couple, as if they came into this world painted. The couple held hands, just like us.

I would wrap myself around you tight as if we could be born together again. I would hold you on the way out, like Grandma's figurines never stopped holding each other.

I can see the backyard that never ended and hear our giggles, lost in piles of overturned leaves.

I dream we are home again. Where is home without you?

Now we are married. You cried at my wedding as though it was my funeral, made me want to run toward you, break from the union I was about to enter, and remarry you. It could have been our baptism.

You, too, have married, except better. You have a husband who wouldn't leave you. I'm divorced now. I didn't cry at your wedding. I wore the black dress you asked me to wear.

Who is the husband now? The wife? The union is divided but remains the same, in shards. Do we live anywhere?

We will always visit the same house, when we come home at night in my dream. We will be each other there, again. Just like we remember it.

On Saturday afternoon, a few days into Cara's stay, we sat side by side on the front porch. "I want ice cream," she said, cigarette in hand. She wore low-rider jeans and a green tweed blazer cropped at the waist. "This is my smart blazer," she said, taking another drag off her Natural American Spirit. She smiled through a mouth of smoke. "I think my book sucks." She waited for me to correct her.

"I can't say," I confessed. "I haven't read it yet."

"Well, don't even bother," she said. "I have things I want to change before you read it."

"There *is* always time to edit," I countered. The few words I said to her about her book, which I hadn't even read, telegraphed my opinion of her abilities—her prose was too lax and flowery.

"You hate me," she said.

I did believe she hadn't worked hard enough. I was always

thinking that about her. What I feared in myself, I loathed in her. A year later, after I'd painstakingly removed all of her files from her computer, I would discover that she'd been writing feverishly before she died.

That afternoon, though, I only said, "I don't eat ice cream for lunch."

What had become of me? My sister had turned me into a scold. I had always been up for ice cream. I'd abolished my free-wheeling self while I tried to establish rules that I hoped would keep her from the needle. But whom was I kidding? Strict rules about day drinking and dessert would never save her.

She left in a huff and went inside. She walked in a disappointed slouch and retreated to the guest room, then came out quickly, looking a bit more chipper.

"Let's go to the gym," she said, and went straight into the bathroom.

I heard her inside, scrambling around, opening and shutting the bathroom cabinets, turning the faucet on and off. She was making noise, I thought, to cover up what she was doing.

I went to the second bedroom of our house, where Jedediah worked on his novel. I knocked on the door lightly.

"Honey?" I asked through the closed door.

"Yeah, Christa," Jed said.

I turned the doorknob and let myself into his study. "I don't know how to tell you this, but Cara's shooting up in our bathroom."

"Christa, I'm working. Can't this wait?" Jedediah took his glasses off and folded them on his writing desk. He put his hands on my shoulders and squeezed them apologetically.

I sat on his lap and cried. "I don't know what to do." I wiped my tears and nose with the dress I was wearing. "I think she's going to die."

"This is between you and Cara."

"Please," I sobbed. "I feel like her life is in my hands."

"Okay," he said and put down his pen. "I'll try one last time." Jedediah knocked lightly on the bathroom door. Cara opened it just a crack, enough to peek out but not be fully seen.

"What is it?" she asked innocently.

"Are you shooting up in our house?"

"Of course not," she said and tried to pull the door closed; Jedediah used his foot as a doorstop. "I'm taking care of some cat scratches," she said and kicked his foot out of place, closing the door on him.

"I can't do this. I can't help," Jedediah apologized to me. "If that's all you have to say about what you're doing, there is nothing I can do," he said to Cara through the door. "She's never honest."

"Please?" I asked him. "One more time."

I'd pleaded with Jedediah as if he had more power than I to lift Cara from her addiction. Of course I knew that wasn't true. In retrospect, I think I knew he couldn't help. Still, it hurt me that he wouldn't make more of an effort. Later, after Cara died, I'd see how easy it was for Jedediah to turn away from me, too. After we'd divorced I'd often think of this moment in his study. He'd been unwilling to help my sister through her brutal and terrible ordeal, and when it was my turn for mental collapse he'd eventually be unable to help me. He didn't have the right tools to do it. It seemed possible that no matter how I'd behaved, saint or sinner, Jedediah would never have had the fortitude necessary to weather the brutal storm of grief that visited our home.

Cara was raped only four weeks after Jedediah and I were married; the rape became part of our marriage. Jedediah would lie beside me most nights. Or we only spooned, him behind me, his arms wrapped around my waist. We could have been brother and sister. On the rare occasions when we'd begin making love, I'd close my eyes and imagine that I was my sister. I could feel her assailant on top of me. Jedediah was gentle, but to give to him, I had to float out of body. I kept my floating a secret.

I walked back to the bathroom; I placed my ear against the door and listened. There was a lot of noise and then there wasn't any at all. She came out with Band-Aids on the insides of both arms.

I had nothing to say to her when she emerged, except, "Get out."

I packed her suitcase and dragged it out of the guest room.

"You're going to rehab," I said. "I'm not going to have anything to do with you until you go."

I pointed to the door.

I remember how the tailpipe of her car spewed smoke as she pulled out of the driveway. I went to the sink and washed the dishes. I stared at the wall in front of me. I thought: when Cara dies I'm going to get a divorce. When Cara dies, I'm going to move to New York City. When Cara dies, I'm going to be very thin.

Bitter berries cling to the tree I cling to. I am wrapped here. Stuck on the land. Autumn fell beneath the snow. We can't eat the berries. They are poison on red lips. Come and get me. This is the land where you put me. This is the dirt I buried myself in, frozen solid beneath the snow. I ate the berries. If you ask, I will tell you. There was no knowledge to consume. I was naked before I put them to my lips, before I stuck my arms with the things you said would kill me.

If I were to write a letter to you, it would read:

Dearest C.,

Nobody can save the naked on the bloody ground. Please forgive
me. Please forgive yourself.

It's that simple.

*I can tell you what it's like to die. It's blue and it's calm and it
was autumn two years ago and it's not like sleeping at all. I can't
tell you how I got back. I can't tell you about traversing cliffs, traversing life. I can tell you how to hurt yourself because that's what
I got good at. I can tell you about being a bitter berry. I can tell
you about my purple face and how many words my ears can't
hear. I can tell you what a fist feels like. I can tell you how to eat
and shoot and eat. I can show you how to run. I can show you
how to fight. I can show you broken bottles on scattered leaves: It
is my face. It is these branches. It is a landscape within another
landscape. I know your camera. It says, I love you and I am
watching. Your film takes the color of the sky and keeps it alive. You
bleach and freeze my body, pure as white. I pray it's not artifice. I
need these moments, the snow and the winter cold. Berries. Remember not to eat them when you are bitter. What would Grandma
think of our lives? Give me your hand, please. Pick me up.*

Chapter 17

I chose flowers and prayer cards, a casket, the method of internment. I sent word of Cara's death to those who loved her. Mom said I should do the planning. I was the only one, she'd said, who'd know what Cara would have wanted.

"How would you want *your* funeral?" Mom asked. I was the next best thing to having Cara there to do it herself. So I planned my funeral during the second week of June in 2006, a hot and humid seven days when spring gave way to summer.

I went to three flower shops to look for a casket topper: I wanted daisies. The daisies, I argued to the flower shopgirl, must not just *top* the casket, they must look *wild* on it, as if they were growing on the lid of the box where Cara lay. I'd bought the Trappist premier Premium casket in a cherry stain. The Trappist is handcrafted out of hardwood and has mitered joints and raised panels on mortised stiles and rails. The Trappist came with a hinged lid and an optional keepsake cross. The daisies on that casket would have to be chaotic and spill over peat moss or something green that might have grown in a fairy tale.

"This isn't just *any* casket topper." I leaned in over the florist shop's counter, within breathing space of the shopgirl's register. Her brown hair was tied back in a severe ponytail; the braces on her teeth were looped with neon green rubber bands. "This is for my sister, my *identical* twin sister." I was nearly out of breath. "And I don't want any plastic ribbons."

"We don't have daisies in right now." The girl absently counted change. "I'm sorry to hear about your sister," she continued, "but what is peat?"

I turned my back on the girl and opened my funeral-planning guide. "There is another store down the street," I said. "If you can't help me, I'll take my business there."

"I can manage daises, I guess," she conceded. "Let me ask my manager." The shopgirl picked up the phone and spoke softly into the receiver. "He'll do it," she told me, and pulled out an invoice pad from beneath the counter and started scribbling. "We've got peat moss but we'll have to order daisies. You'll have to pay extra; they aren't in season."

After the casket and the topper, outfits were next. I dressed my sister and then I dressed myself.

For her funeral Cara wore the dress I'd asked her to wear to my wedding: the black chiffon dress with the three underlayers of crepe that had swished about as she walked. She'd worn open-toed jeweled sandals to the wedding. We'd bought the shoes together at an Albany shopping mall. The price was high but I'd pushed them her way, urged her to try them on, and then bought them for her, an early birthday gift. I'd looked through her closet for the sandals to give the funeral director, sifting through pairs and pairs of shoes, and couldn't find them. I bet she wore those kitten heels into metal nubs.

Her feet were bare, hidden beneath the closed lid of the coffin. She would have wanted it that way, to be barefooted in the afterlife. The casket opened in two parts and the bottom part was shut. A silvery metal rod propped the top lid. It was not just as I would have wanted. I decided then that I wanted a glass coffin for my rest. I told Jedediah and no one else. Months later, the search history on our home computer revealed that

Jedediah had been reading instructions on how to build or buy such a casket.

Cara looked garish in hers. She wore a glossy, cherry stain on her lips. Her hair was kiss curled and sprayed. She was boxed in, cushioned by the soft shining white of satin padding. Her blood was drained and replaced with preserving chemicals. Her lips were sewn in place, almost shut. Her eyes were stuffed with cotton. Her head was propped—these are the things the undertaker must do to prepare a body.

I knelt beside my twin and stared down at her. Her lips were parted as if she were about to give a kiss. I was drawn to the tiny slit between her lips, a wordless sliver of black that set off the thread that closed her mouth: alabaster complexion, pink cheeks, claret lips with silver stitching. I could have kissed her but I didn't. Her eyes were closed with the same thread spun for her mouth. Her eyelids were made up with sarcoline shimmer and shadow, but the liner was crooked, drawn beyond her lashes, almost to her temples, and her cat's eyes had a smudge. The light shadow dusted at the crease of her lids brought out the sour color of her pallor. She looked yellow and green and blue. Her skin was taut and her rose rouge wouldn't blend. Blush sat on the tops of her cheeks in powdery circles. The worry line on her forehead had been erased by the magic plumping effect of embalming fluid. She would have been pleased to know that death had made her younger.

Cara's was a bare-shouldered corpse. She wore a shawl that matched her dress. It was flimsy, barely there. Heliotrope velour flowers covered it seam to seam. It didn't hide the mole on her shoulder, or the web of bruises visible from her neck to her collarbone—she must have bumped herself or fallen before she died. The velour flowers, the hair style, her makeup had all looked flirty when she was alive; the outfit looked dowdy in death, grandmotherly. She resembled an Italian grandmother in death. The undertakers who prepared Cara's body specialized in that exact clientele, grandmas; they'd done their job well. I would look like this if I were dead right now, I thought. I bent in closer and touched Cara. She felt cold and solid. Her arms had been shaved clean. She smelled like her perfume, *Pleasures!*, and like corn chips and rot. Her corpse was both mine and not mine. They say that the funeral ritual helps survivors acknowledge death. It keeps those who are still alive moving forward so they won't die themselves. The body lives. We look upon the dead and separate ourselves from them. *I haven't died, too,* we can tell ourselves; *this is not me.* The death of an identical twin is just the opposite.

My sister lay in her casket, one hand crossed over the other. The remaining polish on her nails was old, dull, and chipped. Her cuticles were pulled back where she had bitten them. I had never seen such a tacky, hopeful manicure. Coral wasn't the color a person who intended to die would choose for herself. I was looking for evidence, for a clue that said: I didn't do this to you on purpose, with no word or note, no letter.

I dressed for Cara's wake without mascara and dabbed my lips with the same color I gave the undertaker to apply to my sister's cheeks. I wore a black eyelet dress, tea length, with four ruffled tiers. The dress was trimmed, each layer, with a red and white candy-striped ribbon. I pinned two cream-colored orchids into my hair, one above each ear. We'd both fastened two orchids into our veils at our weddings; each represented a sister. I wore black-strapped pumps. Blood vessels on my cheeks had burst from crying. I didn't bother trying to cover the purple-flecked constellations with powder.

"You could wear a trash bag and still look good," Cara had told me once; we were standing in the dressing room of a Salvation Army store. I wore a wool tent dress and an equally hideous matching cap, woven from yarn with a loose pile. "It's really unfair," she'd said, looking at herself in a frumpy pair of pants and a cardigan. We could wear an identical garment and it would look different to us, but we'd look exactly the same to anyone else.

I had dressed for her wake in a fury. If I was to be a living stand-in for my sister, I would take it out on her with my outfit. People glanced first at Cara in her casket and then at me. I saw a flickering horror in their faces that they concealed with hugs and solemn handshakes. I looked like a tart and a circus clown. The confused and curious looks, familiar to me as Cara's twin, were now grim instead of inquisitive. Twins are fun to try to tell apart, but not at a funeral.

Chapter 18

I don't know if I believe in the intuition of twins. The knowing, feeling, or knowledge of the whereabouts and pains of a double have always seemed impossible to me, even having one of my own. But when I found out about Cara, I was driving east on Canal Street in Manhattan. And before the ringing phone in my lap was answered, I knew what I'd discover on the other line. I did.

I'd just gone to a tiny bar on the Lower East Side in Manhattan with Jedediah to hear a reading of his book. The bar was a place where Cara had read just the week before. The woman who ran the series came up to me after and said hello, thinking I was my sister. I was tickled. I loved being mistaken for Cara; it was a game I never tired of. I explained to the woman that I was Cara's twin, and the woman and I both laughed at her confusion. She told me how beautifully Cara had read; I'd had to work the evening she was scheduled to read. I told the woman this, though she didn't ask why I'd not come. The truth was that ever since I'd asked Cara to leave my home, I felt I wouldn't be welcome at her readings. Cara was furious with me; she had sent hundreds of text messages berating me. She was distraught by what she felt was my total abandonment. She had told Mom to call me and say that if she died by suicide it was my fault, period.

I'd fallen on the floor and wept for an hour the night my mother delivered the blow of those words, wondering what spell Cara must have cast to convince Mom I was deserving of such a message. I felt the punch of Cara's threat in my gut as if it were freshly dealt as we said good-bye to the bar owner. The familiar flutter of worry in my chest, a steadily turning pinwheel.

After my husband's reading I stood in the warm evening sunlight and held up a compact mirror to help something out that had blown in my eye. I blinked, trying to free the lash or dust or pollen, and I noticed that the color of my eyes seemed lighter, greener, more like Cara's than usual. My guilt was palpable, and I missed her. I thought maybe it was time to apologize, so I called her. There was no answer. I figured that she still wasn't ready to talk.

I got behind the wheel and pulled out onto the avenue, taking a left onto Canal Street. A pair of sisters, no older than nine and six, laughed and played on the sidewalk. They wore pretty yellow matching sundresses and each carried lazy, drooping helium balloons that chased after them as they ran ahead of their exhausted mother. My heart sank at the sight of them. Why wouldn't Cara answer her phone? Was I so terrible as not to deserve a single hello? I'd tried her many times that day and was transferred each time to voice mail.

I watched the girls skip-dance down the block. Their long, curly, dark, messy hair bounced against their backs. They stopped at the corner and hugged. I smiled at the loving pair, watching as the older girl quickly broke their embrace and made an ugly face at her sister, who promptly cried. The mother shuffled up and took each in separate hand, a silent practiced scold. She pulled them along as the crying girl wiped her tears with the back of her arm and her sister pouted. I'd been trying to call Cara since noon; I knew how the younger sister felt. Cara had shunned me with the scary face of silence.

The phone buzzed in my lap at 8 p.m. and I looked down at the words, *Mom Home*, flashing on the display. Mom and I had talked on the phone every day since I'd left for college. But I was queasy at the sight of her number, even though this was the hour we usually talked—after work and dinner. I couldn't bring myself to answer. I passed the phone to Jedediah.

"It's my mom," I told him. "Could you get it? I have a bad feeling."

"Okay," he said, "but can't you just call her back later? We're driving."

"No," I snipped. "Just answer. Please?"

"I don't want to talk to your mother right now," he said lightly, apologizing. "I'm tired and hungry."

"I think Cara died. Please answer the phone," I said, surprising myself.

Jedediah rolled his eyes. He'd heard this before. Cara was so frequently in trouble that he'd grown used to having to calm me down, to talk me off the ledge of worry. But how could he respond to his panicked wife but to answer the call and put her mind at rest? So he did. Jedediah listened to my mother on the other line. He was quiet.

"She's dead, isn't she?" I asked, begging him to wave me off, to say everything was okay. Instead, Jedediah looked away and at his feet, as if my mother's words were a weight. "She's dead, isn't she?" I said again, not waiting for his response.

"Pull the car over," Jedediah said, pointing toward the curb.

"She's dead, isn't she?" I repeated the words that had so strangely come to me. I jammed down on the brake.

"Christa, listen to me," Jedediah demanded. "Pull the car

over." He put his hand on my shoulder, trying to steer me in the direction of the parking space.

"She's dead," I said. I had believed she might die for so many years and the shock of feeling I had was nothing like I'd imagined it would be. I felt bodiless, as if I had fallen into a great cold bottomless sea, sinking fast as a boulder. A scream started in my chest and roared out from my throat. I screamed again and again, short high staccato stabs. I never knew I could make such a sound. I stopped, my face wet with tears, and looked at my husband wild with fear.

"Yes," Jedediah whispered, and tried to take the wheel with one hand and pull me closer with the other.

I batted him away and felt what I can only name as my spirit rise up and fly through the tiny crack between the window and the door. I was vapor, air, mist, breath. I was wind, a woman without a body. Unmoored and unafraid of the consequences of oncoming traffic, I reached for the door. I unbuckled my seat belt and got out of the car and shrieked, banged my hands on the hood, and ran out in front of passing cars. The light turned green.

I weaved through traffic, shrieking at the top of my lungs in waves, like warning sirens for a fire. Cars blasted their horns. Drivers cursed, hung from their rolled-down windows, and waved angry middle fingers.

I didn't see him, but Jedediah chased after me, apologizing to furious drivers as he went. I stopped finally beneath the changing traffic light, looked skyward, and howled like an animal. The force of my screams snapped both of the thin straps of my sundress. They waved limply over my exposed bra, fluttering up and down as cars sped past. The woman on the sidewalk, the mother, picked up her girls in their yellow dresses and covered their ears. She carried them to safety inside a jewelry pawnshop on the Bowery. The lights outside flashed: CASH! DIAMONDS! LAY-AWAY!

Chapter 19

The morning after Cara died, she came back. I hallucinated her in my kitchen.

Cara wore baggy blue pajamas cuffed at the wrists. She sat with her ankles crossed, on the floor in front of the woodstove, beneath an open window. She had helped herself to coffee; she stirred it with a teaspoon. The soft clink of silver against porcelain, the bell with which she'd summoned me.

She looked just as she always had in the mornings: messy-haired, her face pillow- and blanket-creased.

I fell to my knees before her in thanks, rested my head in her lap. She'd returned to me, just as we'd both promised. When we were girls we'd made a pact: If one of us died first, a sign should be given from beyond, a gesture to say we'd made it, we were safe: a flick of a light switch; a vase pushed from the mantel; a door blown open; a ringing phone; a visit must be paid. That was the rule.

"I thought you might be worried. I know how you are." Cara put her cold hand on the back of my neck and gently rubbed, pressing her small thumb down into my sore shoulders, smoothing knots, kneading like a kitten for momma's milk.

"Are you in heaven?" I asked.

"I don't know where I am. But there are other women here like me." She pushed and rolled her bony elbows tenderly into my back.

"I'll miss you," I begged.

"I like it here. We women eat. We play hide and go seek in the sunflower fields. We hold hands and swing near the water's edge."

"Will I ever see you again?"

"I hope not here. You wouldn't fit in."

"Why not?"

"We compare scars and burns," she said. "You don't have any of those."

"But I do," I argued.

Cara lifted my head from her lap, holding the sides of my face with both hands. "You have years before you, happy ones."

"I don't want years." I was certain of this. I felt I had been cut; I was alive, but only by half.

I twisted from her grasp. I'd loved her as though she would never die. "Did it occur to you that if you went and died I would still have to live? How could you do this?"

"There are things still left to do," Cara said, apologizing. "You'll have to plan my funeral."

"What are you asking of me?" I hadn't allowed myself to consider what would happen to her body.

"I spent years trying to get out of this body," she said. "Get rid of it. Burn it."

"I don't know if I can." How could I destroy her?

"Please. Help me get out of here," Cara was pleading.

"I will. I promise." But I wondered too what would become of me. We'd been one soul in two bodies.

"Take me to Venice," she said. "I could be there forever. When we went together, it was the best time of my life."

Cara told me she wanted to wear a fancy dress and then be cremated and scattered in the sinking city: the other half of me wanted to spend eternity swirling in the Venetian tide.

Chapter 20

Three weeks earlier, a tire on Cara's car had flown off on the interstate. She had been coming home to Mom's from downtown when the tire came loose and then shot straight up into the air like a pop-up ball. The hubcap had rolled to the side, a grounder. She'd lost control and turned the wheel quick to the right to recover, careening sidelong into a guardrail. The wheel had flown to places unknown, and the front fender with it.

June 13 was the day Mom and Cara had planned on driving to Will's Wheels and Hubcap Haven in Middleburg, to pick up a new tire. Will's is open until 5:30 p.m., and it's a forty-five-minute drive from Mom's house. Mom hoped to leave work early enough to get to Will's before it closed.

She'd seen Cara early that morning, just after sunup, as she was leaving the house for work. Cara stood in the kitchen stirring a spoon of sugar into her coffee. Ordinarily, Cara woke after eleven; she slept in like a teenager. Mom asked if Cara planned to accompany her to Will's, and Cara was ahead of her. She proudly handed Mom a freshly printed copy of directions. Mom poured herself a cup of coffee into a tall metal travel mug and kissed Cara's cheek, thanked her for being so thoughtful, and headed out for work. Mom said she'd call when she was ready to leave. She'd see Cara later.

Mom works as a laboratory specialist at a fertility hospital. She helps women conceive. Her day consists of semen washes and injections of ready sperm into waiting eggs. She makes twins at her job, as many babies as can be safely tucked into a uterus to grow. June 13 was busy with babies—typical of spring. She wouldn't be out early.

At 3 p.m., Mom left a message for Cara saying she wouldn't be able to leave work for another hour. She asked Cara to call and let her know if she wanted to be picked up to go to Will's. Mom called several more times, and finally made the decision to go straight to Will's. She didn't want to miss out on getting the wheel. Graham, Mom's boyfriend, had set aside time that evening to paint the fender and start putting the car back together. There wasn't a lot of time. Cara needed the car; she was to begin her summer teaching job at Williams College that weekend.

Mom arrived home at six. Cara's dog met Mom in the kitchen, whined and yawned, scratched at her leg. Mom called out. There was no reply. She opened a window and looked into the backyard. Cara wasn't there reading a book or napping on a lawn chair in the shade. Cicadas sang in the trees. Lilies bloomed. The grass would soon need cutting.

Mom went upstairs and looked to see if Cara was sleeping. Her bed was unmade, but empty. Her favorite shoes were tucked beneath her desk. Cara's diary was open; a pen lay in the crease of its spine. She'd left her perfume uncapped on her dresser, beside a soggy bowl of cereal. Cara's purse was open and rifled through on the floor. Her wallet was missing. Maybe she'd gone out with a friend for ice cream or had a last-minute date? There *was* a new young man in the picture—there were several.

Mom walked to the hallway and looked at the open bathroom door. Cara had scolded Mom earlier in the week for walking in on her when she was in the bathroom; that was still on Mom's mind. There were new rules to follow now that her grown daughter had moved back home. Rule number one: privacy.

Mom had painted and freshly papered every wall in the house. Each room had a decorative motif. Mom had moved from room to room in a circle of remodeling. This was her habit; it had been for years. It still is: She finishes one room in the house just as the first needs remaking. She guts her house with sledge-hammers; she sandblasts plaster. Mom smells like wood stain. She breathes in fiberglass by the lungful. She makes her home prettier than the newest Pottery Barn catalogue. She had made the bedroom upstairs and the adjoining bathroom comfort-able for Cara. The shower curtain was crisp and clean. The bathtub was caulked and the drains clear.

Mom had made everything right in her house, but every-thing seemed wrong to her that evening: It was sunny and warm outside, but inside the house was cold and dim. The dog was frantic and wouldn't follow Mom upstairs. The wrecked Mitsubishi was in the driveway, but Cara wasn't around.

Mom went downstairs to start dinner and stood at the stove; Graham came in, said hello, and wrapped his hands around her waist. He asked what was for dinner. She said she'd planned to cook on the grill, but found it was out of propane. Graham suggested they go out to eat. They could stop on the way to his auto shop and save time.

They went to a diner down the road; Mom had a fish fry. She wanted to go back, felt she must go back, but didn't say anything. She'd been told she was paranoid and she knew that she was. Hers had been a lifetime of fears grown into horrors. Her father didn't live to see her eleventh birthday. Her own mother had passed when she was only twenty-one. They'd just buried her eldest brother. It was trivial, she knew, but the family cat had just died, too, right at Cara's feet. Was this an omen? The proud Siamese was old, but had sickened suddenly, seized, and failed. Cara called Mom at work with the bad news. That was just days ago. In the prime of her life, Mom was surrounded by death. There was always a disaster plan. Her life had trained her to make them.

Mom took a deep breath and thought of the shining new hubcap and sturdy wheel. Cara was fine. Soon she'd be off in her newly repaired car.

At the shop, Mom sanded the fender to prep it for the paint. Graham opened the new bucket and found it was the wrong color. The auto paint store had misread the code and mixed brown instead of blue. Car work ended for the evening.

On the way home, Graham saw one of his friends. The two stopped so he could visit. Mom fidgeted with her phone, called Cara. No answer. She told Graham she wanted to go home but didn't say why. Mom was always worried about something: the iron was switched on, she'd left the door unlocked, the dog had slipped the fence, her daughter was dead and gone.

They got home around 7:30 p.m. Mom went immediately upstairs, first to the bedroom, then to the bathroom.

Cara was on the floor, sitting, half on her right hip, her legs bent at the knees and to the side. Very casual and easy. Her head was bent down so her chin rested on her chest. Her hair covered her face. The sink cabinet supported her forehead. Mom called Cara's name, put her hands on Cara's back; it was warm, a trick of the sun. The sun had risen and set on her back. Mom placed her hands on Cara's shoulders to shake her. They were cold. Cara's arms were in front of her, hands clenched and purple. Mom knew she was dead from her hands. Cara sat on her open wallet. It was stuffed full: appointment cards, saved fortunes from cookies, a book of stamps, two one-dollar bills, five bags of heroin. Graham heard Mom scream and ran upstairs—this was noted in the police report. Mom went for the phone, still calling out for Graham. She dialed 911.

The operator told Mom to lay Cara on her back; she said she'd talk her through CPR. Cara was rigid, propped between the sink and the commode. She was immovable, too heavy for her mother's arms. It was Graham's turn to try; Mom stayed on the phone with the operator, begging her to send help. Mom went back and forth. She alternated thinking—Cara was dead; maybe she was going to be all right. Mom left the narrow bathroom so Graham could get inside. She asked him the same question, skipping like a record in her head: "She's not dead, right? She's going to be okay, right?" He didn't answer.

From the door, Mom saw that Graham had moved Cara from in front of the sink to the wall just inside the doorway. She was still, frozen in position. Mom couldn't look at her face. She'd never forgive herself this moment of self-preservation: a mother should never fear her child's face.

She heard sirens in the driveway, went downstairs to usher in the EMTs, and followed them upstairs. Now she was asking them, "She's going to be okay, right? She's not dead, right?" No answer.

The police found a dirty syringe, cotton balls, a spoon, and a lighter, which Cara had used to cook up her brew. All were tucked into a makeup bag in her medicine cabinet. Along with the makeup bag there were several bottles of Dexatrim, a pile of hair clips encrusted with glitter, and plastic flowered bobby pins. She had a bottle of multivitamins that read: *Healthy Choice Naturals*; *choose to begin the rest of your life.*

The police noted that Cara had started to tidy the room after sitting on the toilet to shoot up and must have gotten dizzy. She simply sat down and closed her eyes and never got up. A bottle of Windex with the top screwed off sat on the floor beside her.

She'd cleaned her needle with window cleaner and then tidied the room. It was clear that Cara intended to go on with her day. If she'd died instantly, she would have left a mess. If she'd planned on dying, she would have left a note. Writers leave notes.

The police and paramedics sent Mom downstairs, first to the kitchen, then to the living room. Mom was not to see them taking Cara out of the house.

A psychic once told Cara that she'd die young, and on the opposite side of the world from where she was born. She took her last breath in the town where she was born. She took her last breath at home.

Chapter 21

Cara's boyfriends came to her wake and her funeral. They vied to carry her casket. Joseph Mario was a painter. He accompanied me in the procession of cars from the funeral home to the church. He was nearly family because he had given her a ring. He was the last boyfriend to propose, the second to do so in Italy. He wasn't her fiancé; he was her ex-fiancé, but he was the last of her fiancés. I invited him to ride with immediate kin at the head of the procession. He'd bought her diamond in Chinatown and had it fastened to a platinum band. We sat side by side in the convoy of mourners following directly behind the hearse. I didn't rent a limousine. I selected a van that was ordinary but large enough for six. Cara wouldn't have cared about the car. I splurged on lavender and tulips and zinnia. The boyfriends grabbed armfuls to take to her grave.

Charlie, Cara's coresident at The Meadows, had also given her a ring. He'd twisted a black-eyed Susan around her finger and tied it, pulling the bloom through a knot, knocking off some of the petals. The band had loosened but she continued to wear it; she'd slip the ring off and re-loop the stem, securing it in place. Cara and Devon met at Bard College during the first week of freshman orientation. He was her truest love. Cara carved his effigy from wood and burned it after he left her. Devon delivered her eulogy. Eric, I didn't know well; he stood at the rear of the church. Jude was an architect and never proposed. She'd met Danny on Match.com. He cued the music at the funeral home. Brian was an attorney; he proposed before any of the others. Cara said his diamond was a chip. She'd accepted it and then given it right back.

A few of her lovers weren't in attendance, and there were some I didn't know well enough to invite. Ethan told me over the telephone that he didn't like death. Kevin's car broke down on the interstate and he missed the services. Jared was a jazz drummer and didn't show. Travis was her childhood boyfriend and mailed his condolences. Ishmael was a lover, not a boyfriend, and couldn't be reached. Kahlil told me he wouldn't be coming. He sent three calla lilies.

The diamond in Cara's engagement ring from Kahlil weighed a fraction over half a carat and was set in a channel platinum setting. It had no visible inclusions. Mom had given the diamond itself to Cara as a graduation gift. She gave each of us a diamond: one diamond necklace for each girl, one diamond from each of her marriages. She had had the necklaces and the pendants modeled after the illusion style of her own mother's engagement ring. The diamond pendants hung on strands of yellow gold, anchored in silvery squares so the diamonds looked larger. Cara had the diamond from her necklace extracted and put into a ring of Kahlil's design.

I stood at Cara's casket and received her mourners. Red roses arranged in the word SISTER were positioned on an easel behind me and stood as high as my head. Mom had bought them on my behalf. Clear glass vases filled with seasonal flowers stood tall on the floor. Notes that accompanied the flowers were propped and folded in front of them like labels on a buffet. A kneeling pew sat in front of the casket. Some people approached, ignoring Cara's body, coming to me instead. Others walked directly to Cara and touched the edge of her coffin, kneeling in front of her. I thought of them as the bravest of the grievers.

The funeral home had faded pink carpets. The end tables were decorated with inspirational cards and tissues for weeping, boxes and boxes of them. The thermostat was kept low and the pinch-pleated drapes were drawn. The windows were closed and topped with stiff sage valances. Metal folding chairs with padded seats formed twelve rows, divided into two sections by an aisle that led to my sister. My mother asked the funeral director to display some childhood photographs of Cara. He had obliged, scattering the images around the funeral home on waist-high viewing tables topped with lace doilies and propped on stands beside plastic potted ferns and bowls of peppermints. Pictures were plentiful: Cara at three, feeding a goat with a baby bottle at a petting zoo, my mother beside her, holding Cara's hand steady so that the goat could suckle; Cara at five jumping up and down on her bed after a bath, in our Barton Avenue apartment, her hair cut like a boy's; Cara cradling a beloved doll; Cara in a grade-school headshot wearing a light blue shirt studded with rhinestones; Cara smiling for the camera as she got ready for prom. Cara beaming with pride after her turn as Mrs. Bedwin in our high school production of *Oliver!*, her arm around Fagan's shoulder. The funeral home director displayed the grad thesis images I'd taken of me and Cara, exhibition style. These photographs—large, 32 x 40 inches each—were strung with wire, hanging from the ornate picture rails of the funeral home's ceiling molding. Landscapes of blazing white snow looked stark against the paisley wallpaper.

Our father had missed all of the years displayed in the photographs. Cara and I had maintained some careful contact with him throughout our twenties, though not enough to invite him to either of our weddings or graduations. I'd told him that I loved him and he'd done the same. But my words felt false. I didn't love him. I only thought that I should. He hadn't earned my trust, let alone my love. When Cara died my budding relationship with our father went with her. I can only say in retrospect that I must not have wanted it enough to forgive him his abuse. The question of his attending the funeral was a difficult one. Part of me felt that even though he'd been a terrible father, he had the right to say good-bye to his daughter. The other part of me worried for my mother. I didn't want him to come and make a scene. That had always been his way. Perhaps I was cowardly in my choice to exclude him from the services. I asked Jedediah to call him in Florida where he lives and tell him I didn't want him there. And that command was both true and untrue. I *did* want my father to console me in my loss, our loss. But he had never been that type of father. That father might have kept Cara from her elegant casket.

Jedediah had made a CD of Cara's favorite music for the funeral home staff to play over the loudspeakers: Jonathan Richman, the Magnetic Fields, Indigo Girls, and Otis Redding. I greeted Cara's attendants to Jedediah's sound track. Attendants took turns visiting me casket-side, bringing me glasses of water.

Few of Cara's girlfriends attended her funeral. She hadn't had many. After Kahlil left, she'd spent most of her time trying to win the affections of men. She didn't want to be "a barren old maid," she'd told me; she'd said I'd better learn from her "mistakes as an irresponsible wife" and hold on to my own husband. "Don't do what I did and go out and cheat and lie and run around. You'll be sorry if you do."

Those of Cara's girlfriends who did come to the service stood at the back of the room. One told me she "was there for my sister, not for me." Cara had spent hours, I imagine, telling her how I'd kicked Cara out of my house and abandoned her in her time of need, and Cara's friend had believed her. Her friend was right, I thought. I'd made the wrong choice, toeing the hard line. Now I was going to have to live or die with my tough love, once and for all, with no love left to give anyone. One of Cara's friends from graduate school brought her baby boy. She passed the serene infant around a circle of guests: our high school teachers, my mother's colleagues, relatives I'd only seen once or twice in my life. My distant second cousin kissed this woman's baby. The little cherub brightened the room of death. I wondered how many friends Cara had exhausted and run through by the time she ended her life.

I greeted all of Cara's guests, including one that was difficult to recognize.

Mike the Marine, our ex-stepfather, came to pay his respects. He knelt on the viewing pew beside Cara's casket, making the sign of the cross, bowing his head in prayer. His mouth moved as he recited a Hail Mary in his head. Mike never once looked at the dead daughter he'd left in the haze of Jacksonville, North Carolina, when she was an impressionable twelve.

I'd not laid eyes on Mike since the day he'd pulled out of our driveway and never come back. It had been fifteen years.

I interrupted him in prayer, knelt beside him, moving close enough that I felt his breath at my ear.

"You're a little late," I whispered. "I think that means you should leave."

Mike nodded, stood up from the pew, and paid his last respects with a blank stare at Cara's sympathy flowers. Did he think the answers to his long absence could be found in a wreath of tightly bound pink carnations?

This is how it is: We were always who we were, only together. We were girls who made a language about time and memory. We feared being ourselves because it meant being alone. We are bound in our own bodies and share one mortality. One day there will be one of us left with just the memory of the other. We prepare and we age.

If you are a twin, you watch yourself live two lives—yours and hers. It's constant comparison. I am never as good as the bad I wanted her to be. I was the only soldier I needed. We couldn't have known what splitting would mean. Time speeds past fast, scattering like shrapnel, and is quiet as cobwebs. We wait for the ambush. Sister will find out first; she'll be my living memory. She will be the body left standing.

I fragmented into the loved and the pitied and the loathed; it took me five years. I became a deafening danger bomb, a tick you couldn't find if you hadn't buried it in yourself. I refer to myself as "her," "that girl." Nobody wants to look me directly in the eye. Sister still sees me.

At Cara's funeral, people saw in us the same person: one dead, one half-living. Through me, Cara's ghost came to life. I was her specter. If she hadn't already died, I'd have killed her for doing that to me. I pulled a stray thread from the hem of my dress. I pulled the limp orchids from my hair and crushed them.

I told each of the boyfriends at her funeral the same thing; I told each of them something different.

"I'm sorry," I said. "Cara loved you more than she loved any man." The boyfriends nodded in thanks.

"I wish you'd seen how she'd light up over you," I mentioned to some.

"She told me she wanted to marry you," I said to one of the boyfriends who hadn't proposed. Cara had said that about all of them, hopeful that one would eventually make her a wife again. "You were the one," I said.

"She would have made a great mother," I lied to one of her more attractive boyfriends. "She wanted nothing more in the world than to be a mother. Your children would have been beautiful." She'd wanted a child. I stood and gazed down at my sister. She'd never hold her own baby.

"We'll both be mothers if one of us has children," Cara used to say to me.

"Our babies will be half-siblings, actually," I'd counter. Identical twins are born with exact genetics, which makes their children related in the same way they would be if they shared a parent.

A few of Cara's boyfriends asked me to hold their hands. I gripped their palms and squeezed. I gave the boyfriends my ghost hand, Cara's gift from the afterlife. Holding my hand was like holding hers. We used to hold each other's hands. We'd done it since we were girls. We wanted to know what men felt when they touched us, so we held on to each other. Our rings are size 4, and our fingers are short; women's bodies, children's hands.

I took care with the boyfriends at her funeral. I knew they'd shown her the love I couldn't in the last years of her life. It was no small thing to enter into the fold of our twinship as a lover. Lovers had to pass the tests we administered. She'd ask them to dinner and call to invite me. I'd ask endless questions and dip my fork into their entrées. At the end of her life, they'd tolerated Cara when I needed to retreat from her. The boyfriends provided her with companionship; she slept beside their warm bodies.

We ate ziti and meatballs at the after-wake gathering. I couldn't eat; I chewed my ziti into tiny bits and spit it into a napkin. I sat wordless in a corner, my plate on my lap. Mom looked at the plate and then at the wadded-up napkin on the floor. She left the room crying.

I'd stopped eating so I wouldn't look like my sister. I cried and heard her sobs. I looked at myself in the mirror after she died and pulled at the tiny roll of her fat on my stomach. I ran my palm down the curve of her hip. I was more Cara than myself, so I starved her away. The smaller I made myself, the farther I traveled from her. The more the bones on my back showed, the less it was hers. I needed to rid myself of her likeness to travel back to my own self. I was the original egg; the doctor had said so.

It was simple: When an egg splits in two, the division is never equal. The splitting egg pulls essential nutrients as it goes and makes itself into a second functioning body of cells. The original egg remains, fighting to survive; it's been stripped of more than half of itself. The egg that splits becomes dominant; it drains more of the shared placenta, requires more space in the womb. One twin grows larger and stronger at the expense of the other. This twin is always bigger at birth. The twin who makes herself out of her sister must do so by nearly killing off that sister. Cara outweighed me by a pound; she'd begun her hungry taking, her killing of me, from the very start.

The Unitarians were on a national retreat in the Midwest the week my sister died. It was nearly impossible to find someone to conduct a funeral service. I paged through the phone book and called each of the ministers to try to secure their services. I left messages on the congregations' answering machines, but not a single message was returned. After several days, I was desperate and settled on our cousin Larry, a born-again minister at a church in Altamont. Larry agreed to hold a service but voiced his reservation. My sister was "unsaved and a junkie," and "God wouldn't look kindly on such a life." My mother invited Larry to dinner. I dished some chicken out of a foil roasting pan onto a plate for him; three legs, a thigh, and potatoes. Larry ate hungrily. I poured him a glass of milk and gave him the program I'd written for Cara's service.

"These are not God's prayers," he said and handed it back to me, grease spotting its top right corner. I'd included some Sufi scripture and readings from Shakespeare and Milton and Toni Morrison.

"What about our selection of music?" I served him seconds.

"I'm not familiar with it," he said.

"It's just a few things she liked."

"Your sister died outside of God's plan. Your service will be standard. A conservative eulogy should be given, mentioning your sister's better qualities." He drank his milk in one gulp. "You can feel free to ask some people to read some of the scripture I assign."

Cara's funeral procession gathered at DeMarco-Stone Funeral Home early in the morning. Devon was a pallbearer, along with two uncles, a family friend, and two first cousins. We sat in the rowed chairs at DeMarco-Stone and waited. Mourners filed down the aisle from the back of the viewing room and stopped at my sister's body. Some of them walked past quickly, giving her a short nod, and then headed to their cars to line up for the procession. Others stopped and gazed down at her. They bowed their heads in prayer and looked as if they were trying to force themselves to remember how she looked, just as she was, in her coffin. The pallbearers stood at the back, hands crossed in front of them. Mom and I were the last of the mourners left in the room. I watched Mom hobble to Cara. Stooped and exhausted, Mom jutted her shoulders forward. Her long black hair fell in her face. Strands of hair caught in her mouth as she sobbed. She got to the pew and faltered, oblivious to others. She held a hanky.

Our uncle sprinted down the aisle with smelling salts. It

seemed absurd to me that he'd brought them. Throughout the wake he'd passed me at my post and slid them out of his pocket, nudging me with his elbow. The salts were tied in a cheesecloth bundle. He showed Jedediah how to use them. "This might get ugly," he'd said. "These women are likely to work themselves up into hysteria." Jedediah intercepted my uncle on his dash with his salts. My husband was the barrier of sanity that separated my mother and me from our crazy family.

Mom looked at my sister and straightened the shawl Cara wore. "We're never going to have more moments? Are we?" Mom looked up and opened her mouth to cry out; no sound came. She rested her forehead on the closed bottom of the casket lid and went back to her vigil. I knelt beside my mother, offered my shoulder to her; she held on to me.

I was the last to see Cara before we closed the lid of her coffin. I knelt down beside her. I clasped my hands. I wept. My tears fell on her face and made lines in her makeup. I saw my sister for what she was. My muse was a corpse. I felt her alive in myself, with all of her troubles.

I left her alone to be carried. I watched from the doorway. A drape that covered her casket was removed to expose a gurney. The funeral director unlocked the gurney's wheels with his foot and pushed my sister's casket down the aisle, toward the door where I was standing. The gurney creaked and moaned. They wheeled my sister to the door. The pallbearers knelt to shoulder the burden of her coffin. Some of her boyfriends stood alongside the hearse. In the back of the hearse, standing sprays, wreaths, and bouquets were assembled neatly around the casket. The undertaker plucked roses from an arrangement and handed them to mourners. A line of cars curved through the parking lot; Mazdas, Toyotas, Fords, and BMWs, all with orange funeral flags tied to their radio antennae.

We all made our way to the church. Larry gave Cara the eulogy he'd promised.

"I want to leave you with this thought," Larry said at the end of his service. He stood at the front of the church, the mouth of the nave. "If Cara could speak to you now," he said to the room of mourners he'd held captive with his sermon, "the one thing she'd want to tell you was that you must take Jesus Christ as your Lord and savior."

The room gasped. I felt their eyes on me, both in pity and in plea. Jedediah squeezed my hand and I nodded to him, whispered that I was going to fix Larry's wrong.

I stood up and walked to Larry's lectern, asked if I could take the floor. He graciously gave it to me, allowed me my words.

"If Cara were here today," I managed, though my voice was shaky, "she'd want to tell you that she hoped you could live each day of your life with joy."

The room breathed a great sigh of relief.

"Cara wouldn't want you to be sad that she's dead," I heard one boyfriend say to another outside of the church, after the service. They'd made friends in their shared pew. "She'd want you to be dancing."

"She did that to you, too?" the other boyfriend answered. "She always had to be dancing. I hated that."

"Did you take her out dancing, or what, man?" the first one asked, slightly competitive.

"You know I did." The boyfriends slapped five.

They were wrong, of course: Cara would have wanted mourners to bang on the lid of her casket with their fists, a gospel choir singing in a minor key. Dancing was for weddings.

"What do you think she'd make of all of this?" one of the boyfriends asked and held a prayer card out in front of him.

He'd taken it from a table at the entrance of the funeral home, after signing the guest book. He read the card and folded it into quarters, tucking it into his back pocket. I'd selected the Sufi prayer that she'd asked the entire congregation to recite, in unison, at her wedding. The front of the card was an image of a bright blue sky and rolling white clouds:

I offer you peace.
I offer you joy.
I offer you friendship.
I hear your needs.
I see your beauty.
Our wisdom comes from a higher source.
Our wisdom comes from a deeper source.
I honor that source in you.

Part II

Chapter 22

One night in late November, five months after Cara had died, I got out of bed and went into the kitchen because I couldn't sleep. Our cottage was dark except for glowing embers in the woodstove. The fire there, at the far end of the kitchen, needed stoking; it barely warmed the house. To the side of the stove, a drafty window whistled wind. I could see my neighbor's darkened home. Everyone else in the world was sleeping. I knelt down and pressed my forehead against the floor, my face so close to the ground that I breathed in my exhalations. I listened to the sound of my breath over the hum of the refrigerator.

Jedediah refused to share our bed. In the summer and early autumn months after Cara died, I'd been unfaithful more than once, the first time with a man who said he loved me, the words I needed to hear. Although I didn't reciprocate his sentiments, I gave him my body. The sensation of his hands on me was more of a sting than pleasure. It was the hurting I needed, the punishment for having allowed Cara to slip through my fingers.

As I crouched on the kitchen floor in the night, I heard a low tapping, the familiar sound of our house's eaves settling in the cold. I looked up. Following the flicker of light from the woodstove along the length of the kitchen, I saw something.

It was no further than six feet away, lodged firmly in a crack between the floorboards. I crawled toward it and pried it out: a pill. Covered in dirt, scratched where the writing with the identification code should have been. It was one of Cara's. She must have left it behind.

I rolled it in the palm of my hand, put it on my tongue, and swallowed.

For Christmas break, my mother, Jedediah, and I took a trip to Hawaii. Cara had always wanted to go to Hawaii. It represented the "big vacation" for her—drink umbrellas and tide pools, flowers and rum, escape and rest. For me, Hawaii with its bright emerald sea would be like living in a giant antidepressant. On crystal shores, locked in on all sides by glittering ocean, silky sand, and frozen rum daiquiris, I'd be forced into a state of good feeling.

The Poipu coast of Kauai, I'd read, had the most swimmable waters of all the islands and the fewest sharks. The cost of the trip seemed reasonable, though an empty bank account worried me less than the prospect of spending the brutal gray winter weeks between semesters weeping in a psychiatrist's chair.

Still, I packed bottles and bottles of pills.

I also packed a Ouija board, an antique designed by Elijah Bond in 1890 with block-lettered type of the alphabet and numbers and a creepy sun and stern-faced moon hovering over the simple answers: yes and no. The Ouija board's paper was worn and peeling up from the slab of cedar on which it had been dry mounted. I laid the Ouija board flat on the bottom of my suitcase. Its planchette, carved from wood and embedded with a small magnifying glass that singled out the letters on the Ouija, had to be in perfect condition to glide across the board. I wrapped the triangular planchette in Cara's favorite white flowing scarf: a scarf of fragile silk and muslin; a scarf that still smelled, distantly, faintly, like my sister; a scarf as dramatically long and easy to bow and drape as Isadora Duncan's famed noose.

I'd been wearing that scarf everywhere and even slept with it on. I'd managed to fashion it into an accessory that went with all of my outfits. It tickled the flesh of my bare knees in summer and was dirtied with soot and ash from sitting on the floor in front of the fireplace in winter. It was filthy and ridiculous. It was as excessive and unnecessary as my three-week Pacific Island vacation. But it also worked well as a protective cover for the Ouija's planchette, my earpiece to Cara, wrapping my direct and only line to her in her "energy." Cara had insisted that belongings, especially clothing and jewelry, were the truest and fastest way to the dead. She'd said the dead missed their things and wished for them back; keeping the objects and making them yours would bring out the fight in a spirit. Cara said the dead would come sailing back into life to claim their possessions.

In Hawaii, my fingertips barely touched the planchette. According to the directions printed on the inside of the top of the game box, fingers should only brush the planchette and allow the spirit to whisk it across the board. This is how spirits talk. Also, two living people are needed for a séance, but I attempted to channel Cara by myself in Hawaii. I broke the rules of Ouija. I thought Cara might overlook my oversight and gift me with her grace. In Hawaii, I worked the board alone, in a back bedroom of the three-bedroom cabin we'd rented, while Jedediah and Mom made dinner. I lit candles and sat on the floor. If I heard someone coming, I'd blow out the flames and slide the board under the bed and appear to have been napping or reading a book. I asked Cara:

How do you feel about Jedediah?
He's a coward.
How will I survive without you?
You'll breathe.
Are you okay?
Yes, but I'm so sorry and stupid.

I thought my sister was egging me on to ruin my life and join her. I see now that she was after a different goal entirely, that she wanted something else, something better for me.

I told her all about my day, as I always had. I spelled out what was happening in my life:

Today I had a Mai Tai and cried, swam.

Last night I didn't sleep. When I did, I dreamed of you.

Tomorrow, I will make photographs.

Once, Jedediah asked if I'd been talking to someone in the back bedroom. He'd heard me laughing but hadn't wanted to intrude on a private conversation. I told him I'd only been talking to myself.

On Christmas Eve, Mom and Jedediah and I hiked the Nepali coast on the Kalalau Trail, the edge of a dormant volcano. The steep trail has been crudely cut through the rain forest. Its vegetation is lush, nothing short of magical. Banyan trees with hanging vines grow stout and wide along the path and down to the water; their roots weave in and out of the red-clay sandy soil like jungle snakes. Mom feared the edge of the path, the vertigo-inducing ledges that overlooked the sea. She hung to the side, while Jedediah and I stood as close to the edge as we could, looking down at a family of whales that had gathered not too far from shore. They floated and turned around each other.

I'd barely eaten that morning and afternoon, but I was beyond hunger. My stomach was so empty, had I had any food I would have been sick. So I moved up the mountain hungry, running on fumes, weaving back and forth and stumbling along. Jedediah's hands were quick to reach out and steady me as I tripped over a rock or twisted my foot in a muddy hole. He took my picture when we reached the summit. I sat on the ground with my hair pulled back in a turban I'd fashioned from the white scarf, chin up to the sky, eyes closed, bony shoulders back and sun-speckled.

I'd heard there was a cove with a beach of volcanic rock on the other side of the summit, an hour or two hike down from where we sat. It was a sacred place where people honored their dead. We'd have to move quickly to make it before sunset.

My purse was a white Prada with studs, which I'd bought right after Cara died. Didn't I deserve nice things if I was going to have to go through life feeling like I'd been sawed in two? In the Prada bag, I carried a museum of remembrance for Cara: her lipstick, hair clips, perfume, and a portion of her ashes were always there right beside my wallet, inhaler, and cell phone. The cap of the lipstick had come loose. Its bright red stain had smashed into the bag's liner and melted from the Hawaiian heat.

At the summit of the Kalalau Trail, I rummaged through the bag and pulled out a pale green silk box stitched with angular white cranes. I looked inside. It was stuffed with a plastic bag full of Cara's ashes. I allowed myself to check the contents of this box several times a day, for fear I'd lost her. I saw that Cara was still there in the opulent box she would have liked. I fingered the bag full of my sister and closed her inside and dropped her back into my purse. The ruined Prada wasn't only a museum. It was a mausoleum.

"What was that?" Jedediah reached into my bag and pulled out the box. He turned it over, studying it.

"Oh, that's Cara." I picked up my inhaler and took a puff.

"Let's hurry down to the beach, before dark." I pulled Jedediah along.

When we reached the cove, Mom walked right to the water's edge, her feet sinking in the smooth white sand. Cautious steps. She pulled her own baggie filled with Cara's ashes from her pocket and pinched it between her middle and index fingers; it swung like a pendulum. High tide was coming quickly; the waves pummeled the shore, obscuring the sound of my mother crying. When she turned around and mouthed something, her hair flew wildly around her face, sticking in her tears. I couldn't hear her over the raging water. She barely kept her footing but, slowly, she made her way to the mouth of the sea, which was lined with knee-high, jagged black lava rock. There were small toeholds in the lava and she used them to climb the rocks one after another, until she reached a sandbar. I followed closely behind. Tiny blue crabs scurried sideways up the reef around us, skittering to hide and burrow into the sand. Mom opened the bag and cast Cara out into the pounding waves. Her ashes flew up into the air, and dispersed like mist. They funneled up, up, up and vanished.

My sister believed that death was a minor inconvenience to keeping up contact with loved ones. She tried her best to demonstrate her gifts at this when we were in college, and not only by using the Ouija board; we both took jobs, at her insistence, as telephone psychics. The company patched a telephone line into our apartment that rang from midnight to 5 a.m. Our spiritual training and qualifications were nil. Our new employer sent a contract and W-2 to fill out, including a handwritten note on a Post-it:

Not a psychic? No problem.
Don't believe? Who cares?
The object of service? Revenue.

Company mission? The customer is always right.

Was the customer right even when they demanded access to the world of the undead, a world that didn't exist? I mulled the question over and asked it during my phone training session the following week. The training consisted completely of techniques to hold a caller on the line as long as possible—my new employer was clear: "Give the customer what they want, just keep them with you. Phone sex, therapy, tarot, past life regression, advice—it's all part of the job."

We were to provide slow reflective answers, a beat or two longer than we'd use in normal conversation, and ask leading questions. Callers should be encouraged to do most of the talking—the surest way to raise their bills.

Cara was a good psychic. She read Tarot cards for the callers and summoned their departed relatives. Several times she was able to describe these men and women in detail, down to their favorite outfits and bad habits. The phone was passed to me when a gentleman requested phone sex or got rowdy and rude.

"What am I wearing?" One caller breathed into the phone. "This is a psychic line, right? Why don't you tell me where I'd like your hand on my cock?" I obliged, and let the phone toll go as high as it took the man to get off, which wasn't terribly long, just fifty dollars' worth of filthy talk.

I learned that when I tried to talk to the dead there was nothing but silence. I also learned that the callers who paid $3.95 a minute to talk to college coeds could have saved their money and gotten the same service in many a local tavern for the price of drinks.

For me and Cara, the job was not tenable, fiscally or emotionally. Our pay rate was ludicrous, only a small take of the per-minute charge. Cara quit first. She reasoned that she could get a higher commission striking out on her own in

Woodstock in a boutique, or in the town square in warmer months, though she never did psychic work again.

When I resigned, it was because I held on to the voices of callers long after we'd disconnected. Trying to drift off to sleep after work, I still heard them crying, begging, moaning, chiding. I wondered about their credit card debts and divorces, their thoughts of suicide, their harmless crushes on colleagues and hopes for fame. Their losses through death had haunted me. I couldn't bring people back. The callers' sad voices had played in a loop in my head. Their need had been too great.

On Christmas Day, both Mom and Jedediah left Hawaii; as planned, I would stay on for another week. Jedediah stayed a few hours later than Mom did and he and I had a Christmas dinner of sushi before he flew home.

The restaurant where Jedediah and I ate had elaborate plating. Sprigs of hibiscus and thin zigzagging colorful sauces were the beds for our dinners. I remember the garnish well; it was easier to stare down at my dinner than look at Jedediah, his rejecting eyes. I pushed my food around with my chopsticks and asked him to consider staying longer. He couldn't, of course. He'd made plans for New Year's Eve with friends at home; ever since he'd discovered my infidelities of the last months, he was eager to do his own socializing. He wanted to leave the marriage but he felt he couldn't leave, because he worried over me. He was also concerned that his need for retreat, distance, and most probably a divorce might be the thing that pushed me over the edge and caused me to take my own life. This was the reason he'd made the effort to indulge me in a trip to Hawaii; he'd told me this before we'd left Massachusetts, adding then that I was lucky to still have him in my life at all.

We exchanged gifts over dinner. I don't recall what I gave Jedediah—probably a game, a book, or a new pair of pants.

Jedediah handed me an envelope with a piece of paper folded inside. He reached out for my hand over the table and squeezed it and wished me a Merry Christmas.

He'd typed up a quote on the top of the piece of paper.

"It's the dedication for my book."

I read out loud the line of my Christmas present:

For Christa and Cara—I saw in a closet in Alkmaar a terrestrial globe between two mirrors that multiplied it endlessly—Borges

Later, after we divorced, he changed his mind, his dedication.

Valium erases memory, though I do remember well one day in Poipu, the afternoon of the day after Jedediah left, when I crossed the line. I see flashes of myself under a straw umbrella. I'd decided I deserved a hamburger and as many dark rum punches as it would take to help me forget that Jedediah had gone home. The effect of the rum was mild, so I added two or three Valiums an hour and fell asleep in my beach chair.

A manager from the bar and grill woke me, standing over me, shaking my shoulders. It was getting dark outside and I'd lost my room key in the sand or in the sea. I told the man I needed help finding that key. It might have been driven down into the sand with the force of nearly a dozen dropped plastic cups, all of them empty save a stray maraschino cherry in one or two. It would have been easy enough to find the key if the manager didn't insist I leave immediately. It was simple, he said. I was scaring the children on the beach and disturbing people's dinner. I had to go. He told me I'd not be welcome back and that he was calling the police to come and drive me home. I was that woman, the one making a scene, flapping her arms, asserting her sobriety as she stumbled and fell and gathered her things. I made it off the beach before the police arrived.

I sulked down the two-lane highway to the hotel. I walked in my bare feet down the center of the road, traversing the single yellow line, my balance beam. Cars sped past and some stopped, their drivers checking to see if I was okay. There were a few men who asked if I wanted a ride or more of a good time. "I've had enough of one, thank you," I replied, waving them off as the road dirtied my feet and rocks split my skin. I walked with Cara's scarf tied around my waist, dragging behind me on the ground like a tail of feathers. The scarf picked up pieces of stray trash, mostly wrappers, and blades of dry sea grass. I was a castaway: my shoes had been swept away in high tide. I was marooned, locked out of my cabin, totally alone. I picked the lock on a window and hoisted my way over a bush of blooming crater flowers. Their petals fluttered down: pink, yellow, white, and red. I stomped over them. I landed on the floor of my room and passed out, waking to the mocking cry of the farm-less wild rooster.

I'd arrived in Hawaii very thin and had done my best to avoid indulging at luaus. I'd gone from 115 to 85 pounds in six months and didn't want to spoil my work. There were disadvantages to malnourishment. The plastic of subway seats banged my tailbone until I couldn't sit. The yielding cotton of my mattress bruised my thighs from the weight of my sleeping frame. My hair fell from my head in clumps. Downy hair covered my body to warm it, like peach fuzz. My teeth became loose. It had become impossible to do even small things but I found my new slip of a body worth it. When I was good and ready and paper-thin, I'd die an individual, not a twin.

I stayed on in Hawaii through the New Year.

I wrote Jedediah a note on New Year's Eve on a postcard I'd found in a nearby gift shop. The card pictures a hula dancer facing the sea, her hips tilted, head to the side, and arms out.

She dances beneath a full moon in a cloudless sky. The card reads: Lonely Lola Lo.

I sent that postcard the day before I drove the red clay mountains in the north of Poipu and buried some of my sister's ashes in the sandy soil there, beneath a tree. This was the only time I'd let part of her go by myself, touched what was left of her alone. Her ashes were a lucent blue in contrast to the vivid red soil, like a swatch of the night sky pulled down from the heavens, laid out on earth. The ashes were mingled with bits of white bone; those were the stars. What used to be human—flesh, fingers, legs, blood, and hips to bear children—was now a coarse powder that fell through my fingers.

I spat on the ground beneath the shrubby tree. I'd found the farthest place from home I could to conceal what was left of Cara. I got down on my knees and pressed my cheek against the hot red earth and screamed until I no longer had a voice. I shouted down into the ground, into the hole I'd made for Cara. I cursed. I swore at God, Jesus, Edgardo, ex-husbands, undertakers, lovers, disappointment, and drugs, and most of all, Cara. All of them had allowed for half of me to be taken and left, like a person forced to try to survive without a heart or will.

Chapter 23

In March, nine months after Cara died, I flew home to Massachusetts on a direct flight from a failure of a trip to Rome intent on killing myself. I'd planned it all out: To die at home would be cruel to Jedediah; he'd have to find me and clean up. To die at Mom's would be to destroy her, but I couldn't live just to keep from upsetting her. To die in a cheap motel would be to die in a cheap motel. To walk into the forest and die would be to be eaten by animals. To shoot myself would mean the possibility of missing. Starving wasn't working; sex partners worked even less well. A flight seemed like just the thing.

I boarded the plane and settled into my seat, the window seat. I watched the baggage crew scramble around the tarmac, struggling to fill the belly of the plane with luggage. I saw my bag hoisted into the plane, a tattered leopard print zip-up with worn wheels, pink ribbon tied around the handle. I wondered who'd claim the bag at the other end of my flight. I pulled down my tiny plastic window shade and it blinked shut like a sleepy eye.

I counted the full bottles of pills in my purse: three. They rolled around beside the small box of Cara's ashes. There were enough pills to kill, enough that there would be no rescue. The flight attendants would assume I was sleeping, and not bother to try to wake me for food or drink. I'd be left alone to die, discovered only when it was too late for interventions, when all others had left the plane to meet waiting relatives or to attend corporate dinners. The plan was seamless. This neat and orderly way to perish required no directly gruesome involvement for Jedediah or for Mom.

At takeoff I gripped the armrest, feeling the familiar rush of fear I always got when an aircraft jerked up into the sky. I had a ritual at takeoff that Cara had told me made a crash impossible: surround the plane with white light, watch it rise up like a steady bird into the air, see it glide from one safe place to another, imagine the plane lands in the destination and that migration is over. I placed four pills into my mouth and swallowed, one for every step of my ritual that I was about to neglect. I was ready never to see the ground again.

I looked over toward the aisle, meeting the gaze of my neighbor, the woman in the middle seat, seat B.

"Whatcha doing?" she asked. The woman was young, no more than twenty-five. She tipped her head to the side, her long straight blond hair brushing her lap. She adjusted the strap on her flowing flowered dress and looked into my purse.

"Nothing." I turned away as best I could, closed my eyes, and rested my head against the window. I listened to the hum of the jet's engines and imagined the turning propellers.

"Doesn't look like nothing from over here, but what do I know?" She grabbed my bag from out of my lap and took out one of the bottles of pills. "Fear of flying? I had that, too, before I found God."

"I've had a really bad time in Rome," I heard myself say. "Now I just want to be left alone." But then for some reason I cracked. Confession wasn't part of my plan, but I couldn't stop myself from telling the clement stranger everything. I told the young woman all about my trip: how there'd been a man and a breakup and drinking and drugs. I told her how I'd been to the

Vatican and then to dinner with a dear friend and her partner, a famous painter, and how my friend had asked me to join them both in bed, after. She thought this would save their relationship, to give her friend and herself to this lover. I said I would, even though I didn't want to.

I told her how I'd left the tryst quietly, during the middle of the whole affair, and let the lovers finish. I told her how I scrambled to find my long black dress on the floor of their bedroom. I hadn't realized I'd been crying until a tear landed on my bare foot. I told the stranger how I made my way to the sofa, in the living room, and that the man followed. I told her how he lay down beside me on the sofa and wept. He wept for his brother, who he said was a fuckup and a drug addict. He told me that he understood why I wept, that like him, I mourned my sibling.

I told the woman on the plane how he'd been wrong, that I was crying for myself, for giving myself over to a man while I was married, and because I thought it would please my friend. I told her how I no longer had care or will. I told her how the man had said he admired my photographs, that he thought them beautiful, that he wanted to have for himself the beautiful living woman in those photographs. I told her about the pictures I'd taken and about Cara and how she had died.

I told her how the man had looked into my eyes and declared to me that he should have the image of me he'd seen in pictures, how disappointed he was to meet me and find that I was not at all beautiful, that I no longer looked like either twin in my photographs. I told her how he'd been perplexed by this fact, the fact that men wanted me even though I was not much to look at. He included himself in this group.

I told her how I wanted to throw myself off of his balcony

that night and just be done with it, this life, this body. I told her I didn't believe in God but that I wanted to join my sister. I told her I changed my mind as I stood on his terrace and looked down: I saw a pile of what I imagined to be ripped-up canvas and discarded paints. I refused to die on his terrible paintings.

I told her I called Jedediah instead of jumping. His voice had a gravelly quality, like sandpaper words caught in his throat. I'd woken him up. I hadn't remembered that from this great distance, his night was my earliest morning. "Jedediah?" I answered, relieved to hear his gentle voice. "I can't do this."

"You can't do what?" he asked. He sounded worried and tense but also distant. He had the familiar sound of fatigue that I recognized from my own voice. I used to take this tone with Cara when she'd call me from one of her nights.

"Live," I told him and started to weep. "I'm calling from another man's bedroom."

"Where are you?" he sighed.

"I'm still in Rome," I said. "But I need to come home. I have to change my ticket."

"Do you think I can save you when you're all the way around the world if I can't even do it from our living room?"

"Probably not," I answered quietly. "I just needed to hear your voice."

"You can't keep calling me like this," he said. "Just tell me you're going to be okay, that I'll see you at home. Can you do that?"

"I'll see you at home," I told him and hung up, even though I wasn't sure that was true. I told the woman on the plane that I imagined him coldly holding our phone in his hands. I told her it no longer mattered to him who I'd lain beneath. I'd hurt him so much that his heart had gone dead.

By the time I had told the woman everything, we were in

mid-flight. She sat beside me and cut the food on my dinner tray into tiny pieces. She buttered my bread and asked the attendants to bring water and hot coffee. The woman nodded and listened. She listened until the plane landed and I had lived.

Chapter 24

I kept my teaching job throughout my first year of mourning but I dressed in Cara's clothes. I wore them down to holes and stains. I dated a handful of men I'd met on the Internet, though I was still married. All the while, I was perfectly convinced that I could talk to Cara, and that she was asking me to become her, to give her life and ruin mine, to join her in death.

There hadn't been a single day since she'd died that I'd been without medications. As more time passed, the drugs grew in number and dose. There were pills to wake up, to stimulate appetite, and to mollify. Pills to keep me upright, and pills to put me out, deep into sleep. I kept them in a line on the windowsill in my bedroom. I identified which I had in hand by shaking the bottles. I knew the proper pill even in complete darkness by the sound they made as they rattled against the bottle's lid. The medicines worked their magic: I hadn't walked in front of a bus, even though I so wanted to. But the pills made me hard to live with.

My job was our ruling battle. Jedediah had been planning his departure from our marriage since we'd returned from Hawaii and, understandably, he feared I'd lose my income. Neither of us had much money. Jedediah wouldn't be able to support me even for a short time, though he would have if he could. My unemployment meant he'd leave a very sick wife with no financial means of her own. He couldn't bear to do that, so he gently and sometimes not so gently pushed me into work.

In the early hours before teaching one morning, the autumn after we lost Cara, I woke up peeing the bed. And when the spring semester was near, it was this incident that fueled my argument to Jedediah that I shouldn't return to work. I was clearly no better off than the semester before.

I had been a bed-wetter as a child; Cara used to joke that I'd flood her out of the bed we shared. She had a recurring dream that a monsoon would sweep the landscape of her nocturne. Cara clung to a life raft. No matter where she was in her dream, she was washed away.

Without her, I was doing it again.

This time Jedediah was awake and drinking his morning coffee in the kitchen. I cried out from our room and he ran in and pulled open the drapes. The morning light exposed me. "I'm scared," I said.

"What's going on?" He sat down beside me and then jumped back up. The seat of his pants and his palms were damp.

"I wet the bed."

"I can see that." Jedediah looked down at his hands in disbelief. "It'll be okay." He took me into his arms.

"I don't want to go to work today," I said. "I don't feel well."

Jedediah walked across our bedroom and drew the curtains closed. The bedroom had a wall of windows, each of which was tricky to close in its own way: a loose hinge, a broken spring, chipped wood where the window met the sill; a gap that invited the chill of winter. Drafts had always been a problem in that house. We learned to hold each other close during the coldest months to keep warm.

Jedediah slept soundly with a thin blanket and a hard pillow. I favored down comforters and velvet shams to cover goose feather pillows. Jedediah never snored, he only purred and sometimes talked in his sleep, although I can't remember what he'd sleep say. There was a time when I was able to recount each and every word; I savored them and I'd tell him what he'd said the next morning. Now I'd peed the bed and my young frightened husband slid the top drawer of my dresser open. He looked carefully through the garments that lay before him in the drawer and took out a fresh nightgown. Jedediah motioned gently for me to lift my arms; he pulled the soiled nightwear over my head. I sat naked in our pee bed with my arms extended, waiting for Jedediah to serve me my clean dressings.

"Get up, honey. We've got to change the sheets and get you into a shower. I don't want to put this on you until you're clean." He looked at the stain I'd made on our white sheets. I stood up and walked naked to the bathroom. Jedediah waited patiently for me in the kitchen; he slipped the new gown over my shoulders.

"I can't call in." I hugged him, a plea hug. "Could you call the administrative assistant for me and tell her I have diarrhea?" That was our nearly decade-long joke. Diarrhea was a sure-fire, nonnegotiable reason to skip a workday. Who'd take issue with it? It was best in a call-in situation to try to disarm your superior with a little bit of self-humiliation. I wished Jedediah would shush me and change the sheets, send me back to bed, and keep the curtains closed. Maybe I'd sleep it off. I could wake in a couple of hours and forget it all, start the day at noon and sip coffee with him; in my fantasy we'd both pretend I'd been faithful. I wrapped my arms around his neck and pulled down tighter than I should have. He dialed the phone and left the message.

"Christa won't be in today," I heard him say into the phone from the other room. He hesitated on the reason. "She's not been sleeping. Actually, she's not slept for days."

Chapter 25

At last, Jedediah decided to move out. I sold our house and moved myself and all of my things to Keene, a small mill town in rural New Hampshire. I would teach at Keene State College.

I taught a full load of photography classes that year: three courses in the fall and three in the spring. I was known, at the time of my hire, to be competent and reliable—if a bit intense and flamboyant. I had good recommendations and the right language for critique. I was young enough that my students trusted me as one of their own, pretty enough that they thought me harmless, and old enough that they understood I knew something about photography that they didn't yet know.

Keene is quaint, as long as you're not a newly separated woman in her early thirties with a long-distance love prospect and no local friends, and as long as you enjoy kayaking and mountain biking. All the shoes I brought were pumps. I owned a badly house-trained barky Chihuahua that I'd procured from petfinder.com, a pair of Siamese cats I'd bought in my early twenties and no longer had the wherewithal to care for, a collection of hundreds of etherized exotic butterflies, wings pinned with map tacks and stuck behind glass. I'd bought them from a junk shop and spent my entire faculty moving allowance on the five-case collection. The owners of the store had tried their best, in earnest, to discourage my purchase: a single woman ought not to spend that kind of money on extravagances; a single woman might find herself in an uncertain economic position.

Somehow I did not fully realize that I would be a single woman in Keene. I moved into a sunny yellow, wood-sided Victorian with white painted shutters and doors, and I considered what a perfect place it would be to bring a baby home to. I fantasized that D, the man I'd just begun to date, would appear on my doorstep on bended knee. I pictured a winter wedding, followed by an autumn baby.

The house was directly across the street from an elementary school. The school rang its morning bells and began the students' day at a surprising 6:30 a.m. Jaw clenched, hands gripping my down comforter, hung over on Ambien and Valium, I'd lie in bed in the early morning and listen, learning to distinguish the piercing trill of girl screams from the low vibrato of boy yowls.

At 7 a.m., my alarm would go off. I'd groan into my pillow, put a foot on the floor, an arm through my dress sleeve, and drive to work with my brain still sleeping (the pills having not worn off yet). I'd coast the car into the faculty lot and grab the parking hangtags from the glove box.

Gradually, combing my hair in the morning became out of the question. Brushing my teeth began to take the kind of effort that, say, taking the bar exam might require. I hadn't opened my mail in six months for fear of delinquent bills. When I did not get to work on time, my students knew to tack up their photographs and wait for me. I'd trained them to do it with care, without putting holes in the corners. They used the tacks around the edges of the photographs to keep the images in place and preserve them from the damage of display.

If I had an anxiety attack during the fifteen-minute class

break, I'd hide in my office to cry. I'd crouch bomb-drill-style beneath my desk. I'd extend the break to a full half-hour— then get back to my students.

My classroom at Keene was on the third floor of Fern Arts, a sand-colored brick building with tract windows running its perimeter. Fern Arts also housed a professional-level theater program and a nationally recognized art gallery. Equipment wasn't brand-new, but it functioned. And floors were swept. Chalkboards were wiped clean at the end of each day. Chairs and desks were reset into neat rows.

I came in early one morning and observed a man from the maintenance department drilling a green placard with my name on it onto my office door. I sipped my coffee in a quiet panic, drinking the only calories I allowed myself for the day. I weighed the responsibility that came with such a public decla- ration as a placard, and then spent the morning drafting and redrafting a letter of resignation, explaining why I wasn't deserving of such a public acknowledgment.

I called the dean's office and spoke with the administrative assistant. "I'm not sure I deserve to have my name and title listed on a door," I said.

"It's your office, Christa. It's only a formality," the dean's assistant answered with a twinge of annoyance.

"Basically," the assistant went on, "that nameplate isn't an 'acknowledgment,' it's just a way for students to find you easily, so you can sign their add/drop forms."

I drafted dozens of resignation letters during the months I taught at Keene, filing them in the metal cabinet under my desk. One of them read, simply: Dear Dean: I'm dying and I'll not be able to fulfill the duties of my position upon my death. Regards, Christa Parravani.

But beneath my name placard, a colleague had congratu- lated me on my hire by tacking a hand-typed Henri Cartier-

Bresson quote into the wooden door with a single sewing pin: "Photography is to place head and heart and eye along the same line of sight. It's a way of life." And as my students were helping to keep me alive by requiring that I get out of bed each morning and go somewhere outside myself, I tried to give them my best performance.

They brought in pictures that revealed courage: drunken family members, posing in cluttered living rooms, first sexual encounters and bashful studies of the body, attempts to describe lost loved ones through landscapes or crumbling homes.

They'd also bring in some of the same pictures class after class, different students photographing and then printing the same places. The covered bridge as subject reappeared most of all. The rickety wooden Queenpost bridge was over two hundred years old. It had been painted red, though the paint had long since chipped and peeled. Winter snowstorms and driving spring rains and summer mold had eroded the bridge. It is now bowed and unsound; the decrepit bridge feebly provides passage over a shallow arm of the Ashuelot River.

My students centered the bridge in their pictures, put its wooden plank road directly in the middle of their frames. They set their cameras low, which caused a tunneling effect. It's an amateur's mistake to overlook the left and right sides of an image. All four corners are important, more important than the middle square. But in every bridge picture light glowed from the end of the tunnel; the saving grace of every bridge image was this quarter-size ethereal spot, an orb that eased the failure of bad technique.

My students' projects were endless and I encouraged each one. I inspired them to snap their shutters, to expand and contract the diaphragms of their lenses. They brought their lives into the classroom through their picture making: eight-by-ten-inch, double weight, and printed on fiber glossy paper. The pictures my students made were personal and often missed the mark and, at other times, didn't miss it at all.

During a late October group critique, I stood at the front of the classroom and studied a collection of images that a female student had tacked to the wall. All of her pictures were of young women posed in positions that suggested suffering or malaise. I pointed at a picture of a blond woman who sat on a linoleum floor. The girl in the picture appeared to be reading a handwritten letter. She shielded her eyes from the sun with one hand; her elegant fingers, her visor. She clutched her willowy neck with the other hand, a sign of difficult news. The cursive script of the letter she read was legible in the photographer's print.

I congratulated the student on her darkroom technique, and then went in for my composition kill. "If it looks like a Paxil ad it's not working," I said. "The woman in this photograph is too aware of the camera and of the photographer to properly articulate the kind of anguish over love or loss that the photographer is trying to convey. It's contrived. Your self-conscious approach to the camera creates an uncomfortable feeling for the viewer." The student eagerly took notes and set her pen dolefully on her desk. "You'll have to try harder to be invisible next time," I said, "to make your model comfortable enough to be herself."

I moved on to the next image. "This photograph *is* working." It was a picture of a young woman with black hair, styled in a Louise Brooks bob that sharply framed her face. Thick straight bangs cut across her forehead, made a harsh line just above her eyebrows. The woman was too thin. Her shoulders looked like weak, bent hangers that could barely hold her clothes. She wore a dark dress and a tightly fitted, cropped black vest. She sat on a table with her legs crossed, looking down at a thick, open book on her lap. She had drawn one hand up to her forehead, touching the place right above her nose. "The woman is looking at the book but she isn't reading it," I said. "You can tell by the way she's averted her eyes from the page. She's looking at the book but she's somewhere far away from it. The photographer was able to capture this woman in a telling moment of reflection. Her thinness and her gesture tell us something true about her possible life situation. Is this woman going through something wrenching?" I asked, proudly.

I'd been looking at pictures long enough to know I was right on the money with my reading of the picture. The woman in the frame was fucked up; it was obvious from her body cues. The photographer had done an excellent job of being invisible. She'd found a subject who was comfortable enough to show herself—or who was so entirely strung out on pain that she'd been unaware that her image was being taken. "Am I right?" I asked. I received no response. I'd hoped I'd been able to intuit what the young photographer had asked me to see in her photograph, but nobody in the class made a sound or moved an inch. I turned back to the picture of the frail woman and studied it. The woman in the photograph was me.

Chapter 26

The bearded lady and I watched romance movies in the television room.

It was just the two of us most of the time. The other patients on the fourth-floor personality disorder wing were usually too agitated or sedated for movie privileges. The personality disorder wing at the Payne Whitney Clinic housed patients who fell into categories ranging from dissociative identity disorder to psychosis; major depression could land you in there, too, if you'd lost an identical twin and had bouts of turning into her. I spent a week with a handful of the seriously disturbed. I did the *New York Times* daily crossword puzzle, made origami swans, and painted ceramic reindeer in craft group, and I'd go into my room and write poetry in my small clothbound red notebook.

I'd checked myself into the Payne Whitney campus in White Plains several days before Thanksgiving the year after we lost Cara, after I'd flipped open a bottle of Zyprexa and swallowed all of them. My doctor had told me to take two a day to relieve anxiety; swatting an elephant with a newspaper, that's what my dose was. I'd talked her into giving me a sixty-day supply so I wouldn't have to get refills, but I hadn't taken a single one of the medium-size, smooth-coated, baby blue pills, not until my impromptu end night. Each of the pills was imprinted with a stamp that read: Lily 4415. I was visiting my boyfriend, D, in Brooklyn, when I Googled "How to overdose on Zyprexa" on his computer; I followed the directions carefully. D was out at a business dinner and I knew he wouldn't be home until nearly midnight. I'd have time to spare if I decided to die.

I weighed my options at 9 p.m. on the blustery, preholiday Sunday night. The prospect before me was an early rise and the long drive north to my afternoon class at Keene. Faded autumn leaves blew in hurried gusts through the Brooklyn below D's apartment, scratching the sidewalk with their dry pointy lobes. I assessed: students, or a poisoning? I choose death over teaching undergraduate photography.

I lay down on D's soft white carpet and waited for the pills to kick in. According to the Internet, it would take forty-five minutes to feel anything. It never occurred to me that D would find me lying dead in his living room when he arrived home. I couldn't consider anyone, not even myself. D and I had been seeing each other on and off since Jedediah and I had separated. We'd even recently gotten serious enough that I had my own set of keys. But I wouldn't allow myself to feel happiness over our new commitment. I was still wracked with guilt that I'd failed Jedediah. Although I couldn't see it then, there was no way I'd make a decent partner living with those regrets. I think D knew that, too.

That night the thought of leaving D's apartment and returning alone to Keene was like a vise grip twisting my heart. Pain radiated in waves that thumped with its beat. I couldn't breathe. If I have a soul, it was floating just outside of my body, an inch or so above my shoulders, kept from traveling to the ceiling only because anxiety, rage, and panic had frozen me in place. Hours, days, and years had brought me to this: sisterless, divorced, and without a clear idea of where I'd escape to fix myself. I must die, I thought. Even if I had to do it by my own hand.

And then, in a stroke of luck, my cell phone rang, interrupting my suicide attempt. It was Jedediah. I'd called him earlier that day and begged him to take me back, to reconcile. He was resolutely opposed. It wasn't the marriage I craved, but the solace of habit, the peace of our home. I'd found myself raging over the phone at him for not wanting me, raging in the exact way Cara had raged at me for my not wanting her. I'd wanted her though; just not the part of her that didn't allow me any other life. Now I couldn't access Cara or myself. With infidelity and pills and harsh words, I'd crushed down the good-enough person I'd once been. Why? I'll never really know. But I *was* that raw and pained, like a naked woman in a winter whiteout.

Jedediah had called to apologize for his rejections. He said he hadn't meant to be harsh and regretted that we'd had to part ways. There was no way to articulate my real worries in my poisoned state. I didn't really want the marriage back. I wanted Cara. No man could be her or provide her return. And because of that, I punished them all.

"Whatever you say," I slurred. "It's not like you loved me anyway."

Jedediah's voice shook. "Please, don't—don't say that. I did everything I could. You were everything to me."

The pills were working. "Soon you'll be sorry."

"Have you taken something? You don't sound like yourself."

"I took lots of something."

"Where are you?" He was frantic. "You've got to tell me where you are."

"That's not your business anymore." I couldn't tell him I

was at another man's house. "It doesn't matter where I am. You don't need a pathetic ex-wife, a beggar. You don't want me," I said. "I get that now."

"But I do. I need you alive. Maybe we can fix this."

"Really?" I regretted the pills for the first time. "You'll do that? You love me enough to come back?" I pulled my shoes on and walked out of the apartment, wobbling down the three flights of stairs to the street. "I don't want to die." I tripped and fell on the sidewalk, scraping my knee, blood trickling down my leg through the run in my tights.

Jedediah stayed on the phone. "Steady," he said. "One foot in front of the other."

"We can have a happy life," I managed through my Zyprexa cloud. "I love you. I forgive you for leaving when it got hard."

"We both did regrettable things."

"We did?"

"Where are you now?"

"Outside of the emergency room."

"Good, get in there." He was calm. "Give your phone to the receptionist."

"Thank you, Jeddy," I whispered, thankful. "We'll be okay." I gave the nurse at the information desk my cell phone and she spoke with Jedediah for a minute. She finished and handed it back.

"He wants to talk to you."

"Christa, be safe," he begged through labored breath, crying. "I won't be able to come back to you like you want me to. I needed to say that to make sure you'd get help. I'm sorry."

"I understand," I said and hung up on him. I couldn't expect him back; I'd done too much harm and ultimately it was my responsibility that our marriage was blown. I'd lost the two people in my life that I truly loved and, at that moment, I felt the losses were all my doing.

* * *

When Jedediah had finally moved out, eleven months after Cara died, I'd stood, defiant and physically frail, at our front door and handed him the last of his boxes.

"If I'd been sick with cancer, would you still have left?" I asked him.

"You don't have cancer. You have a problem keeping your clothes on."

"But I'm sick," I pleaded. "I hate what I've done to our lives." I tried to explain that my encounters had had nothing to do with sex. I was on my hands and knees. I was crippled and everyone was telling me to walk. But there was no remembering how. There was no getting up.

"It's always about you," he'd snapped. "I've thought of nothing else but you since we married. I must think of myself, cancer or not."

In the emergency room, dizzy from Zyprexa, I repeated the word *cancer* to myself over and over again. It distracted me from the waiting room filled with patients who stared at me shamelessly—the young woman wearing four-inch wine-colored suede heels and ripped leopard-print tights streaked with blood. I gave in to the pills. My legs folded and I hit the floor. I was falling down into a well with no bottom, no water.

When I came to, in an emergency-room bed, having just vomited the last of the charcoal dispensed to rid my stomach of pills, I was thinking not of Jedediah but of Mike.

In 1988, our neighbor had adopted a kitten, a fuzzy black ball with white-booted feet named Sebastian. Cara had grown so fond of this kitten that she'd traded her only pair of designer jeans with a classmate for a larger litter box and a harness and leash for him. She carried him in a pouch she had fashioned from her book bag.

One whole afternoon, she had played with the kitten at

the neighbor's house, trying to convince him to lap some milk from her hand instead of from his bowl. Cara and the kitten sat together in the grass beneath a shady tree; it was a perfect Sunday spring afternoon. Cara was about to head home when the kitten caught sight of a squirrel, and chased after it just as our neighbor backed her car out of the driveway. Cara leapt after the kitten, but he was too fast. He was crushed beneath the car's back tire. Yowling in pain and fear, he sprang from the car's undercarriage to find Cara's comfort. He died at her feet.

Mike heard the ruckus and ran like a good solider to survey the threat. He found his stepdaughter crying inconsolably over her lost friend's twisted body.

"Why did this happen?" Cara sobbed to Mike, needing a father's consoling answer.

"There's no telling," he said, and wrapped his arm around her shoulder, pulling her close. "I *will* tell you," he added, "you'll be lucky if this is the worst thing that ever happens to you."

As years went by, Cara's pain from losing Sebastian faded until, finally, her memory of the day was centered around how absolutely pitiless she'd found Mike's advice. "Can you believe we were raised by that man?" she'd ask me rhetorically. "I mean, who says that?"

It is the job of the Marine to keep his men safe, to watch their backs when they're "in the shit," as Mike would say. We two girls were Mike's men, like it or not. In winning my mother's hand, he'd also taken ours: rambunctious, curious, dirt jammed beneath our fingernails from digging for worms in the herb garden; he'd hold our dirty hands as we crossed the street, pull us back at even the hint of a car—the low purr of an engine or a twinkle from headlights. He'd stand guard, manning the living-room window while we romped in the yard, watching from the safety of air-conditioning. He kept a good eye on his brood, ready to rock 'n' roll, to pummel and destroy any invader: stray dog, storm, stranger. He was armed and ready: pepper spray, umbrella, or his fist, as solid as stone. It wasn't only weaponry Mike deployed. He was chock-full of advice, and he didn't care about a warm and cuddly delivery. As much as we'd troubled him, he must have loved us.

Nearly twenty years later, alone with beeping hospital machines and my frantic desire to die, I found myself thinking that Mike had been right. Cara and I had both been very lucky the day the neighbor's kitten died.

Would this worst thing ever end?

On my dash out of D's apartment to the emergency room, I'd forgotten to close the computer, exposing my search for Zyprexa overdose instructions. D came home late that night to find the empty pill bottle tipped over on the floor next to the computer. He sat down calmly and called all of the hospitals in Brooklyn and New England until he located me, at 2 a.m. I woke in the early morning from my Zyprexa hangover, D standing at my bedside rightfully glowering down at me. He stood, hands in his pockets, next to the guard they'd assigned to my cubicle to make sure I didn't try to run. D was still wearing his early-winter navy wool overcoat with the smooth wood buttons. He'd wrapped his favorite yellow cashmere scarf around his neck and it hung in a blazing drape over his collar and down onto his chest. He was tall and handsome. I was certain he hated me. He didn't. He went on loving me in his own way for years. He loved me until I was no longer sick, neither of us knowing what to do with a sane me.

"I love you," I said, and lifted my hand to my mouth and wiped. Charcoal smudged the back of it. My light blue paper hospital gown was specked with vomit and tears. I was drowsy and not in complete control of my speech. My unsteady heart was unforgivably on the sleeve of my flimsy hospital dressings.

D and I hadn't even weathered a flu yet. I was certain this health emergency would be our end.

"I love you too, C." He brushed the side of my face with his fingertips, tenderly, paying no mind to my absolute filth. "But," he conceded, "you're not coming back into my apartment like this." He'd spent months making his home into a place where I'd be safe from my own ideation. I'd just defiled that. "I can't have you at home anymore, not without help," D worried. "You need to be someplace with professionals, doctors who know what they're doing. I'm a writer, for Christ's sake."

"I don't want to be locked up." I pouted. "I have nowhere to go, D. Please?"

"I can't risk another episode like this." He pulled the thin hospital blanket up over my shoulders, tucking me in. "You might not make it next time. Losing you would be maddening. I can't risk it."

"Fine, then. I'll figure it out." I turned away from him and stared at the hospital equipment on the wall. D hadn't slept all night and was near tears. I pushed him further. "If I can't stay with you, would you mind moving my car? I'm parked in a tow zone. I don't want to get a ticket. The keys are in my purse."

I was discharged from the emergency room late in the morning and though D kindly escorted me to my committal, I'd made the choice to be hospitalized. I had ideas about a particular hospital this time. Marilyn Monroe and Robert Lowell had gone there for treatment, for exhaustion and for clinical depression. Payne Whitney is a sprawling, idyllic campus scattered with mortared stone buildings that look like castles. I imagined therapists wearing herringbone suits with elbow patches, rushing in and out of the residences, holding patients' charts. I pictured the interior of the hospital as highly and regally decorated with floral wallpaper and gilt wood settees. I was right about the look of the campus, for the most part. But the offices are staffed by workers slumped over desks piled high with paperwork. The decor is Victorian and the furniture is a mix of richly colored wine and paisley fabrics. Romantic land-scape paintings and realist portraits of the founding doctors of the hospital hang in the foyer. The ward, in contrast, is stark. The floors are linoleum tiled for easy body-fluid cleanup; the place is lit entirely with fluorescent track lights with flickering, dim bulbs.

With D alongside me, the doctors and nurses kept asking if I'd like my father to be informed of my treatment plan. I corrected them at first but grew tired of explaining to new staff members, who observed D weeping like a frightened parent in the waiting room. "I don't think my dad needs any more information." The admitting doctor pressed a stethoscope onto my bare chest. "I think he's had enough."

There were enough of us at Payne Whitney then that I don't remember the bearded lady's name. She wore a knit brown hat and cargo jeans. I looked at her cap and thought about the rebellious brain beneath it. She sprouted opposing personali-ties. Her beard grew in black wooly wisps; she didn't fuss over it, but stroked it in group therapy the same way my male col-leagues had stroked their beards in our art department faculty meetings.

The common room at Payne Whitney was also the group therapy room, the arts and crafts room, and the room used for containing us whenever they hauled a new, resisting patient into the unit by force. They'd signal us in by blowing a whistle and usher us inside single file. We'd wait in a confused mass of medication-induced twitching, nervous chatter, and, in the case of the youngest patient on the ward, uncontrollable skin picking.

Sleeping through the night is difficult in a mental hospital. Fifteen minutes after lights-out, there is bed check. Nurses go from room to room to observe patients while they're sleeping, to make certain they've not gotten up and tried to hang themselves, or stolen a spork from the cafeteria, fashioning it, while they should be dreaming, into a shiv. Doors are left open a crack, tapped lightly, and patients are viewed. Sometimes there is a small square window at the top of the doors covered with a thin curtain. The curtains on most of the doors at Payne Whitney were light blue and strung up with thin silver hooks that resembled fishing line. The nurses slid the curtains open and observed. My door was curtainless and cracked; it creaked open. I anticipated the noise; lying on my side, I stared through the semidarkness of the room at the opening door. The night nurse looked in. She closed one of her eyes, as if she were staring at a distant planet through a telescope or glimpsing me through a peephole. She took pity through her open eye.

"I'm awake," I said to my peering nurse. "I need more meds."

"It's not time," she said. "Meds are taken at seven a.m., you know that." The door whined closed, as closed as was allowed.

The door opened, again. "I'm still awake," I said.

The nurse came into my room and sat on my bed. I was lucky. I was one of the few patients who didn't have a roommate. "See yourself on a beach listening to the waves break," she said. "Rest. Feel the sand beneath you, holding the weight of your head." I closed my eyes. I thought of Cara full of formaldehyde. My fluttering lids and medication-puffy face didn't just resemble hers. They *were* hers. It's like the adult moment when you understand that you've turned into your own mother or father, except it's psychotic. "If that doesn't work, take this." The nurse handed me an orange pill.

"Why did she have to die?" I asked.

"God always takes the good ones," she said blankly, as if she'd practiced it. "Now, try to sleep."

I imagined again that I was Cara in my Payne Whitney bed. I took my hands and held them out in front of my face. My bitten-down fingernails were painted red and they were Cara's hands, my twin hands. I tried to change the visual; I saw myself as a skinny tiger stalking through a jungle full of poachers. They'd need a blow dart to take me down.

Fifteen minutes passed.

The nurse peeked at me through the slit of the open door, careful.

"I'm awake," I said.

"Still?"

"Please?" I sat up. "I need something more, another pill." I was wearing the brand-new pajamas that my mother brought me during her day visit: black yoga pants and a red T-shirt, both soft from washing and perfumed with fabric softener.

"Let me make a call." The nurse came back with a paper cup with a couple of Benadryls inside. "You can't have anything more than this." She shook the pills from the cup out into my hand.

"Thanks." I took the pills without water. I started to cry, sorry for myself. "Will I ever get better?"

"I can't say I know that," she said. The nurse put her arms around my shoulders and rocked me.

On my third day on the ward I was alerted that Dr. Otto Kernberg had taken an interest in my case. He'd devoted his life's work to defining and discovering borderline personality disorder, the illness Cara had been diagnosed with while at The Meadows. Kernberg wanted to meet with me to assess my condition.

A young medical student, a woman who wore a tight pencil

skirt and matching pumps and wore her long black hair knotted into a bun at the base of her neck, delivered the news with a hushed voice. She told me of Kernberg in such a way that I was to know that what I'd just received was near an invitation from God himself and I must accept. She took great pains in explaining why I ought to meet with Kernberg and consider staying at the hospital indefinitely to remain in his care.

I asked if I'd be allowed to leave the hospital and go outdoors for the visit and was told that there was a short walk across campus to Kernberg's office. I accepted immediately.

I was no longer the witty professor who sparred with students over composition and photo theory, or the artist full of fire and cutting compassionate vision. I wasn't the loyal friend, loving daughter, or faithful wife I'd once thought myself. I was a fugitive and a schemer. I hadn't been at Payne Whitney long enough to earn the privilege of walking the courtyard; meeting with Kernberg could help me make a break.

The young doctor and I walked the campus grounds to Kernberg's office in a small stone building. I'd layered myself in two pairs of pants and wore three long-sleeved shirts—all I'd packed in my bag to Payne Whitney. I wore slip-on flats and my feet were bare inside of my shoes. I'd forgotten to take socks to the hospital, counting on tights to keep warm. My stockings were confiscated at check-in: they were too easy to fashion into a noose.

I looked for holes beneath the fence of the campus or a strait on the winding path where I could tear off. I could outrun my escort. I'd sized her up and determined that although I had asthma, she had been the kind of girl in high school who was still running the mile in gym class when the next period's bell rang. I imagined she moved slowly so as not to ruin her hair. Her pumps stabbed like spikes into the wet ground.

And then it started to rain. A drizzle fell first and picked up quickly into hail. If I ran now, I thought, I'd freeze.

The resident pulled a collapsed umbrella from her shoulder bag and opened it over us. "Hurry in," she insisted. "You'll catch your death in this wet and cold. You're too thin for pneumonia."

I hadn't the courage to flee. I realized as I stood in the rain sharing the resident's umbrella that I had expected to die, as surely as I expected that Cara would die. Having to live, I realized then, my feet wet and teeth chattering—that was the most unexpected and terrifying and impossible thing about surviving.

I know what you are thinking: I'm on thinning ice. You are always one step behind me.

You could fall in, too, and we'd freeze before taking in mouthfuls of cold water. We agree drowning is the best way to die: the bitter cold euphoria of what it is to stop floating. To sink and float, sink and float, and press against the ice until a thaw. A man would find us on an early spring swim, our identical bodies preserved by the cold. What a story he would tell about being tangled in identical limbs as he tried to do the backstroke. "And there were two of them!" he'd say. He'd bend ears into old age. We could be a litany of death. We could go on and on. Death would laugh and say: those who are born together die together. The man, years after the backstroke, would irrevocably ask into his late years, "What were those dear girls thinking?"

The medical student and I met Kernberg in his office. I sat in a green leather studded chair pulled up to the far end of a rectangular table. Kernberg sat at the opposite post. Medical residents, scribbling notes on yellow writing pads, filled three chairs on both sides of the table. Kernberg nodded and our session commenced. He appeared small in his high-back chair, and elderly, but he commanded attention with his heavy German accent and few words. He wanted to talk with me about

my sister. He asked me to recall a time before her death that
we'd acted unknowingly in the same way and to recall whether
I'd acted in that same way since she'd been gone. He asked me
to keep it simple: tasks first, then feelings.

I told him about the sinks in Arlington Cemetery.

We were only nine years old and touring D.C. with Mike.
He took us to the tomb of the unknown soldier and had us
salute. We walked the cemetery hills dotted with endless white
tombstones, tablets that read BORN and DIED and SERVED
and were as alike as the rigid military uniforms the men had
worn and fought and died in. Mike walked ahead of us. I
remember the quiet imposed by what I imagined to be the
drama of battle. The silent cries of men before they'd become
casualties were not far off; they were coming from the ground.
I could hear the choppers and artillery fire. I was a girl of nine
with a fierce imagination and a Marine Corps elementary
school education. I knew how to raise a flag and I knew how to
mourn our heroes.

Cara and I were tired from walking so we knelt on the
ground to rest. I rooted my hands through the grass and pulled
it out in bunches, a child's reflex. Mike stopped and turned; he
had an animal's sense for our wrongdoings. I'd not only shown
weakness by resting on my laurels during our remembrance
march, I'd also desecrated his good name and our family name,
the name he shared with our mother while we kept our father's.

Mike yanked me up from the ground by one arm and held
me dangling in the air. He held Cara by the other. I dropped
my fist full of earth, the ripped strands of grass falling down
onto the lawn below. "You're in a place of honor," he barked
and then released me. "Go wash your hands." He pushed us off
toward the public bathroom.

We shoved our hands in our pockets and did as we were
told. Once we'd gotten out of earshot we giggled. "I have to pee

anyway," Cara told me. "Don't feel bad. These guys are too dead to notice."

I went into the restroom first, while Cara stood outside and took a long drink at a water fountain. Inside there were dozens of orange doors parallel to dozens of sinks. I went into a stall at the far end of the restroom and then found a sink and soaped my hands. It was late afternoon on a weekday and the restroom was empty of anyone but me. Cara was still outside. I dried my hands with a paper towel and skipped out to find her. She was waiting by the door.

"Aren't you going inside?" I asked.

"I was standing guard, but I'm not going in alone. Watch my back, okay?"

I followed her in and and she surveyed the stalls. "This place gives me the creeps. I hate the military. They make the bathrooms the same as the graves." Cara walked to a stall and went inside. She opened and used the exact one I had.

She emerged after a minute and then selected a sink, *my* sink. We were wired to make the same choices given any number of options.

I told this story to Kernberg.

"You were little girls who made the same basic choices?" Kernberg asked.

"Yes."

He wanted to know if there was something else, something small that connected us in our choices to each other. I told him about my chair.

Mom had helped me redecorate after Jedediah moved out, and she'd found me an antique sitting chair at a yard sale with arms wide as a hug and a back that was tall and supportive and built to last. The chair was upholstered in smooth black leather but the seat was torn. Mom said she'd like to take me to a fabric warehouse so I could pick material I liked. She'd reupholster the chair. She thought it would be good for me to have a new piece of furniture, something completely mine: not from my marriage, not something inherited from Cara. Mom said she'd done the same for Cara with a chaise longue that had a swan carved into the wood on the back. They'd gotten as far as picking out the fabric, then Cara had died.

The fabric warehouse had many thousands of lengths of silk, fleece, cotton, wools, linen, and tulles. There were rooms organized by design: shabby chic, modern, antique, utilitarian. I went to the most colorful room I could find and browsed the fabrics for an hour, trying to imagine incorporating a new chair into my life, one completely of my choosing. Jedediah wouldn't argue that it was too pink, ornate, or feminine. Cara couldn't want it for herself.

I decided on thick red cotton decorated with tiny yellow elephants wearing sage green riding saddles. I pulled the fabric out of the bin and brought it over to my mother to ask whether or not it was good for a chair, if it was the right density and weight. I handed it over to her to inspect, proud of my choice.

My mother went pale as she looked down at the fabric. "It's perfect," she said. "It's the exact fabric Cara picked out. We already have enough to cover the chair at home."

"You've been taught your lack of free will is what defines you and keeps your sister with you? No?" Kernberg said.

"I don't know. Maybe." He could read me and I feared that. I feared I'd have to let Cara go. "Am I sick, like her?" I asked in a child's voice. I needed to know I hadn't caught what she had when she died, taken her illness.

"I never met your sister. She was not under my care. I can't say what ailed her. I can say with certainty that you are not well, but this state of yours is temporary, acute. My concern is how you navigate as you go along."

"So I can go home? I don't need to be here?"

"Yes, you can go home. But yes, you need to be here."

"You'll sign off and let me go? I'm not a borderline?"

"Yes you can. No, you're not borderline, but we're not finished here."

I called D and let him know that, as it turned out, I was sane and could go home. Kernberg had said as much.

"Kernberg? You saw Kernberg? *The* Kernberg?" D asked.

"Yes. Is that so important?"

"You just saw the father of modern psychotherapy, after Freud. You know that, right?"

I didn't. I was just glad to leave. "He seemed nice."

"Nice? Jesus, C. Jesus. Kernberg? No shit. I just can't believe you saw Kernberg. What did he say?"

"He said I wasn't crazy."

"You mean you're not borderline?"

"No, I'm not."

"I knew it. But now that we've heard it from him, I'm relieved." D took a deep breath. "I told you you'd be in good hands there," he added lightly. "How about you come on back home? I'll make dinner."

I loaded my suitcase into the trunk of my car in the Payne Whitney parking lot. During my short stay, a seal had cracked in the trunk and rain had soaked everything inside. My wool winter coat was ruined; it sat atop moldy dresses and soggy notebooks. The most prized book in my photography collection, a hardbound Arbus monograph with a set of dark-haired identical twins standing shoulder to shoulder on the cover, wearing crisp white shirts, jumpers, and curious frowns, was waterlogged. The cover and thus the twins were split down the center, ripped apart.

I pulled out of the hospital parking lot and headed back to D's in Brooklyn. As I hit the road I recalled a drive with Cara through the center of Northampton. It was January 3, 2003. We'd just had the first significant snowfall of the season. We were on our way to photograph winterscapes. Cara had been raped only a year and a half before. On that drive, she had lifted her chin toward the rearview mirror of my yellow Volvo wagon to check her makeup. I'd created a diva. One arm dangling out of the car window, she smoked a long cigarette; she was dead and breathing.

I was about to take my first picture for *Kindred*. I didn't know what I was doing.

I found an embankment distinguished by a hibernating tree webbed with red berries and pulled the car over. The tree had hundreds of thin, tangled branches.

I directed Cara to stand in front of my camera by pointing at a blank space beneath the berry tree. She tromped out into the snow and knelt down, pushing back the thorny, bare branches. "A real actress never lets anyone see her sweat," she said, and proceeded to huddle on the ground.

She lured a bough of the red berries over her head. Bittersweet climbed the vines she pulled closed. She wanted to be both hidden and seen, peeking out from behind the bough. I stood beside her and lowered a cluster of vines. I pulled the cage of them down hard to cover her. She stared at the lens of the camera as if it were a person familiar to her, someone to whom she needed to reveal her secrets, someone she wanted to lash with her painful truths. She looked down without my asking, hands in just the right place. Her cloak plumed around her legs, a black tulip in bloom. She reapplied the red lipstick I'd brought for her.

We wore the identical black wool coats our mother had bought us for Christmas that year. Cara's coat concealed purple pajamas. She'd refused to get dressed, so I found the only thing she owned that would cover her nightwear. She'd missed a spot for her lipstick on her top lip; a crescent moon of pale pink exposed itself from behind the garish red stain. She sat quietly picking at her ragged manicure and then lit a cigarette. She didn't pay it much mind; smoldering tobacco touched the tips of her index and middle fingers. She wore a mood ring and the diamond from her failing marriage; she never took either off. Dirt and bark lodged under her nails. Her hands were turning blue. She clawed her way into place for the picture.

"Hurry up, Christa," she yelled out over the wind. "If you want me to lie down I'll do it. I always know what you want." She assumed the position, satisfied with herself.

She didn't know. I wanted her giant doe-in-the-headlights eyes back. I wanted the woman who believed that she could win the Publishers Clearing House sweepstakes. Instead, I stood face-to-face with a Klonopin-ed Medusa who'd been stripped of her powers; a fallen goddess, stoned and frozen, who slurred her words.

I heard my own voice counting for the picture. The voice was familiar; it's Cara's voice.

I made pictures of us in snow and pictures of us over bodies of water and on mountains of rock, but I couldn't reach her.

The shutter clicked.

I extended my hand to help Cara off of the ground. She took my hand and stood; she brushed herself off.

"Wait," she said.

"Why?" I asked.

"You need this." She reached down and picked up a handful of snow.

"Don't." I put my hands up and shielded my face. "Don't you dare hit me with that."

She laughed. "You think that's what I want to do?" She took the snow and threw it into her own face in a puff; it stuck in her hair and eyelashes. A frosty queen, she blinked at me. "If you die, I'll kill myself." Cara put her hands on the sides of her cheeks and felt their cold. She waited for me to respond.

I wiped the snow from her face in gentle strokes. "If you die, I'll survive you." I sank to the ground and made a snow angel. Cara got down beside me and made one, too. We moved our arms and legs in tandem, like swimmers.

Chapter 27

I moved back to D's in Brooklyn and started going on dates with Cara's boyfriends. I logged onto Cara's e-mail to find their names and addresses, and tracked down each one of them, calling or e-mailing. I was hoping I'd catch a glimpse of her by setting a boyfriend net. I did keyword searches. Her favorite words: *lovely, moon, twin,* and *zodiac.* Her pet names: *baby, dearest, sweetie, flower,* and the mystifying, *chunky.* I found searching for phrases to be helpful also:

> *I love you.*
> *How's it going?*
> *I want you.*
> *What's your sign?*
> *I'm a Cancer.*
> *I had a nice time.*
> *Bowling?*
> *Dancing at Diva's?*
> *I never do this but—*

I checked the archive of her e-mail tirelessly. She was too much of a romantic to delete a single letter; she'd saved and archived all of her messages in folders. Each was labeled not with a name, but with a type of jewel. She'd even held on to the rejections: "You're too needy," one of the men wrote. "I've gone back to my wife," said another. I savored her notes. I looked for even a hint of flirtation in her correspondence with a man. When I found an inkling of courtship, I'd make contact and ask them to meet me. I told her boyfriends that I'd hoped to pull together a book of Cara's work and needed help piecing together her last years. Not one of her boyfriends said no. There was a common reprieve: "Please don't mention this to my wife." And I heard more than once, "She won't understand this, but I do."

I wasn't cheating on D, I reasoned. It was research. I had no desire to be intimate with any of these men, and I never was. I thought of our meetings more as fact-finding missions.

"Is it crazy to go out and find my sister's lovers?" I asked D one night at dinner. We'd been trying out living together for the summer; we were in a honeymoon period, and though I'd kept my own place, we hadn't gotten to the point where our shared possessions had become more than symbol; we'd bought only the trimmings for a home—groceries and sheets, roasting pans and books—with the intention of defining who we'd become together as we went along. There was always that fear, up until the end, that if we didn't keep up appearances, we'd failed. I baked cakes and he prepared meals; he poured drinks with the precision of a surgeon's hand.

D had made an elaborate dish the night I asked him about the boyfriends: a roasted chicken in a cast-iron skillet that he turned by hand and basted every ten minutes. He'd shelled several cloves of garlic, chopped carrots, potatoes, an onion, and parsnips and arranged them all around the bird. Each caramelized in the chicken fat as it cooked. D didn't own a kitchen table, so we'd picnic on the living-room floor each night. He'd take an expensive, high-thread-count Italian sheet and spread it out. We'd eat on that, and tried not to soil the sheet with grease or wine. We'd sit across from each other, each with our own careful dining styles. D had been raised with meticulous table manners and could eat anything anywhere without betraying etiquette. I took tiny bites and lifted my plate up to my chin. It was my job to set our places, and I happily did so. I carried out plates, paper napkins, utensils, and a small carving station for the chicken stacked on top of a solid mahogany serving tray. I set our table on the floor. This was our eating ritual, which we followed with hours of pot smoking. I went back into the kitchen to see how dinner was progressing.

"Sounds about right to me, Sweet Pea." D opened the freezer and pulled out a half-sized martini glass handblown with a ribbon of tangerine that he'd brought for me from Europe. He placed it beside his larger one and poured us both a drink. The glass was dainty, just the right serving so my cocktail stayed cold. D mixed Manhattans, his favorite, and learned to make a more palatable, sweeter version for me than the mix he liked for himself. He'd served me my first stiff drink, and thought it funny that when I took my initial sips, I wrinkled my nose like a child. But a smaller, pretty glass had made the jet-fuel burn of the bourbon go down smoother; in no time, I was throwing them back and making my own. I was regularly drunk before dinner. "This chicken is nearly done." D pulled a bit of the skin off the top. "Open up, sweetie." He dropped the skin into my mouth. "When I wrote the memoir about Louanne, I contacted her friends and asked as many questions as I could. You're just being a good artist."

"Thanks, D," I answered, mouth full of salty, crispy, perfect skin. I felt for Louanne when he called her by her first name. She'd birthed him, nurtured him, loved him the best she could. She may have been an alcoholic and a nightmare, but she was still a mother.

* * *

Most of Cara's boyfriends made small talk, then explained they'd be happy to help with any "research" I might be doing. Conversations would usually devolve; I became a boyfriend confessor. They were clearly mostly still in the solipsistic "if only I'd" phase of grief. "If only I'd loved her more," "If only I'd spent the time with her that she needed," "If I'd only not left her," she might still be here.

We had more in common than they realized.

They were full of guilt and longing and regret. I'd so hoped to find them that way. I picked at their grief scabs to the point of bloodshed. I took pleasure in it. I was furious with her boyfriends. We should have been able to keep her alive if we'd all worked together, but, of course, we hadn't. The men in my life had not shown up. My father had not loved me enough. My lovers could never give enough. Cara's boyfriends had let us down, too.

Men couldn't be trusted. My mother had made that clear. "They'll fuck you. But they'll never love you," she'd said upon finding my middle school diary, in which she'd discovered that her thirteen-year-old twins had been having sex with their eighteen-year-old boyfriends. "If I never say a word to you about this again," which she didn't, "don't forget what I've told you."

I hear her words as I lie down with a man. I hear them if I love him. The harder I love, the louder her words are.

My body was a machine with No.1. Bones to the grind, my flesh was a slave stone. No. 1 pushed and my back thumped the head-board. The cats kept sleeping. I serviced him like I was milking butter with my mouth.

No. 2 painted pictures. He seduced me and put marbles in my pockets. He mouthed my neck in Union Square. I danced for him and then I cried. He left his marbles in our hotel bed. They were swirled worlds of color, round, clear, and breakable. I woke. No. 2 was not sleeping next to me.

I cheated with No. 3, but thanked him for taking me to the ocean. We celebrated my first un-wedding anniversary and undid my marriage. I cried at Mystic Pizza *and hated him for not being my husband. We fucked hard in the heavy sea air. I held my cigarette on the balcony and sat for hours plotting my revenge. I thought of all of the ways one might finally kill a heart as dead as mine.*

No. 4 had braces and curls matted down from sweat. He rocked me into the wall. My head got sore. I would have kicked him if I hadn't invited him to fill my empty bed.

No. 5 worked on his thesis while I pretended to sleep. I heard him tell me he loved me even though Edgardo made me deaf in one ear. I can make out words and take away their meanings. I can turn words to dust and have them forwarded to my mailbox. No. 5's flowers wilted, waiting. I never came home to get them.

No. 6 wore blue face paint on Halloween. He was older than I, and couldn't save me. He kissed me and we drank blackberry brandy. We ate steak late at night, naked. We finished our meal with sweet tea at sunrise.

Cara had a collection of so many men. She'd ask me to come to her apartment to help her sort them. She called it "man shopping." We'd flip through her Match.com profile, her plenty of fish account, her nerve chat history. "What do think of him?" she'd coo. "He's cute."

"He's broke," I'd say. There were her ever-active other accounts to consider: credit cards maxed out by clothes and by the eBay home decor purchases to furnish her never-ending need for new spaces. Moves to new apartments made her feel better so she kept on making them. There was always a boyfriend to carry a box or lift the heavy end of her sofa. "Let's take a look at the next guy." Cara clicked her track pad and moved to the next potential suitor.

"Oh! Look! He's a doctor," I said. "That's just what you need."

On my first date I met the painter. I took him to a Manhattan bar, Death & Co. I paid the bill. We ordered cocktails and I made eyes at him. I scootched in close to his bar stool to get a better listen to his part of the story. I'd already heard Cara's over and over. The painter didn't know this. I tipped my head a little to the side and batted my thickly mascaraed lashes. I adjusted the hem of my skirt. I asked, "How was she in bed?" or more important, "How was she after?" I thought of myself after lovemaking. I hadn't been able to stop myself from weeping directly after orgasm ever since Cara had been raped. Eight years of postcoital crying. I was sick of it.

I had rapid-fire questions for the painter: "Did she cry? Did she make a scene and try to cloy you back into her grasp? What about her hair? Had she bleached it to straw yet? Did she wear sexy underwear? Any at all? Was her pubic hair waxed and trimmed? Were her nipples pierced then? Tattoos? How many dates to find out?" I twirled my hair around my finger and crossed and uncrossed my legs. "Did she wonder what your children would look like? When was the last time you spoke? How about the last time you went out? What was that like? Did she talk about me?" I knew that in all of the dates I'd had since she'd died, I'd certainly not left Cara out.

The painter moved in close, put his hand on my face. "You don't look anything like her," he whispered. "It's weird."

On my second date I met with Brian. I hadn't seen him since Cara's funeral. He'd told me over the telephone that I'd be surprised to see him now. He'd made a change, in his new position as partner in a law firm; he'd turned into a man who was well paid and well loved.

"I'm getting married," Brian told me.

"Congratulations." I tried to sound happy for him.

"That's sweet of you," he said, relieved. "I'd love for you to be there but I wouldn't want to confuse the relatives. They still remember your sister."

"Of course, I understand." Did I? I did. I was used to making people uncomfortable solely by the sight of me.

"How about we plan to meet up?" I asked hopefully. "I'd like to interview you."

"For what?"

"I'm working on something about Cara. I've got questions."

"We could go and see Amma?" Brian suggested. "She'll be in town next Saturday."

"Amma?"

"I go every year. She's at the Manhattan Center in midtown. You've got to get there early to get a token," Brian said. "It's not worth your while to go if you don't get a token to be hugged."

"Got it!" I was perplexed and wondered what a token might possibly be, but didn't let on.

"Does nine a.m. work?"

"I'll be there," I promised, even though I hadn't been up that early in months.

Immediately, I researched Amma. She is a curing saint, born to a family of farmers in a small village in rural India. She's reported to have come from the womb into the world, smiling. She cooked, cleaned, and reared her siblings. When she met a person in need, she brought them food and clothing. But food was scarce; she rummaged piles of trash from the homes of higher-caste neighbors, brought scraps of bread to feed her family; picked bones clean and scavenged rotten chunks of vegetables to cook soup. When Amma was fourteen, she looked around at the men and women sifting through trash alongside her; she dropped her gatherings and extended her arms, embraced a skinny weeping woman who held on to a fussy, starving infant. After that, Amma hugged strangers on the street. She would not stop hugging people. It was not acceptable for a teenage girl to touch others, especially men, and she was scolded, cast out. She kept on hugging.

The week I was to meet Amma, there was a heat wave. With an air conditioner that was low on Freon blasting, D and I didn't bother getting dressed and spent our days and nights in bed drinking port, eating takeout, and making love. It was good to sit shoulder to shoulder in bed and eat. With D, food tasted good again.

But the night before I met Amma, I barely slept. And I woke the next day just as I'd woken most days in recent years—at late morning, stiff and agitated, hair stuck up on one side, pillow creases on my cheek, head heavy and full with foggy hangover from a nightmare.

I was naked except for the crisp white top sheet wrapped around my legs. I'd stolen the sheet with my nocturnal tossing and turning. I glanced over at my sleeping and completely naked boyfriend and felt a pang of guilt. Uncovered, he looked cold and vulnerable. He snored lightly; I tiptoed to the foot of the bed and flapped the sheet up in the air. It floated down on top of him.

The night before, I'd gotten carried away talking with D and had spilled a glass of wine on myself. I looked down and touched the sticky purple wine stain that ran from my breasts to my belly. I'd paid my spill little mind the night before. I'd pulled my dress up over my head and tossed it quickly and excitedly into a corner, wiggled over to D, and straddled him on the sofa. He brushed me off of his lap. "You're drunk, C," he said. "Later?" I sat naked on the sofa, beside him, rubbed the back of his neck. D adjusted his glasses and put his arm around me, pulled me in closer, lit a joint.

At a quarter past five, we'd made our way to the bedroom. I lay on my back in bed. The sun was rising, lighting the sky from behind the day's early smog. The brick exterior of a neighboring building had begun to glow. D and I were discussing how one day soon I'd be taking pictures again, and he'd finish the novel he'd started years before. I tried to focus my eyes on his but couldn't. I was looking toward him but not at him.

"Pop out of it, kitten. I'm here." He ran his hand along my shoulder. He'd gotten to be a pro at redirecting my drifting thoughts, sensing my unease. I could hide nothing.

"I'll try," I said and turned away from him, pretending to fall asleep.

Our relationship had begun on faulty footing, as an affair, and I had grim imaginings of how it would all end. We'd spend the rest of forever talking about living together in D's Brooklyn apartment, but never really do it. Because he was twenty years my senior, D and I would continue to think of our age difference as an obstacle to settling down together.

I looked over at the dresser by the bed. I'd crammed all of my clothes inside of it, so many clothes that they pushed open the bottom drawers. I wondered if there'd ever really be room in D's place for me. I saw everything through the veil of loss. Loss, I reasoned, was the inevitable consequence of love.

D had lived in the apartment for two decades, the first longtime location he'd been in since his childhood in rural Virginia. He'd made himself a sweet home, decorating it with cheerful art deco pottery fired in orange and lime glazes. He had a full library of books he'd collected over the years; hundreds of volumes of poetry and rare first edition novels filling bookshelves from the floor to the ceiling. It was the kind of home I'd fantasized about in high school; it was a sweet breezy walk-through in a bustling city. But I couldn't bring myself to fully live there, and I couldn't trust that D wanted me to.

"We're at the brink of marriage," he had said once, "and I am nearly selfish enough to go ahead and do it. I just can't bear thinking of you in this world alone."

"Oh, D," I'd sighed in frustration. "Don't even think it."

"I'd understand if you took a younger lover. I could handle it. Fidelity isn't negotiable as much as it is flexible," he said, keeping the door open for his own out.

I was both over- and underdressed to see Amma; I wore a purple silk dress with a lotus flower print. I'd washed the dress in hot water in D's bathroom sink the night before, and draped it on the back of a kitchen chair to drip-dry, actions that didn't adhere to the care label sewn into the dress. The garment bunched up at the waist, riding up in a way that made my chest appear too big, and its thick regal purple shoulder straps had warped into long elastics.

At noon, I ducked out of D's apartment in my shrunken silk and made my way onto the subway, into midtown, and then marched toward the Manhattan Center to meet Brian, looking for him through a swarm of Amma hopefuls.

Other women crowded outside—New Agers, drum circlers, hacky-sackers, cancer survivors, unfaithful wives, job seekers, midlife transitioners, and spinsters. Their shoulders and heads were covered, or they were dressed in slacks, long skirts, blouses that buttoned at the elbows. I looked more hooker than worshipper. Sweat dripped from my armpits, circled out onto my dress. I kept my arms down and made a half wave at a man I thought was Brian but wasn't.

The terrible heat had stopped the city in its tracks. Sidewalk eateries were empty, flies flew logy, hair went limp. But the convention hall for Amma's gathering was booked to capacity.

Hippies and cultists leaned up against the gray stone exterior of the Manhattan Center, counted prayer beads, tranced in the shadows. Sage and nag champa faded sweetly down the block, falling off somewhere between the avenue and the aroma of a storefront Chinese take-out operation. The greasy food smelled delicious to my growling belly. I'd gotten better at feeding myself in the last year; I'd gained back nearly all of the weight I'd lost. I was up to 115 pounds, my fighting weight. But I'd forgotten to eat breakfast in my dash to see Brian and my blood sugar had dropped. I *was* hungry.

"Hey, do you want a rebirthing?" A monastic woman put her hand on my upper back, moved it to my naked arms, undeterred by my sweat. She leaned in close, pointed to a small trailer that was parked curbside. "There's a Cherokee woman in there giving them for sixty bucks," she whispered.

"No thanks," I told her. "I think that's the last thing I need." It was really, probably, the first thing. I pushed my way through the crowd gathered at the doors and went inside. A flurry of people moved through the convention center. Women danced in broomstick skirts that skimmed the ground; kids sat in circles and chanted; vendors sold beads and prayer cards.

A token was really a single raffle-style ticket lettered in black ink, its crisp green paper stock bowing at the edges, that admitted you into Amma's arms; I hadn't arrived in time to secure one.

I found Brian on the third-floor balcony of the convention center. He was meditating with a group of middle-aged women he'd traveled with from White Plains. The group was dressed in yoga wear. Brian wore wide-legged cotton pants and a white shirt with a mandarin collar. He'd grown his hair; it fell in russet-colored curls just above his shoulders, sprung out in waves he tucked behind his ears. Brian sat calmly in tripod position with his hands extended out onto his knees, palms up. He was chubby but cherubic; shorter and stockier than I remembered him, but lighter in aspect.

"Bri?" I interrupted his meditation. "I'm here," I said. "I haven't got a token."

"I knew you'd make it," he said, lifted from a trance. He reached into his pocket and pulled out his own token and studied it, as if this would cause another to appear. "Well, we'll need to get you one." I grabbed his hand and pulled him to his feet.

We made our way through the crowd to a booth where a woman sat behind a table of Amma-related goods and a cash register. "This is my friend, Christa," Brian told her. For a moment I thought he'd known her, been her longtime friend, but it became clear that the two were strangers. This was merely a transaction and not an introduction. "She doesn't have a token to hug Amma."

The woman looked unconcerned. "I'm so sorry, but we haven't any left to give."

"Her identical twin has recently passed away. She's in need of a token."

I didn't correct him. I hadn't seen him since the funeral, so this apparent lie must have been truth for him. As I stood before him my loss was as fresh to him as the day Cara had died.

The woman smiled at me in a way I'd come to recognize. She pitied me. She reached into an envelope that sat beside stacks of cash in the register and pulled out a token. "These are reserved for special cases," she said and handed one to me.

I looked away from her and toward the convention floor.

I'd made a picture once of Cara and me atop a frozen field, beneath a gnarled apple tree, on a red blanket, kneeling, holding hands. In the picture the red of the blanket is radiant, floating magically off of the bright white snow like a flying carpet. We posed kissing on the lips, porcelain urns turned in to face each other. It was the coldest day I can remember being outside in all of my life. The two of us held still, face-to-face, our breath freezing the other's rouged cheeks. Our eyes stung from the bitter wind, tears pooling at their corners. We blinked them away as best we could, but I left the shoot with a frostbitten tear duct.

"Sexy, sexy," Cara teased, trying not to move her mouth so the picture would be sharp. We put our hands in each other's pockets to keep warm between exposures. Cara had forgotten her gloves, so I gave her mine, a bright red pair with short-cuffed wrists. In the picture I hold her red-gloved hands tightly, my Lady Macbeth. We laughed as we tried our best to pose seriously, waiting for the timer to wind down and the shutter to click. We giggled as we harmlessly pecked our twin-lipsticked mouths.

It looked as if Amma was doing the same face-to-face, leaning-into, hand-clutching, and loving, but with strangers, and while we all watched.

Amma, tiny, in a blazing green sari, hunched over a man who clung to her as she swayed back and forth with him in her arms. His arms were bony, arthritic; he wrapped them around her waist as she held him; he lunged forward into her arms, pressed himself with force against her. His head hung down over her left shoulder; his face turned in toward her neck.

It appeared from where we stood that Amma had cronies. Pairs of men stood on either side of her, collecting hug tokens, like ride operators at a carnival. Stiff backed, they lined people up single file in front of the saint, escorted one person at a time to Amma, hurried people along. It was an assembly line of touch. The men seemed to be timing each embrace. After a few seconds, one walked over to Amma and bent down, put his hands over the shoulders of the devotee she held, and ripped the person out of Amma's arms. One person was pried out of a hug and another was promptly pushed into one. Push. Pull.

Push. Pull. Worshippers emerged from Amma's embrace shell-shocked, shipwrecked.

Brian and I went downstairs and waited our turn. We stood in line and were cattled forward. Brian was at the front of the line and turned around to face me; he grabbed for my hand and held on to it, squeezed. He was pushed forward into his hug, went down on his knees, and accepted it fully, buried his face in Amma's breast. Amma patted his back. Brian was up as quickly as he'd gone down. I was next, pulled forward and pushed down onto my knees, directed with force into Amma's embrace. She spoke quietly and in Hindi, ran her hands over my bare arms. She held me the same as she did all of the others, until she didn't.

She stopped her hug and put her hands on my chest, thrusting me away from her as if she'd made a mistake. The move was cold and deliberate, certain. She looked at me and shook her head, motioned to one of the men standing beside her to come over to us. He seemed to understand what this all meant; he pulled me up by one arm and forced me down onto the floor, beside Amma.

"Don't get up," he said. "She wants you to watch." He put his hands on my chin and turned my gaze to face the line of people waiting for Amma.

For twenty minutes I watched. I studied the scene as people made their way to Amma. I viewed their faces. I looked on as people wept on her shoulder, snotted on her dress sleeve, begged her not to let them go, to hold them for a second longer. The room was full of need, and I shared it. Person after person approached the saint with looks of relief, only to be forced away in even greater need: the necessity for another hit of solace, another hug, and another chance. We were all starving; there was no end to our urgent hunger.

"You're done now," one of the cronies said, helping me to my feet, brushing the hair out of my eyes. I was weeping, too. "This is for you." He placed an apple, shiny and red, into one of my hands, a Hershey's kiss wrapped in silver foil into the other. "Amma wants you to consider *how* to eat the apple," he said, directing me back to the busy convention floor. I took a bite, and then another; I ate the apple and all its seeds.

Chapter 28

PSYCHIC: Before we get started: Some of my clients are very focused on connecting with people that are passed. Some of my clients are not interested in that; they are more interested in a psychic reading about whatever is happening in their lives. But I like to know if you have a strong focus in one direction or the other, so I know how to focus for you.

ME: My focus is on making a connection with a lost person in my life.

PSYCHIC: The way I like to start is I like to begin by tuning in to try to see who I'm picking up. Keep in mind, like it says on my website, the person that you want to communicate with might not be the first person that comes through. . . . There is usually a group of people, so it's really important to just be open to whoever comes through, because we don't have any control over that. If someone wants to say hi, they will.

ME: Okay.

PSYCHIC: One of the reasons I give you the recording is because it's also really, really common that at the time of the reading I may bring through people, or I'll talk about events—things that you just, you just can't identify what I'm talking about at the time of the reading. . . . Please do not dismiss it as wrong—I've been doing this a long time for a lot of people. . . .

ME: Okay.

PSYCHIC: Spirits will often bring through things that you don't know at the time of the reading on purpose, to prove to you that I'm not some sort of mentalist or mind reader, and that it's really them talking to you.

ME: Okay, great.

PSYCHIC: [Clears her throat.] Okay, so the way I'd like to start is I'd like you to close your eyes for just a moment and I want you to take a nice deep breath. I want you to pick one person who is passed over to the spirit side. I want you to focus on connecting with that person, get a good picture of them in your mind, as you remember them last—when they were really happy and healthy and well. . . . While you're focusing, I want to take a few seconds and be quiet and focus in on the energies that I'm picking up around you. [Psychic pauses. Waits several seconds.] Immediately I'm picking up the energies of three females. The first thing I want to ask you, is your mother passed over?

ME: No.

PSYCHIC: I've got a mom with three sisters. Do you have a grandmother that has passed who had two sisters that would be passed, too? Like, two great-aunts to you?

ME: Yes.

PSYCHIC: I feel like she's connected to your mother's side of the family. Is she?

ME: Yes.

PSYCHIC: I see her very much connected to your mom—I wasn't sure if it was your mom, or your mom's mom. But, I definitely have her here. I have her coming strongly through with two sisters. I see one standing on either side of her—if that makes sense to you?

ME: It does.

PSYCHIC: She's acknowledging a little small dog. I don't know if this is her dog, your dog, your mother's dog—but she's showing me a little small dog that to me looks either like a Yorkie or a terrier, or a kind of Benji-like dog. Do you know who that dog is?

ME: Yes, I do.

PSYCHIC: Is that your dog growing up? Or, is it your mom's?

ME: My mother's.

PSYCHIC: The woman I have here wants me to acknowledge that she has the dog with her. It's one of those little details that only you and she would know.

ME: Well—I never met her. She died before I was born and the dog died long before she did. But, I think the dog was my mother's childhood dog.

PSYCHIC: She's also showing me a Persian cat, a very fluffy-looking Persian-type cat. I think it's either white or very light in color.

ME: [Laughing.] Yes, yes.

PSYCHIC: Whose cat is that, Mom's?

ME: Yes.

PSYCHIC: Is the cat passed over or still with Mom?

ME: The cat is still with Mom.

PSYCHIC: Okay, she's acknowledging the cat that Mom still has. It's really, really fluffy. [Pauses.] Do you have a fiancé that has passed? Or a boyfriend?

ME: I don't think he's passed, no. But I did have a boyfriend who was a drug addict. I don't know if he's alive or not.

PSYCHIC: That's interesting. She's showing me this image of a young male that to me feels like a boyfriend. Do you have a brother that passed?

ME: No.

PSYCHIC: So, it's not a brother. Hold on, let me see. [She pauses, sighs.] Yeah, she's showing me this man. She's telling me that he's still alive but her words are, "At the rate he's going, his days are numbered quickly."

ME: Oh, good.

PSYCHIC: I don't know how much longer he's going to live. Was he a heavy user, specifically of hard drugs? I see him crushing up prescription pills and injecting them—pills like OxyContin or heroin.

ME: Yes, that's right.

PSYCHIC: There is also a young female here.

ME: Okay. [Voice lifts and breaks.]

PSYCHIC: Is this your sister that has passed?

ME: Yes, yes. [Crying.]

PSYCHIC: First of all, I'm really sorry because I know this is really hard and very emotional for you. [Psychic pauses.] Did your sister die by suicide?

ME: [Sniffling.] It's unclear.

PSYCHIC: Okay, so we are going to talk about that. She is talking about having a history of eating disorders. Are you aware of that, that she had that? Wait. Is she talking about herself or is she talking about you? I see somebody battling with anorexia?

ME: That's me.

PSYCHIC: It's you?

ME: Yes.

PSYCHIC: Are you still having that problem or is that something from the past that she's talking about?

ME: It's in the past but it comes up.

PSYCHIC: Yeah, all right. I understand. That is the kind of thing that will never really be gone.

ME: [Breathing heavily into the receiver, weeping.]

PSYCHIC: Okay, take a deep breath. I know this is hard. Your sister, she's just as emotional as you are. She's very upset. Is this pretty recent? Did this just happen six or eight months ago?

ME: No. It was four years ago.

PSYCHIC: Okay, what's been going on recently, like in the last six or eight months to a year? Are you going through a divorce or something?

ME: Yes, I'm divorced.

PSYCHIC: Did that just happen in the last year?

ME: It happened a year and a half ago, legally.

PSYCHIC: She's talking about there being a lot of intensity in your life. She's telling me that it's pushing you into a place of being overwhelmed. Does this make sense to you? She's keeping a close eye on you. I want you to know that she's always around you. She's watching out for you. She's telling me that maybe not at the very end of her life—but for most of her life—the two of you were really very close, very bonded. Is she your older sister?

ME: No.

PSYCHIC: Okay, you're older. Are you about three to four years apart?

ME: No.

PSYCHIC: Oh my gosh! You're twins. No wonder you're so incredibly bonded. [Psychic pauses.] I'm not sure what this is about. Did either you or your sister use a bronchial inhaler?

ME: Yes! Yes!

PSYCHIC: Who uses that?

ME: I do.

PSYCHIC: Okay, so were you prescribed that for asthma?

ME: [Answers nearly inaudibly.] Yes.

PSYCHIC: She says you're really having panic attacks. Do you recognize you are having panic attacks?

ME: Now I do, yes.

PSYCHIC: Sometimes you get so you can't breathe, right?

ME: Yes.

PSYCHIC: Have you tried to go to any kind of counseling?

ME: Oh God, yes.

PSYCHIC: Is that helping at all with the panic?

ME: Ugh, yes.

PSYCHIC: Okay, good.

ME: You can tell her—you can tell my sister that I'm doing much better.

PSYCHIC: She's talking about how when you feel like you're out of control, have the feeling of an overwhelming lack of control, or when you're fearful that things will happen outside of your control—she's saying, that's when you can't breathe. When your sister passed did they find a bunch of pills, prescription pills?

ME: I don't know, probably. I just don't know.

PSYCHIC: Did they find her in bed?

ME: No.

PSYCHIC: I don't know if she's talking about her or you. She's showing me a bedroom. Next to the bed there is a little night table. She's pulling out the drawer and she's showing me all of these bottles of prescription pills. I'm seeing a lot of pills. Is that you or is that her?

ME: It's the night table that I have right now.

PSYCHIC: And that's you with the pills in the night table?

ME: [Softly.] Yeah.

PSYCHIC: Are they for a bunch of different things? She's telling me that there are some for antianxiety; some of them are for sleeping—sleeping aids. I don't think you're taking any narcotic painkillers, are you?

ME: No.

PSYCHIC: Your sister is saying, "No, there's none of that."

ME: Okay.

PSYCHIC: Your sister wants me to give you a word of caution. She's saying, "Be careful with those pills because you're walking a very fine line." There is a thin line between having them help you and making everything worse. Don't take more than you are prescribed to take, okay?

ME: Yeah.

PSYCHIC: She says, "It's a delicate balance." You know? "Pills can calm you but they can send you in the opposite direction from calm, too, if you rely on them." Be careful.

ME: Yeah, right. I know.

PSYCHIC: She's telling me that you are a very sensitive person anyway. She's telling me emotionally you're very sensitive.

ME: Right.

PSYCHIC: Even if your sister didn't pass, even if your life was wonderful and perfect—you're a very emotionally sensitive person.

ME: Right, right.

PSYCHIC: So, for people like you—and I'm one of those people, it's a little harder to maintain balance in your life. It's easy for people like us to get thrown off balance, especially when bad things happen in our lives to the people we love. So, she's saying that she feels like it would be a good idea for you to go into behavioral counseling. . . . If you need somebody there is a wonderful man I work with—he wrote the foreword to my book. He works with people who have lost people to sudden death. He's been doing that work for over twenty years.

ME: [Annoyed.] Okay.

PSYCHIC: If you feel like you need someone, I can give you his number. He can work with you by phone. [Psychic pauses.] Do you have a little boy at home?

ME: No.

PSYCHIC: Do you have a son at all?

ME: No.

PSYCHIC: Did your sister leave a son?

ME: No.

PSYCHIC: Why do I see one single boy? Is there a single boy in the family—like, does someone have a son? He is appearing to me at about—

ME: I had an abortion when I was younger.

PSYCHIC: He's appearing to me at about ten or twelve years old. So that means to me that there is either someone in your life that age or passed at that age. It could also be a termination of pregnancy that was that many years ago.

ME: It was exactly twelve years ago.

PSYCHIC: Okay, well your sister is showing me that she is there with him, your son. And whether a baby's life ends, or a pregnancy ends naturally through miscarriage, or termination of pregnancy occurs, the soul is immortal. The soul lives on and the spirit lives on. You can't destroy a spirit. Your sister is acknowledging him there, and she's showing me that he's okay.

ME: Thank you.

PSYCHIC: This is kind of specific. Did your sister either fall from something or jump from something?

ME: No.

PSYCHIC: Do you know somebody who ended his or her life by either falling off of something or jumping off of something?

ME: Yes. I knew someone, but not very well.

PSYCHIC: Is that person like a cousin to you?

ME: No. It was one of my best friend's boyfriends.

PSYCHIC: I have that person here. I have that young man here, also. Is there a question of whether he fell or jumped?

ME: I don't know. I didn't know him well enough to say.

PSYCHIC: This young man wants to let his partner know that he's okay.

ME: Okay, I'll let him know.

PSYCHIC: Did that happen in New York City, the suicide?

ME: Yes.

PSYCHIC: Was it the Brooklyn Bridge or one of those bridges that goes over to New York?

ME: It was the Queensboro Bridge.

PSYCHIC: Yeah, I'm seeing that. This man just needs to get the message through to his partner that he's okay, that he's sorry. If your friend ever wants to talk to his boyfriend, he can always call me. Will you let him know?

ME: Fine.

PSYCHIC: Your friend's boyfriend says to tell you, "I'm sorry. I didn't mean to interrupt your reading." He just really needed to get that through.

ME: [Laughing.] Okay.

PSYCHIC: Let me come back to your sister. You have some questions about the cause of her death?

ME: Sort of, I do.

PSYCHIC: She's saying that the police and the medical examiners deemed it an accident but that you're not so sure and that you think there is some kind of foul play.

ME: I think that it was an accident. She got bad drugs from my ex-boyfriend. That's what I think happened.

PSYCHIC: Is this the same ex-boyfriend that we were talking about earlier?

ME: Yes it is.

PSYCHIC: So that's why they were bringing up the ex-boyfriend then. Was she injecting drugs with a needle?

ME: Yes.

PSYCHIC: Because, I'm seeing a speedball. She is talking about a speedball. I'm seeing her with a needle. Is that what it was? A mix of cocaine and heroin?

ME: It was a mix of heroin and fentanyl.

PSYCHIC: She's saying, "Yes and yes." To me that means: yes, it was an accident. It definitely wasn't a suicide. But yes, she got bad drugs.

ME: That's right.

PSYCHIC: "Too strong," she says, "too potent." It's not so much that the drugs were contaminated with something, but they were too much for her, for anyone. The drugs were lethal in the mixture she got.

ME: Right.

PSYCHIC: It stopped her heart.

ME: [Softly.] Yes, that's right.

PSYCHIC: "It was a stupid, stupid mistake," she says. "But, it's not his fault. It was mine. I insisted, I insisted," she says. "He warned me not to take too much. His exact words were, 'This stuff should come with a warning label.' He told me how potent it was, but I didn't listen." Her intention wasn't to end her life. Her intention was to get high. I see that now. [Pauses.] Is your ex-boyfriend's name either Max or Mack?

ME: His name is Sean.

PSYCHIC: Did she know a Max?

ME: That is the name of a cat we had. The cat died a couple of days before my sister died. My sister watched the cat die. The cat was twenty years old and had a stroke on the kitchen floor, at my sister's feet.

PSYCHIC: Oh! Then she has the cat. Is it Max or Mack?

ME: Maxine.

PSYCHIC: Maxine? But you called her Max?

ME: I didn't, but my mom did. She called her Max Cat.

PSYCHIC: His days are numbered, I'm telling you. This guy,

your ex, is—he's an addict. I mean he's like a shooting-up addict, this guy. She's showing me that he's run out of good veins and he's shooting up between his toes. He's pretty bad.

ME: I don't know. I don't have anything to do with him. I haven't for many, many years.

PSYCHIC: You sister says, "Forgiveness, forgiveness, forgiveness. Please forgive." She says, "Christa, you hold a lot of anger and a lot of bitterness in your heart. Not for me, for him." I think that you blame him and I can certainly understand why. Your sister wants to say, "I take full responsibility for my death. I'm the one that's accountable."

ME: Right.

PSYCHIC: "I knew what I was doing. It was like playing Russian roulette. You think, this will never happen to me. On some level I thought I didn't care if it did happen to me, because I wanted it so bad. I wanted relief." She's telling me that at the end you and she had started not to get along—I wouldn't say you were estranged, she's not saying that. She's saying that you were getting on her about the drug use and she did not want to hear it.

ME: [Crying.] Yes.

PSYCHIC: That's what she's saying.

ME: Yes.

PSYCHIC: "It's important"—these are your sister's exact words—"that you recognize that you did everything you could for me and I know that now. I know that. I know everything you did was because you loved me. You told on me," she says. You told your parents what was going on with her?

ME: Yes. I told my mom.

PSYCHIC: She was really mad at you. How could you do that, she said then, but not now. She totally understands now. She says, "I'm so grateful that you loved me enough to risk our friendship. I know how much you tried to help me. Christa, there was nothing more you could really do. You did everything you could." She says your family had been talking about having an intervention right before this happened.

ME: Yes, that's right.

PSYCHIC: One thing that I'm definitely picking up around the time that she's tuning me into—your sister would have had none of it. Your sister was not in a place where she wanted to get help or wanted to get clean—

ME: That's sort of true and sort of not true. She'd gone to get methadone on the morning she died.

PSYCHIC: So she went to get methadone, but she was still taking drugs.

ME: Yes.

PSYCHIC: Yeah. [Drawing out her words, sighing.] She wasn't really ready. Well, you know—a lot of drug addicts use methadone. I mean, they go to the clinic and they get it, and then they turn it around and sell it on the streets—

ME: My sister would never do something like that. She was a good girl. She probably just wanted to get drugs she could use more consistently, or legally.

PSYCHIC: Exactly. That's what that is. It's not a cure for addiction; it's a controlled substance. But, tuning in with your sister during that time in her life—no matter what she was saying to anyone around her, she was not in that place where an addict says they've had enough and want to get well. She just wasn't.

The reason I bring that up is, no matter what you would have done—if you and your parents had forced her into a clinic, she probably would have kept on using.

ME: Right.

PSYCHIC: They have to get to a place in their own minds where they really want it for themselves.

ME: I know.

PSYCHIC: I have addiction in my own family. I've seen it. It's an awful feeling, because you're watching someone basically kill herself. [Voice breaks.] You can't do anything. You can't get through to them. I just feel like you did everything you could have done—even if you took more drastic measures, she just wasn't there yet. You couldn't have changed the outcome.

ME: Will I be alone for the rest of my life now?

PSYCHIC: As far as the divorce, you mean? As far as having another relationship come in?

ME: Yes.

PSYCHIC: She says, "She's very depressed, my sister." Are you very depressed? Do you feel very depressed lately? Your sister is telling me you're like, clinical depression. Have you talked to anyone about it?

ME: Of course I have. I lost my identical twin, for God's sake. Anyone would be depressed. It's fucking depressing.

PSYCHIC: Yeah, yeah.

ME: I'm getting better.

PSYCHIC: Yeah?

ME: I'm sorry. This is just emotional.

PSYCHIC: I know it is. Your sister is telling me you're having a real struggle with depression. [Psychic pauses.] I think you might really want to consider calling my colleague.

ME: Right. [Irritated.]

PSYCHIC: I know he'll talk to you initially at no charge. He'll talk to you about what he does and the two of you can go from there. I'm only telling you this because I've worked with him for five years and he's worked in grief recovery for twenty years. He's fantastic. . . . It is possible to get better.

ME: Right, right. I know that and I'm getting there.

PSYCHIC: Yeah. [In disbelief.] You know if you need help, you should definitely get help. Sometimes we need an objective person to put things into perspective for us. What she's saying to me is that it's still really raw for you, the loss of her. Even though your sister has been gone for four years, your grief to me feels very raw.

ME: Right.

PSYCHIC: I can tell you that there is no formula. . . . You are still very raw and I think you need time to heal. I think that that is going to affect relationships coming into your life, in the short term. . . . Let me just see what your sister says about romance. [Pauses.] Are you in your late thirties now?

ME: I'm in my early thirties.

PSYCHIC: You're in your early thirties, okay. Were you recently dating someone that you met through work?

ME: Yes. We met at an artist's colony five years ago.

PSYCHIC: She's showing me that that was never really going anywhere, right?

ME: No—well, I don't know.

PSYCHIC: You've been on and off for five years?

ME: Yes.

PSYCHIC: Is he still married? Was he married when you met him?

ME: No.

PSYCHIC: You were married though?

ME: Yes, I was married.

PSYCHIC: He was not?

ME: No. I had an affair with him.

PSYCHIC: Was he living with somebody? I see him living with somebody.

ME: He had just ended a relationship when we met.

PSYCHIC: I'm seeing some overlap, though. I'm getting the feeling that he's not been honest about that. He wasn't clear with her or with you. This is the kind of guy who does that. Am I right?

ME: Maybe.

PSYCHIC: He's moved on from her and you've moved on from your marriage?

ME: Yes.

PSYCHIC: But you guys are still in the same place that you've always been. You haven't really advanced much farther in the relationship zone, right?

ME: Yeah. Yes.

PSYCHIC: The sense that I get from you guys is that—well, your sister says you definitely love each other. There is real love there. But, I'm almost getting the sense of like a sibling or really good friend energy. You have a really good friendship and a very close connection. You can confide in one another, even about other people. Like you guys date other people and talk about it.

ME: Right.

PSYCHIC: It's kind of a complicated relationship, isn't it?

ME: Yes.

PSYCHIC: It's very complicated. There are a lot of facets to it. I'm going to tell you, you have a really strong connection to this guy—I think you've been together before in previous lives. I almost get a feeling, a really strong sibling kind of energy with the two of you. I really kind of wonder whether in past lifetimes you haven't been siblings.

ME: Right.

PSYCHIC: I think there is some physical chemistry there, but I don't think it's that strong. I think the strongest connection you have is very good caring friends. Would you say that's true?

ME: No. We have a very strong sexual chemistry. It's hard to leave because of that. It's complicated because he's twenty years older than I am.

PSYCHIC: It's definitely complicated. There is a lot of mixed-up energy there, and—you know, there is something there that is really positive. You are really there for one another when you need one another. I think that you have a certain trust together and you can count on one another.

ME: Yes.

PSYCHIC: There are some limitations on that, though. It seems you go to a certain point and that's it.

ME: Yeah.

PSYCHIC: This seems to be his doing. You want more and he won't give it. Like, he doesn't want things to go much beyond where they are.

ME: Yes, he's afraid of that.

PSYCHIC: Uh-huh. Well, there's something about his connection with you that makes him think that this is not marriage material, like a rest of his life kind of relationship.

ME: Okay.

PSYCHIC: I don't know that I would spend your life waiting for him. But I don't think that you are. It's interesting. I feel like he could be in your life for a long time. I feel like it could be one of those scenarios that ten years from now, even if you've not talked to him in five years, you might pick up the phone or he might pick up the phone and just call you. There's something interesting and connected about the two of you. I don't see it ending in marriage, though. I see you being in each other's lives for a long time, as friends.

ME: Oh.

PSYCHIC: Your sister is telling me there are some other choices for you on the horizon. There are some other men. I'll tell you that this older man has been in your life for a very important reason. The one thing that he does for you—there's something about him that provides a feeling for you of security. He somehow, even in his ambivalence, gives you a feeling of security and some stability.

ME: Yes.

PSYCHIC: He makes you feel safe. Gosh, he's even got a little bit of a fatherly energy. I have to say, he's the kind of person who is meant to be in the background of your life to help keep you on track. He's there for you and provides for you a kind of emotional support that you have really needed throughout this time in your life, through your divorce and the loss of your sister. Do you know what I mean?

ME: Yes. That's exactly the truth.

PSYCHIC: He's not a bad guy. He's just not the one for you. Your sister is telling me that it is very likely you will marry again.

ME: Okay.

PSYCHIC: There is definitely going to be the opportunity for marriage. If you didn't marry it would only be because it would be your choice not to. Somebody is going to put that out to you. . . . And, I think you will say yes.

ME: Okay.

PSYCHIC: I've got to say that there is something very important that you need to accomplish first, before you love. I think this phone call might be part of that. You need to finish up the healing process before you really move forward with a relationship. Does that make sense to you?

ME: Yes.

PSYCHIC: You need to get some closure and peace. You need to close the book on your grief.

ME: Could you ask my sister if she knows anything about a book?

PSYCHIC: Yeah. Is this a book you put together yourself, a handmade book, something that you put together, your creation?

ME: [Silent.]

PSYCHIC: Like a scrapbook or a book of photographs?

ME: I made photographs of my sister, yes.

PSYCHIC: Is it a book you did for her? A memorial book?

ME: No. I'm writing a book about her. Her book is in my book.

PSYCHIC: Okay. She's talking about it like it's your creation. The book is your creation and it's somehow a memorial of her. So, yes, she knows about it.

ME: Mmm hmm.

PSYCHIC: Mmm hmm. She's been helping you with it a little bit. As you've been writing it, I don't know if you can tell this— but she's almost been writing through you.

ME: Yes, that's correct.

PSYCHIC: Yep. I'll tell you—I don't know, did you read my book?

ME: No.

PSYCHIC: Well, my book is a lot like your book. There are spirits that I talk about in the book that literally wrote right through me. I mean, I was pretty aware that I was not writing it. As I was writing it certain sections were just coming to me and I didn't know where they were coming from. Does that make sense?

ME: Yes.

PSYCHIC: I'm definitely getting the sense that your sister is doing that in your book. I mean, she's telling me that you can literally hear her talking, hear her words.

ME: That's correct.

PSYCHIC: Well, that's really her. Just like she's speaking to me and through me to you, she is doing the same thing with you. It's called clairaudience.

ME: Right.

PSYCHIC: You're kind of, in a way, doing a type of automatic writing.

ME: Right, right.

PSYCHIC: She keeps showing me—and I don't know if you've figured out the front cover of the book or not, but, I keep seeing a collage of photos. Like you'd lay down a bunch of photographs and photograph those and put them on the front cover of your book. It has a very scrapbooky look to me.

ME: I don't like that idea at all.

PSYCHIC: She says, "It's a tale of two hearts."

ME: Really?

PSYCHIC: A tale of two hearts, yes. Have you thought of the title?

ME: No.

PSYCHIC: Yeah! She kind of shows me that as a title.

ME: I'd actually picked something else out I like better.

PSYCHIC: Better than a *Tale of Two Hearts*?

ME: I call it *Her*.

PSYCHIC: I think you're planning on publishing this, aren't you?

ME: Yes. I hope so.

PSYCHIC: Your sister definitely knows about the book. She's helping you with the book. Did you have some other things you'd like to ask her?

ME: I don't have anything else to ask her.

PSYCHIC: She misses you very much and she loves you. "It's not as hard for me as it is for you," she says. For her she can really be around you and visit you. The dead can see us. They don't feel very far away from us themselves—they don't perceive it that way. . . . I can tell you that she is definitely around you and she's definitely helping you with the book.

ME: Does she think that the book will be okay?

PSYCHIC: "It's a bestseller. I think it's a bestseller."

ME: Yes!

PSYCHIC: Your book is going to do really well. "There are a lot of different publishing options," she says. Do some homework and shop around. If you need any help with that, you know, I can help you with that. I have a great publisher.

ME: I guess those are all of the questions that I have. Does she have anything else she'd like to say to me?

PSYCHIC: She says, "I know it's kind of a cliché, but mostly, I just want to tell her, I'm sorry, how very sorry I am. For the poor choices that led to my untimely and premature death, I'm sorry. The funny thing about being here on this side is you are painfully aware of how much your actions and your choices affect the people around you. I am painfully aware of how much I hurt the people in my life, the people that loved me. From where I am it's the hardest pill to swallow, no pun intended. It's the hardest thing I have to live with every day, how much pain and suffering I've caused my family. Nothing can ever change that. In a way, it's my cross to bear in this life, the spirit life. My only salvation for that is not forgiveness from God, but forgiveness from the people I've harmed."

ME: I'll give her that. I forgive her.

PSYCHIC: You might want to read my book. I actually talk about that, what she's talking about. I really explain that and how the spirit side works.

ME: Yeah, right.

PSYCHIC: She says, "For the most part I'm just sorry for the pain and suffering I've caused, especially with my mom." There isn't a day that goes by that your mother doesn't think of her, you know?

ME: Of course not.

PSYCHIC: "It's hard for me to live with," she says. "I lived a very selfish life. I was self-absorbed." She says, "You know, all drug addicts are narcissists. There's no beating around the bush about it. I'm not saying I didn't have my share of problems. But it still wasn't an excuse for the way I behaved." She says, "I'm not as much sorry for the damage I did to my own life, I'm okay where I am now." She has a lot of regret for the collateral damage that she caused. She says, "You know, I spend most of my time here trying to figure out ways to clean up the mess I made." She's trying to get through, get through to you and your family. She's working behind the scenes, doing what she can. . . . She says to tell you that she loves you. The most important thing for her is for you to live your life to the fullest and to be the happiest you can be. For her to know or feel like you can't be happy in your life without her, or because of her—that's the worst thing she can imagine. "I have to live with that fear," she says.

ME: I know. I'd just feel better if I could find a real partner and have a family.

PSYCHIC: You will. He's coming or he may already be on the scene, but you will have someone. The thing is, you have to let the pain of losing your sister go. One thing I know, because she's telling me, is that the only way for her to be relieved of her burden of guilt for dying is to have you release her from it by moving on.

ME: I'll try.

PSYCHIC: About the book—she believes it's very cathartic. Do you know what *cathartic* means?

ME: Yes, but I don't think that's the right word for memoir writing. Vacationing in Hawaii is cathartic. Writing a memoir is like getting clanged on the head with a frying pan.

PSYCHIC: You should read my book. Not because you should buy my book, but because I think you'll connect with some of the experiences I went through and talk about in the book, with writing the book. I went through a whole process also. . . .

Some things I couldn't understand until I put them down on paper. I feel that happening with your book and with your sister.

ME: I'll keep that in mind.

Chapter 29

I dispersed Cara's ashes in Hawaii, Thailand, Germany, and Hollywood. I'd scattered her worldwide even before D and I traveled to Venice. My sister has no grave marker, no memorial plaque, no stone with her name carved above a date. It was my choice that she have no resting place.

Our family plot is in Schenectady, New York. Acres and acres of rolling hills that once abutted the forest are now directly beside a suburban shopping mall. To visit a relative there means also to be in full view of Macy's and Sears and shoppers rolling their filled carts to waiting SUVs. I refused to abandon Cara in a dismal scrubby plot, in full view of mall employees and bargain hunters.

There was simply no place to leave her, so I took her everywhere.

I divided up her ashes and kept them in multiple bottles, urns, boxes, and satchels. I carried her for three years in my pocketbook. I have one container of ashes saved in a storage unit at the funeral home. I can visit a drawer full of Cara there.

I found three glass bottles in a gift shop: two purple and one clear. These little vases stand three inches high and are wide enough that I can hold each in my palm. Their handles serve as arms. They slide into grooves that I have attached to a black iron hanging rack. I poured some of Cara's ashes into each bottle and corked them with purple wax from one of her candles. The iron rack was meant for votives, but I hung my sister there instead, securing her with wire.

I took her to California only a week after she'd passed. I was traveling for a photography assignment, photographing a heavy metal band from the '80s. I rode with them on a tour bus through the West and watched them ready themselves for shows: four men who used curling irons, hairspray, and eyeliner and wore leather pants that laced up the sides of their legs. They called themselves Poison and after twenty years on the road they looked as if that's what they'd swallowed. I hoped to spare them this judgment with my camera. That observation was crueler than they deserved. They were good family men and kind and all took great care with me in my grief sickness. Cara and I had loved them as girls and had worn their concert T-shirts and memorized the lyrics to all their songs. I stood at the side of the stage and watched them night after night as perplexed onlookers wondered how party anthems could bring on such tears.

At the end of my time with them, the drummer took me for a ride on his motorcycle in the desert. We drove through yellow sand and I held on to his waist with one arm and tossed my sister in the wind with the other.

I brought her next to an artist's retreat in New Hampshire. I tossed some of her ashes into a ravine from the open window of a writing studio.

When I traveled to the White Mountains with Cara's friend Danielle, we set her loose in a cold, black trout stream behind Danielle's in-laws' house, down a hill, past stalks of blue wildflowers and a ditch of tiny stones. Danielle cried for Cara with quiet tears. We sat beside the quick-moving water and each let go of a single handful of ashes. We fed her to the fish. Cara and

Danielle had not spoken for years, their friendship a casualty of Cara's drugs. The two women had loved each other since high school. Cara would have been pleased with their final parting. In the end, her best friend had been able to hold her, to say she was sorry.

I mixed her ashes into eye shadow and dusted my lids. I dipped a wet finger down into a baggie of ash and tasted her bones. I dropped an urn of Cara, spilling her, and vacuumed her up. I thought of stirring her into my coffee or making bread from her bones. I kept her in my glove box and beneath my bed. I showed her off to strangers. I stared at her ashes for hours and marveled at the way they sparkled and at how light and free she had become.

Lastly, I brought her ashes to Venice, as she had asked me to do.

It was D's first time in Venice. He followed behind me with our luggage as I found our way from the train to the hotel. It was the first time that D and I had been out together in a Mediterranean city, and here, I was the one of proper height. D's head poked over the crowd, higher and balder and whiter than the rest; I was at one with the sea of people, just another dark-haired traveler.

We checked into a small room in the center of the city, unpacked, fought, and then made up. We did it all in what seemed one long breath. We were practiced.

In the heart of Venice, there is no direction or time; there is dark and light; there is sun that disappears into shadow behind shabby stone buildings; there are curving, confusing, seemingly endless, glinting gray water streets. And for me, as perhaps for others, Venice had become a city of memories. It was exactly as I'd remembered from my trip with Cara: Venice was alive as if time hadn't touched it. As I walked hand in hand through the winding alleys with D, looking for the perfect place for Cara's final sleep, I could hear her laugh, see her sampling strawberry gelato on a tiny plastic spoon, watch her begging a gondolier for a free serenade, or reaching her arms out wide, hoping to land pigeons. I remembered how she'd thieved.

With every turn of a passageway I was lost for a spot to leave her. One place was too closed in, another was too public, a third was frothy with gasoline. I'd crossed the world; still, there was no perfect tomb. D and I wandered the maze of the city only to come full circle, arriving back at our hotel. I needed a guide. Then I saw him, a well-dressed man in tweed, holding a pocket watch: the innkeeper from the trip I'd taken with Cara. He walked down a stone staircase and over a slim bridge. I pulled D's hand and we followed the man, our white rabbit. I told D who he was and why I needed to track him. D said I must be mistaken. It was unbelievable, impossible, and it was, but it was also true; it *was* him. We followed him all the way to the front door of the hostel where Cara and I had stayed.

In front of that hostel was our plaza, and from the plaza were steps that led down to the water. Cara and I had picnicked there. We'd taken a meal of bread and cheese and had finished a bottle of red wine. Glittering light reflected from the water onto Cara's face as she chewed. I'd teased that she looked like a ghoul or a goddess; I wasn't certain which. Those steps were nearly a square, enclosed by homes with immaculately tended gardens and with window boxes full of fragrant flowers. Excepting one narrow pathway that led out into the Grand Canal, here was a private ocean.

On the way to the watery steps, I stopped at a flower shop. I pulled a long-stemmed iris from a bucket of water and paid the shopkeeper. D and I found the square and I knelt on the steps. I pulled Cara from my purse. I emptied her from a stoppered glass bottle into a wave, the wake of a boat. Her ashes floated iridescent on the surface of the canal. I set sail with them the iris, just like the one tattooed on her forearm, and I cried for both of us.

I was finished.

I dipped the empty bottle into the water and took a sample. The silt that was left of my sister floated up and whirled in the bottle and then fell to the bottom; it was alive. Cara had become a snow globe, in a bottle that had once been hers. She'd had a collection of such bottles from around the world. She'd dipped them in all of the oceans she'd visited. She'd filled them with sand and water and kept them on her writing desk.

D asked if we might find the Tiepolos at the San Marco church. He looked down at my dusty, tear-streaked, ashen hands and helped me to a café where he bought us each an espresso while I washed. I closed the door on the café and turned the spigot on the faucet. I watched what was left of my sister on me circle the drain.

D and I stood in silence for over an hour in the church, craning our heads back to look at Tiepolo's ceiling fresco. I was taken with his cherubs: valiant, insistent, dazed, plummeting through the clouds. They looked at war with the sky, shot down by God's grace and wrath. A pair tumbled hand in hand.

Chapter 30

There wasn't anything special about the listing in the insurance pamphlet. I had only one criterion for a shrink: I should see a woman. I settled on one whose name sounded like it belonged to a solid person, a woman of strong conviction.

I described the problem at hand on Katherine's answering machine: I was thirty-two years old. I'd suffered the loss of my identical twin sister four years earlier. I'd recently quit my job as a professor and moved from New England to Brooklyn. I was in a troubled relationship with an older man whom I loved dearly. I'd been hooked on Valium for so long that going without sent me into treacherous withdrawal. I'd found myself fighting the urge to jump in front of a speeding C train the week before, though I certainly wanted to live. That about covered it. I recited my list to Katherine's answering machine as matter-of-factly as I might tell D what I'd bought at the supermarket for him to prepare for dinner.

Katherine quickly returned my call. I was seated in the center of the plush sofa in her office on the Upper West Side of Manhattan the very next day.

She was short and tiny; frail, with narrow wrists and jutting collarbones. Her wavy brown hair hung, blunt cut, to her waist.

She wore tailored gray tweed slacks and a black cotton leotard with a scooped neck. Strings of beaded necklaces dangled over the collar of her flimsy cardigan. She smiled at me with sympathy and curiosity as I explained the mess of my life. Her perfect smudge of a nose hung over her lip when she smiled. Her gaze gave her a pointy and sunken look of her own. We matched. Her arms and legs were among the thinnest I'd ever seen.

She told me in our first meeting that she'd been a dancer. An injury had caused the early end of her promising career with the New York City Ballet; a strained ankle had been her truest blessing, she said. It caused her to reconsider her life path, and she'd gone back to school to study psychology.

"Sometimes tragedy alters the course of our lives and we are freed in our traumas to live according to our true passions and desires," she said in response to my long, guilty monologue on having abandoned photography. "We are free to write the new story of our lives, or so it seems."

Katherine's observation seemed so generic and well rehearsed, I was certain she used it with all of her clients. "I guess so," I said. Hadn't it been obvious I'd tried to think that? Couldn't she tell from my message how I'd wished that cliché were true? I'd given up my job, my camera, and my home. I'd taken plenty of risks of passion after losing Cara, as if throwing caution to the wind would somehow give her death another ending.

Among the constellation of motivational posters that hung on her wall was one quoting Robert Fulghum. How could I accept help from a woman with such stock advice and strange decorating proclivities? I'd never given my own mother the same consideration.

Mom had hung one of the *All I Really Need to Know I Learned from Kindergarten* posters in our dining room during the author's wild success when I was in high school. I'd passed it each morning on my way to the kitchen, rolling my eyes. He seemed so obvious, so uncool.

"Can't we just take this lousy thing down," I pleaded with my mother. "I don't want my friends to see it when they come over."

"I like it" was all Mom said in response to my arrogance. She swatted me off like a horse does a fly. Cara always left Mom alone in her tastes and that was dignified. I took them as a declaration of war.

Mom's Fulghum poster read: "I believe that imagination is stronger than knowledge. That myth is more potent than history. That dreams are more powerful than facts. That hope always triumphs over experience. That laughter is the only cure for grief. And I believe that love is stronger than death."

It had amazed me, even at sixteen, that my mother could address the summation of her problems, all of our storms, with a trite poster.

I recited the Fulghum poem in my head in Katherine's office and cried. It felt like being brought to tears over a dog food commercial, but there you are. "Love is stronger than death," I said to Katherine, seemingly out of nowhere, and I believed it then, for the first time since I'd read the silly line on Mom's wall, the sturdy walls we'd all slept and dreamed beneath as a family of women, free of fathers and husbands, the safest place I'd known in all my life. And now I was replicating my mother's ways. I lived alone and, though I was involved with a man, I was lonely. I had held on to my mother's advice for a very long time: "Men will fuck you but they'll never love you."

The truth was: I hadn't needed any of their love until Cara died.

"Love *is* stronger than death," Katherine repeated.

That was exactly the problem. Love is stronger than death. I was wrestling all my love against Cara's death, and I was losing: I was obliterating myself because in the face of her death I had nowhere to put my love.

I needed to believe Katherine. "I hope you're right," I said and laughed flimsily. I looked around her office and took note of a shelf of books on feminist psychology. I recognized some titles from an undergraduate seminar I'd taken freshman year with a brilliant professor. The posters and books canceled each other out. I focused on Katherine's windowsill. There was a line of small photographs turned facedown. I looked at the smooth felt backs on the frames and wondered why she'd flipped them over. There were exactly four of them.

I returned the following week. I started hesitantly at the beginning, with Mom and Dad. Katherine listened with great care as I tried to describe the violence in our home; Mom's blackened eyes, her smashed jaw.

"Do you think this has anything to do with your relationship narrative? Your choice of men?" Katherine asked.

"Probably," I said, resenting her question. This was D's consistent refrain. Again and again he asked me to consider whether or not I was using him as a stand-in for my father. But to me the story of my father had grown so old, it seemed as harmless and irrelevant as dust bunnies in an abandoned house.

"How do you think your mother feels about that?"

"My mom has very little sympathy for men."

"Was it always that way?" Katherine asked. "Has that happened since her divorces?"

"There was an overcorrection, I think." One evening when we were in high school, Mom sat at the kitchen table and waited for her date. Hours ticked by. His headlights never warmed the driveway. Mom quietly removed her earrings—silver hoops—and kicked off her uncomfortable shoes and retired for the night.

The next day the phone rang. It was her date.

"Were you abducted by aliens?" Mom asked him plainly, giving him no time to respond. "How about your children? Were they abducted by aliens?" Cara and I eavesdropped on our mother's conversation, mouths open wide in disbelief and pride. I gathered from the way Mom listened that the man must have told her that no, neither he nor his kin had suffered such a fate. Mom calmly cleared her throat. "I guess we have nothing to discuss then. Please forget my number." She hung up the phone and resumed folding a pile of warm laundry. No one said another word. I wondered why Mom couldn't give the poor guy a break. I vowed then and there to keep an open mind on men and a forgiving heart. I would be nothing like her. She was harsh and cutting, so Italian, so immovable. I would be more permissive; this had become my downfall.

I thought about how to explain to Katherine what had happened in my mother's life since Cara had gone. "There hasn't been anyone worth mentioning in her life, no love at all." Mom had broken up with Graham. She lived alone. She kept up the yard cheerfully herself and was busy with work and friends. She liked to go for cocktails and walks on weekends and Thursdays; other than that, she was home. I tried to visit her often and it was always the same scene. Mom watched *Law and Order* on what seemed to me to be the *Law and Order* channel. No matter the day of the week or the time of the day, the show played. Mom favored the more gruesome episodes, ones where young women were abducted, defiled, murdered, and then tossed in the trash. Was this Mom's way of trying to occupy Cara's terror? Repeating it again and again, as if by learning it play by play, she might take on some of the fear and humiliation Cara suffered and carry it herself?

Cara had been my torch in our dark house. I couldn't have survived it without her. And where was she now? It seemed impossible to be in a world without her. All of our stories and hurts were now mine alone. I'd grown so used to stories being shared that without Cara it was as if neither of our lives had ever happened. With her death, my history had been erased.

"There is so much I can't remember," I told Katherine.

It wasn't simple for me to begin therapy with our early days. There was too much ground to cover; there were too many boulders in the way of what was happening now and what I felt really needed talking about. I wanted to rush through the story of our girlhood. But Katherine slowed me down. As the weeks went on we seemed to be getting somewhere. She understood something about twinship that nobody else had.

"I get it," she told me. "I'm single and I'm in my forties. There's no love like family. I still live with my sister. It's easy to feel like we're just two old maids, but we have each other, and that makes a home."

I wondered what relevance her sibling had to the matter at hand, but I agreed. "My biggest fear, aside from her dying, was that Cara and I would be spinsters together, like Marge's chain-smoking twin sisters on the Simpsons." I laughed at my own joke. I imagined Cara and me side by side in some crappy apartment, old as goats—that once greatly feared fate now seemed such a luxury. I wasn't making any kind of home comfortable for myself because I'd never thought, even though I'd been married, that I'd have to have one without her.

"At least you wouldn't have to pretend to laugh at someone else's jokes," Katherine said. "I can't tell you how unfunny these guys in Westchester are."

I looked up at the clock and saw that our session had run over. Therapy was going better than I'd expected. I left her office with the great big hope that if I kept going on my path, I'd wander into the right life, somehow.

I was surprised to hear from Katherine after our eighth

session. She called to say that we needed to have a talk to "clear the air."

I considered her words on the subway ride to her office. Had I possibly pocket-dialed one of the monologues about her hokey observations that I'd recited over a joint with D? Making fun of therapy with Katherine was so easy, and I liked to make D laugh. My favorite poem of Maya Angelou's had been penciled onto the white wall of Katherine's waiting room, behind a fern, beside a rack of month-old magazines with the delivery addresses scratched out. The words were written in such small, winding script that they were nearly illegible. I often wondered who had put them there. I decided it must have been a teenage girl. Her As were round and her Ms sloped like dull mountains. Was this her prayer to herself? An attempt to memorize for an exam? An act of vandalism and boredom? A mantra?

I flapped my arms like a giant bird when I recited the poem for D, dancing through the cluttered living room. "I know why the caged bird sings," I sang low. D smiled up at me and flicked the ash of his roach into an open CD case. "The caged bird sings of freedom," I hummed, feeling the tickle of the words vibrate from my tongue until I landed on the floor. I was so stoned; it wasn't out of the question that I'd accidentally called Katherine from my back pocket.

Katherine greeted me in the waiting room and we walked together to her office. She sat down quietly at her desk and shuffled through pages of notes. When she finally swiveled to face me, my stomach jumped to my throat. "Would you like a cup of tea," she asked politely. She'd never offered me tea before.

"No thanks," I said.

"I hope you don't mind if I do," she said and ripped open a pack of raw sugar and stirred it into a steaming cup.

"Not at all," I said.

"I've been unsure how to tell you something that feels very important to our ongoing relationship," she said, nervously sipping her tea. The rim of the cup covered her nose and mouth. She looked over its white porcelain lip; two worried eyes of Horus stared me down.

"I hope this isn't about my co-payments?" I apologized. I hadn't paid her a single one, hoping that she'd overlook the hundreds of dollars I owed.

"No, that's not it at all," she said. "I've made adjustments in billing your insurance. There is no need to worry about the co-pays."

"Good," I said. "I'd hate to have to end our work here. I can't afford extras right now." I sounded exactly like my mother did when she explained why she couldn't join me out for dinner or a movie.

"I don't exactly know how to tell you this," Katherine said, "but I have an identical twin sister, too."

"Oh?" I tensed up and grabbed the handle of my brown leather purse and squeezed. Katherine gazed at me as if she were looking into a mirror while trying to rehearse a speech. "That's a coincidence, I guess," I replied, trying to stay casual even though my heart was racing.

"My sister is dying," Katherine told me shyly. She was looking at the yellow, lined writing tablet in her lap. "I feel I've been out of bounds in seeing you," she said. "I allowed my curiosity to cloud my judgment."

"That's okay," I said, though I was the farthest place from okay I'd been in a very long time. I felt weightless and invisible, a familiar feeling. Cara and I had called this our faraway place; we'd gone to it since the first time we saw Dad hit Mom, and often after that. The two-foot distance between Katherine and me grew to what seemed like yards and then miles. She was a tiny dot at the end of a sentence, a speck of dirt on my shoe.

"When you called I knew I needed to see you. I wanted to know what will happen to me when my twin dies," she said apologetically.

This was simply impossible, but it was happening. There wasn't a single person I knew who would believe this story. But I was already crafting a plan to tell it. I'd learned from Cara that relaying a story didn't make it sting less, but it did make it survivable.

I thanked Katherine for her hard work and opened up my pocketbook. I unsnapped my change purse and pulled out a double dose of Valium. I washed it down with the last sip of her warm tea. I closed the office door without saying a word.

Not long after I walked away from Katherine's office, I closed the door on D's apartment for the last time.

D had been preparing to cook a salmon. I'd had too much to drink, enough to muster the courage to ask for the millionth time why we hadn't managed to try to move in together again.

"Isn't salmon enough?" D asked, sipping a Manhattan and stirring a skillet of leeks simmering in a fragrant broth. He wiggled his nose and his wire-framed glasses slid easily down to the tip.

"Not really," I told him. "I want stability, a family, to change diapers. We don't seem to be moving in that direction."

"Who said I don't want that, too?" he said casually and turned the heat down on the vegetables.

"I said it." We'd been dating for nearly four years. "It's not just you. I haven't made the great leap either."

"Fuck, C," D yelled and flung a raw slab of succulent Alaskan salmon at my head. I ducked and it slid down the wall and flopped onto the floor. "Get out of my house. Now. You think you'll ever find a man who will cook you such delicious fish?" he roared ridiculously.

"You don't want me because I'm getting better," I said. The words *getting better* used in reference to myself seemed foreign but rang oddly true. I was getting better.

I walked down the hallway to the front door and sat on the floor before it, listening to D bang around in the kitchen. I promised myself that if I left, if I set one foot out into the hall and toward the stairs, I'd never come back.

"I've got to go," I said to the whirl of D's clanging pots and pans, the scrape of a fork pushing a ruined dinner into the trash. "I'm sorry." I closed the door quietly behind me. I ran as fast as I could down the stairs and onto the street. I hailed a cab home. I decided to take a trip to the Hudson Valley to visit Grace. I packed my bags.

This time would be different. I couldn't put my finger on it, but I wasn't the same.

In D's closet I left behind a wardrobe of dresses that were two sizes too small, several pairs of broken-down high-heeled pumps, a freezer full of film, and my prized Celeste green bicycle with licorice-red trimmed wheels and a straw basket attached to the front. It had been the nicest gift from Cara that I'd bought myself, a birthday tradition I'd started when I realized I would never be able to part with the indulgent treasures Cara gave every July. I saved up all year to buy myself something nice from my sister. I'd fled in such a hurry that my perfect bike was left at D's.

The next morning, I pulled a shirt over my head and laced my shoes and off I went to see my friend Grace in her rustic, converted barn in Rhinebeck. I have made that drive in little more than an hour and a half, but that day I made it in just under three, stopping off to pick apples from an orchard. My gift to Grace was a bushel of shiny, tart red and yellow Empires. In exchange for the apples we were to have one of those kinds of evenings: sitting around sipping tea, eating takeout from cartons, nibbling gross amounts of chocolate, downing bottles of wine until we forgot the reason for doing any of it: swearing off men. I promised Grace I'd never go back to D and she nodded and listened, not believing a word of my oath. We'd done this before.

I had a habit of running to Grace, fretting about what to do with D. I'd gone to the barn just two weeks before when I'd discovered recent images of a woman he'd had an affair with in Germany. I'd retaliated each and every time he was unfaithful. For the woman in Germany, I'd traveled to France with a man I barely knew. I brought back a single piece of yellow crockery for D, a pitcher with a chipped handle. That was my thanks to him for his European affair. I was absolutely no better than he. Still the image of the German woman who posed for D stung. She bent over seductively in front of her camera in a transparent white swimsuit, hands on her knees, ass in the air, smiling as if to say: "I wish you were here."

"I don't need his salmon," I said to Grace, not sure if I meant it. "He has something he calls 'the lobster trap theory,'" I added. Grace was slouched over her laptop on the sofa, slippered feet and crossed ankles propped on a coffee table. Her smooth black hair was trimmed into a no-fuss-or-frills bob. It fell softly toward her sharp chin and over her eyes as she leaned toward her computer, squinting. She was reading through her catalogue of music, trying to find a decent album to play to sooth my broken heart. She settled on Morrissey.

"It's not that he doesn't want to commit. He just needs options," I said, trying to make D's big sea plan sound less harsh.

"A lobster trap theory? What the fuck is that?" Grace

chirped. She has a gentle and childlike manner. Almost every-thing she says is delivered in an upbeat, chipper, airy tone. Swearing, cursing, hexing, or calm: there's a quality to her voice that resembles song. "I don't know," she added, the words drawing out in tuneful notes. "It just doesn't sound healthy."

"He says that men like to know that they've got options, even if they don't act on them, like a lobsterman." It sounded ludicrous as I was explaining it. "He says he just likes to make sure he can cruise around and pull up his traps and reset the bait if they're empty, toss them back out into the sea."

Grace laughed. "I think you need another glass of wine." She filled my goblet to the top. "How about we watch the sun-set on the porch and swat mosquitoes?"

I was fortunate to have found such a friend in Grace. We'd met years before but had come closer after she lost both her sister and mother to suicide within months of each other. She was two years behind me in loss and I easily traced her path alongside mine. She'd moved from the country to the city and now from the city to the country and soon she'd move again, she'd told me. She just didn't know where.

She wanted not to be burdened with her mother's Shaker furniture and her sister's pages of song lyrics, many guitars, and T-shirts. She wanted nothing more than to carry just a shell on her back, so she moved frequently enough to make that possi-ble. Of course, I understood. I'd logged a move a year, some-times two, since Cara had died. It was a way to rid myself of her things. Each moving truck seemed to carry fewer and fewer of Cara's possessions.

Grace and I found in each other a most enormous kind of relief: it wasn't clear which of us had suffered more severely. It was an unspoken code between us that we were welcome to feel as if it were the other. We gave, through our camaraderie, the comfort of knowing that there was someone we knew actually—

not from the TV news or radio or newspaper—worse off than we were individually.

"I have problems of my own with men," Grace said. On the horizon only a sliver of gold sun remained and it looked as if it was kissing the meadow before us. "I've met a man so fierce I fear I'll be tempted to sleep with him." She smiled mischievously and sighed like a happy schoolgirl. She took a long drink of wine and then jumped to her feet. "I have an idea!" she squealed. "I'll have to fix you two up now that you're single." She clapped her hands, applauding her idea. "That will solve my problem." It was the beginning of night, and the steady hum of crickets and cicadas buzzed loudly in incandescent twilight.

The next day Grace and I went for a walk through the forest. We bravely plowed through an uncut path, pushing through briars and short prickly brush. Grace kept her head down, eyes on her feet. She watched her shoes crunch against leaves, not paying any mind to the husks of field stalks that whipped her legs. She walked quickly and kept up a good pace until she was far ahead, just a little spot of black hair and blue jeans in the distance.

I counted steps as we went, a ritual from childhood walks with Cara. We had a game we played called Fewest Steps to There and Back. The twin who arrived home from a stroll with the smallest number won the other's dessert. I'd found myself playing the game alone since she died, on walks on city streets, down apartment hallways, through parking lots and offices. I tallied my steps and compared them against my own last best try. My award for having kept going was still dessert. I shoved my hands in my pockets and counted my way through the forest, remembering how good Cara was at Fewest Steps. She'd won every round.

"Chocolate or vanilla," I shouted to Grace.

"What on earth do you mean, dear bird?" she called out.

"Cake." I ran up beside her. "Let me make you one." I'd started the venture of learning layer cakes just a couple of months before and discovered I had a talent for them. Why not practice on Grace? I liked the rules of baking, the rigid codes that left you with little room to improvise. Cakes had become my meditation, a place to retreat when I thought anxiety might get the best of me. I'd traded Valium for baking soda and whisks, and this was my secret for now. I didn't want to tell a soul in case I decided to give it all up, my newly found health in calories and cholesterol.

"How about olive oil cake?" she asked. "I have all of the ingredients at home." The wind picked up and blew Grace's hair back, exposing her pale neck. "I forgot my scarf," she said sadly. She could turn on a dime. Ethereal happiness and dark despair sparred within her, a fight so close to my own.

"Take my scarf," I said and draped it over her shoulders. "I'm warm enough in my sweater."

A hollow pop echoed through the trees, like a car back-firing.

"Did you hear that?" I asked, though I recognized the sound from my years at Camp Lejeune. Artillery fire. Or it could just as easily have been a clap of thunder as a gun.

"Let's get home," Grace said. "I'd hate for you not to have enough time for our cake. Also, we shouldn't be out so late this time of year. It's hunting season and we're both dressed in black."

Chapter 31

I waited nervously for Tony at the bar. He'd agreed to meet me in Manhattan for a drink. I'd finished a second cocktail when he pushed past the floor-length red velvet curtains that hung at the doorway. In daylight I'm certain the drapes are ridiculous, shabby, possibly puke splattered or torn or moth eaten. At night, after a strong drink, the drapes are a magical portal. They swayed from the bustle of patrons in for and out from drink, muffling laughter, arguments, and conversations on cell phones. They separated the doorman and the noise of the street from the speakeasy ambience of this candlelit water-hole. They swished open to welcome Tony to our second date. Our first date hadn't really been a date. We met on a blind setup with Grace. We three had dined together at a Mexican restaurant upstate. Tony and I had been so caught in the electricity of our attraction, we'd forgotten Grace joined us.

I jumped from my bar stool and hugged him, clasping my hands and hanging my arms in a trusting circle around his neck. I gave him some of my weight and he held it nicely. Tony stands just under six feet tall and has broad muscled shoulders and arms. They're the arms of a man who's spent many hours at the gym, though long ago. The shape of the muscle is there, the girth and outline, though his middle is a soft round belly.

"I'm so glad you could make it," I said.

"Me, too."

Tony pulled off his glasses and rubbed the bridge of his nose.

"Sorry I'm late," he said, though he was early. "What are we having?"

He folded his glasses and tucked them into his front shirt pocket, smiling boyishly. He knew what he was having.

"I'll have a Jive Turkey," he told the bartender.

"And the lady, what will she be having?" Tony asked me sweetly, looking at my empty cocktail glass. His steel blue eyes cut through the dark of the room; they were both warm and cold, welcoming and questioning, eyes that looked like they hid another, exhausted pair.

"I'll have a Pick Me Up," I told the bartender, after scanning the list of whiskeys and sours for something fruity but not too much so.

Tony looked good in his neatly pressed pink button-down shirt and blue jeans. How could a woman resist a big strong man wearing pink? I'd learned from Grace that Tony had been a sniper in the Marine Corps during the First Gulf War and had written a memoir about that time in his life. Could I be a match for a man who could shoot a gun, lay himself bare on the page, and wear cotton candy pastel?

Through e-mails and conversations over the telephone we had discovered that we had much in common. We'd both been raised by strict military fathers; had young marriages that ended in divorce because of the affairs we'd had; spent the same years on Camp Lejeune, but in different capacities—Tony could have been one of the young handsome privates I'd try to flirt with on weekends at the Jacksonville mall.

We also had both suffered the loss of a sibling in our late twenties. Tony grieved Jeff, his older brother, who lost a short battle with non-Hodgkin's lymphoma in his mid-thirties. He told me he still had Jeff's ashes in an urn on his desk. There was no place he'd found that had been right to scatter them. I'd met him just in time, he said. He'd traveled the world and found himself flat out and exhausted and running out of money and hope: he'd moved to a tiny cabin in upstate New York to try to make sense of his life, to reassess.

"So Grace says Cambodia is the next stop for you?" I asked, nibbling on the rind of the orange wedge from my drink. "Is that trip work related?"

Tony laughed. "I think I'll stay where I am," he said, "or move back to the city."

"Why Cambodia?"

"It seemed like the farthest place away from Manhattan I could run," he said and repositioned himself on his bar stool. "But now I'm not so sure I want that, to run."

"I understand," I said, and looked at him for a long time, wondering if he saw in me what I'd seen in him. I'd heard the legend of love at first sight, of just knowing you'd met the person you were about to share a vast love with, and I'd thought the idea was as jive a turkey as Tony's drink. I wasn't so sure anymore as I sat there and observed in this man a depth and kindness, a kinship and openness that moved me to feel I'd known him all my life.

"I had a feeling you would," he said, and looked down bashfully.

I leaned in. The musky scent of soap on his collar sent a thrilling charge up my back. I couldn't resist the man in pink. I kissed him quickly on the cheek, then fully on the mouth.

We stayed out until daybreak.

As we made our way out of an all-night restaurant, men with briefcases who were early to work hurried to their offices. "What's next?" Tony asked.

I held my arm out to hail a taxi. One quickly pulled to the curb and Tony opened its door. "I'm going to take this cab home, alone," I said. "I'll see you soon."

Tony drew his hand down to the small of my back and pulled me away from the taxi to face him. He squeezed my hips tenderly and slid his fingertips just beneath my waistband. We both grinned wide and then kissed in the street.

"Let me make you dinner over the weekend," he said. "And then breakfast and lunch."

He was confident I'd accept his invitation, though there was something else in his tone that was a bit uneasy, weary. "I'm an excellent cook," he quickly added. "It would be my pleasure to prepare a meal for you."

"Only if I can bring a cake," I said, knowing I'd find a recipe I could spend a few days and all my nervous energy on.

For a time in college I'd fancied myself a poet: I was a poet and Cara wrote fiction. We were a word team, a double threat, and competitors in a duel. In our shared dorm room we stayed up late scribbling in notebooks, imagining our romantically impoverished future selves writing side by side by the light of a single candle, cupboards bare. I'd make popcorn in an air popper and we'd write and munch until the snack was gone and we'd wrung ourselves of every last letter and punctuation mark. We were writing for our lives. Words were our way out of Albany, our family, our dual struggles. Sometimes we'd read what we'd written out loud. Nearly everything we wrote during those years could be boiled down to love notes to each other.

We shared one story, and we argued over who would tell it first. These fights were like the ones we'd had as little girls. All of a sudden we'd break into brawl: hair pulling, rolling around on the floor, laughing and crying at the same time, biting each other, beating each other with our fists and with other weapons—a broom handle, a toy plastic horse with sharp hooves. I'd toss that horse at her like a throwing star. As children we'd fought for toys and attention. As adults we fought over memories and words.

At first, Cara won. I didn't think I'd ever have the chops to beat her. She would never have told me to stop writing, but she did instruct me about which subjects were off-limits to my poetry. Those subjects turned out to be almost everything that had ever happened to either of us. It was unspoken that there wasn't enough room in the universe for two Parravani writers. During the summer before our junior year at Bard College, I picked up a camera and stopped writing.

Then, in late April of our senior year, we were in our rusty black Saab, on the way to school to turn in our theses. We shared possession of the car, but when we were together, Cara always drove. On this afternoon, we each sat with a stack of papers cradled in our laps. Cara had written a novel and I had completed a paper on photography, a document that I barely cared about. Sitting with it, beside Cara and her novel, I saw that I hadn't come near her accomplishment.

"I hope you don't mind," I said, "but I need to go to the darkroom tonight and print some photographs. I'll need to use the car."

"But there's a party tonight in Tivoli," Cara reminded me, flipping down the turn signal. She pulled away from the curb without looking for oncoming traffic. "You'll have to go tomorrow. I've promised some people a ride to the party."

"Seriously?" I sneered. "Since when do you care about a stupid party with people you'll probably never even see again?"

"I don't know, but I do. I care."

"Please?" I was tired of asking. We'd split the cost of the car, though I used it less than half as much. "We always go where you want to go."

"Nope," Cara said. She looked down at the finished manuscript in her lap, careful to steady herself so it stayed put as she shifted gears. She'd positioned herself stiffly; her legs were the perfect table.

"Fine, then," I huffed. "Let's see how you like having your hard work ruined." I grabbed her thesis and hung it halfway out my window. Its pages bent and snapped wildly in the wind. "If you don't let me go to the darkroom tonight, your thesis is toast," I warned. "I *will* let it fly."

Cara looked at me in disbelief. "Grow up."

"Why don't you make me?" I said, face flushed, hands sweaty. It wasn't the darkroom or the car that moved me to hang her manuscript out the window; it was rage. Hadn't she silenced me? I'd given up something I'd loved nearly as much as I loved her so that she might have it without competition. And as it turned out in the car that afternoon, my gift to her still hadn't been enough. I was full of remorse for having so easily given up the chance at my own manuscript, as if it hadn't mattered. And didn't she now have something I would never have? A story she cared about and had told well and might possibly tell the world.

"Fine." Cara sighed and forced the car into fifth. She narrowed her brows and angrily grabbed my thesis, thrusting it out her window. "Don't play a game of chicken with me. You'll lose." She gunned the gas. We flew past a cornfield on our right. Our car swerved over the median and back, toward a shallow ditch at the roadside. I held on to her pages as best I could, screaming at the top of my lungs, bracing for a crash. Cara's pages flapped frantically outside at high speed, dangerously close to scattering—I didn't really want to let them go. She knew that. She held the steering wheel with one hand and my thesis in the other. My pages whipped back and forth against her arm.

"Stop the car!" I yelled, but she drove on. "Slow down!" I begged, but there was no stopping her. I pulled up hard on the emergency brake to the loud gnawing of grinding gears and squealing tires. Our bodies slammed forward against our seat belts. We fishtailed and screeched to a halt. Thick hot white smoke billowed in a cloud from the pavement. Neither of us had held on.

I see now it was never the car we were battling for. We were fighting for the privilege of having an individual voice and of living a life apart from the other. I finally had those chances, with her death, but then I wanted nothing more than to be trapped inside our bubble together, finishing each other's sentences. That day in our halted car we sat silent, the stench of burning rubber wafting in. It took some moments, but we turned to the other and smiled sheepishly and apologized. Our pages fluttered in a trail on the road behind us, all mixed up together, blowing beautifully toward lush farmland.

A year after my stay at Payne Whitney, I'd been admitted to the graduate program for Poets and Writers at the University of Massachusetts at Amherst with the poems I'd written while in the crazy hospital. I was granted a full teaching fellowship, just like Cara. After Cara died, I found myself mingling our words, just as the pages of our two manuscripts had been mixed together by the wind.

It is very difficult to explain the thing that happened to me through writing. It did what time and therapy and lovers never could. I knew that to write I must have a clear mind. And because writing was the only way to be with Cara, to move again in tandem, writing won hands down over my grief. To write I knew I would need sleep and nourishment and sobriety. At one point in those early writing days, I'd almost practiced my way into a better life.

Soon enough, though, writing became increasingly difficult, and then almost impossibly hard. I'd fuss with a single page for days, unable to say what was needed without sounding exactly like Cara. Was I a fraud? I wondered. Was I hiding in her words, mimicking her, because I couldn't write for myself? That's when Valium became my best friend, when it softened my frustration until it had gone soft as a pillow, diffuse as a dandelion puff.

I became so reliant on pills that if I went without one for a certain number of days, withdrawal set me off into worse panic. I had tremors, and I saw things that were not there. The hallucinations disappeared only if I took more drugs. I'd fill my prescription at the middle of the month, then look down, worried, into an empty bottle two weeks later. D had always helped by giving me his pills to get me through. But finally, I couldn't stand to ask him; I couldn't bear the shame.

I tried to quit.

I sat naked at Cara's desk in the middle of the night, the quivering blip of a passing ambulance sounding on the street below. I traced my fingers over the small carving of her initials in the center of the desk; scratched there crudely by something blunt, like a paper clip. I wondered if she'd been in my place before, trying to kick the drugs. Could the carving have been a smoke signal or SOS she'd made for herself? My half-finished manuscript sat to the left of the carving, Cara's to the right; our words flanked her graffiti.

Withdrawal pounded an iron mallet against my bones. And it froze me: I shivered, shrouded beneath the down comforter I'd pulled from the bed and onto my shaking body. It was high summer, hot and sticky and relentlessly still. Yet I knew no warmth. And I couldn't sleep. I'd read that it would take five days to clear the drug, and five long days I waited, wrapped in the comforter, wide awake at Cara's desk, until the need for those pills left me, like a ghost.

I slept.

I began to write again.

One night I had a beautiful dream: Cara and I sat together in a tree house, looking up at the midnight sky. "What if I'm a star hurtling through the atmosphere?" I asked her.

She considered my words carefully, and then she smiled bright as the moon. "You'll get stardust in your bra," she said, and took both my hands into hers and kissed them.

On Friday, I met Tony at his cottage in the Catskills. The meal he cooked was delicious, as promised: short ribs braised slowly in a luscious red wine and homemade beef stock with an accompanying creamy, peppery potato fennel gratin. I made a coconut cream four-layer cake with a salty butter cream frosting. Before we ate a single bite, we gazed at the clear night sky full of stars, hundreds of shining specks of light. Cara had crossed into the afterlife alone; this was her fate. There are places even a twin can't follow. I stood transformed on a cold night in September, four years after she'd died, my heart pumping warm blood, face flushed with something unexpected: hope. How had I managed to live without her? Tony and I stood together on his rickety porch hand in nervous hand, sipping wine, feeling about as small in the universe as a human should under the magnitude of the heavens.

I was a woman entirely humbled. I'd been spared by the wrathful grip of grief, and not because I hadn't been willing to be stolen into her clutches. I was thrilled and terrified. I was alive.

This seemed such a curious and rare thing, the gift of life I'd been given. I was going to hold on to it as tightly as I could. I had something before me that Cara would never have: years. I would try to cherish each one. They were so hard-earned and they were solely mine, just as Cara's death was hers.

Drunk on pinot noir and thankfulness, I looked at Tony, who was trying his best to find Orion.

"How about we try again tomorrow night?" he asked and smiled timidly.

"That sounds perfect," I said and squeezed his hand.

This man had seen so much suffering: war, loss, dashed hopes. I decided that I would never, if it were in my power, add to the troubles in his pack.

We were married three months later.

Part III

Chapter 32

Cara had gone the way of our grandmothers, and I had won the name Josephine fair and square.

Tony and I knew we wanted a family together; it was only a surprise that it happened so quickly. Four days after we married, on the eve of the New Year, the test was positive. Our Josephine was coming. I was often worried during my pregnancy that I'd birth Josephine into a life of my tribulations and losses. There was also the worry of resemblance. I didn't wonder whether or not she would have my eyes or my smile, or the small Sicilian ears with points at their tips like my mother, sister, and I. I worried that she would look like Cara.

I grew round and robust in pregnancy, looking more like Cara than I ever had, even when we were girls. The sight of myself, my new body, was a jolt. It was hard to trust a body that looked like Cara's. I showed both the promise of life and the fact of death; I tried not to conflate the two.

Toward the end of my pregnancy I stayed up nights imagining Josephine. She had blue eyes like her daddy's and hair like peach fuzz. I didn't go beyond those features in my imagining. There was still a sensation during my pregnancy that Josephine was other, that she was mystery. Although she was clearly living and rumbling inside of me, she was a question mark; she eluded the fantasy of detailed description.

Tony and I played a guessing game. We'd move our hands over my belly and feel for our daughter's arms and legs and head. She bounced around when we tried to tickle her.

"She's got tiny wrists just like Mommy," Tony would say, and loop his fingers around my wrist. Since the week before we'd married, his name had been inked there. It was a crazy lover's impulse we had, tattooing each other's names just over our pulses, as if it would be possible to forget the other without the cursive black letters that ran across our wrists. Tony had gotten my name tattooed first, a game of loving chicken he played with me, a dare I took.

Only eight months later, our daughter floated peacefully in my womb. At night, she'd kick out her foot or wiggle her elbow as Tony read her poems before bed. He was careful with each word, tender and steady, as if a single word or sound had the power to convey to his Josephine how much he had wanted to learn to love her. Poetry was his nurture, his promise. Sometimes she'd hiccup and I'd feel our girl rapping, a quiet, insistent rhythmic knocking. As she grew and moved, my belly rippled with her like a windy lake.

The pregnancy had been easy. I still enjoyed hikes and read and wrote every day. There was very little of the morning sickness or fatigue I'd heard about. I did have heartburn, but the old wives' tale that heartburn meant a baby with lots of red hair had won me. With each flame of the burn, I imagined braiding, washing, or brushing the orange hair from her eyes as she looked at her first great crayon drawing.

By the middle of September I was a week overdue. The signs of her birth were near. Practice contractions had been coming for weeks. My belly had dropped. I wept at my prenatal appointment, begging the midwife to induce the birth. But she shook her head and laughed; she'd seen this bargaining every day of her professional life. "It'll be time soon," she assured me and closed my chart. "You've both been working very hard at bringing her here."

The afternoon before Josephine was born I stood in front of my television screen and attempted the routine of the prenatal yoga video that Tony had ordered for me months before. I'd put on fifty pounds, and I rolled around on the yoga mat grunting and sweating after only five minutes. At Namaste and prayer pose, I'd already given up. I sat and watched the round-bellied women stretch, rubbing my sore legs.

I tried again to join them.

The instructor on the tape asked us all to squat and hold and then to roar like lions. "Stick your tongue out and call to your babies, get them ready to join your pride." I looked around for my husband and didn't see him and roared as quietly as possible, the sound no louder than the growl of a tummy. I thought of my own mother as I did this. She was a wallflower. Even if music fills her, her legs won't allow her to dance. Did mothers teach shyness? I wanted Josephine to be able to cut a rug and twirl and give herself over to joy. "Roar again," the yoga instructor commanded her troupe, and I did. I roared and stuck my tongue out and panted. I growled for Josephine, lifting the lights on all the parties she'd ever attend.

The next morning, early, I lay on my side in the hospital bed and closed my eyes as each contraction bore down. A fetal monitor to my right blinked her heartbeat and charted her movements like a seismograph. Tony stood to my left and held my hand and head. Josephine's beats flashed in white numbers that spiked with each contraction. My own beats pounded hard in my chest, and my breathing was shallow. A nurse fitted me with an oxygen mask.

At first the contractions pulled me in, a relentless undertow.

Again and again the cresting of each wave took me down, crushing me. I abandoned all worry over decency and tore off my paper hospital gown. A nurse quickly presented me with a softer gown of worn cotton printed with pretty blue polka dots. I didn't want that, either.

"I can't breathe. I can't do this," I screamed out.

Mary, our doula, put her hands on my back. "You were made to do this very thing," she said.

Mary had magic hands. She was able to halt the cramping in my back just by laying her hands on me. She escorted me to the shower and stood beside me as hot water washed over my swollen belly. She steadied me as I tried to stand. The contractions were falling one on top of the other.

"I want my sister," I said like a child asks for her mommy. Mary took my face in her hands and held it as the water beat down on me.

"Of course you do," she said. "She should have been here."

I lay back down on my side in the birthing bed, moaning, waiting for another contraction. I'd taken castor oil, and it had brought on freight train labor, and Josephine protected herself by slipping down into birth position quickly, her little spine on top of my own. We gnashed like unaligned gears.

I screamed for a nurse, begging for the epidural I'd requested not to be offered. I looked at Tony and he smiled. He thought it a man's job not to show his cards. He was hard to read and had been since our drive to the hospital. He tried his best to calm me by treating this event like it was any other thing we did. But his eyes gave him up. There was a world of panic and love in them. He'd been waiting his whole life patiently to meet me, and now his daughter was coming, too. He'd been in war, and he'd lost nearly everything afterward. He was unshakable, and he was in awe.

We had this in common, our wars. His had been in Iraq's endless desert, and though twenty years had passed since then, he still jumped at gunfire and explosions in movies, spilling popcorn or soda and a bit of pride. We were two people who'd found each other at the bottom. I'd recognized his weariness even before our first dinner.

"You're strong and you're healthy. You can do this," he urged me, and ran a cool cloth over my forehead.

He had said this throughout the pregnancy, assuring me that I was growing a healthy baby and doing a good mother's job right from the start. He'd not been with me through the hardest years, I'd think. How did he know I wasn't going to go back there?

I still felt the shock of a survivor who walks from a crash mostly unharmed. I was still astounded by every night of good sleep, and since I'd met Tony that had been every one.

I took in the cool air from the ventilator and closed my eyes. In our couples birthing class Mary had told us that during labor we'd find an image to focus on as the pain grew in intensity. The music of the birth mix Tony and I had made for Josephine's arrival played against the beeping of the ventilator and its hissing air. Van Morrison sang "Into the Mystic." Tony hummed along.

My picture came into focus:

First, a parking lot—yards of smooth, coal-black asphalt. But this pavement is cracked in one spot, and the thin stalk of a plant with a single leaf at its top has slipped up through the blacktop. This thin stalk is spare and thriving. It has been ravaged by insects or weather, but it is plucky. Its leaf has stubbornly held on. As each contraction came, wind rushed into my picture, pummeling my rebellious little sprout. And with each contraction, the leaf held on, fluttering tenaciously.

My vine and I hung on together through three hours of active labor.

We made it to transition, the period of labor where contractions are strongest and come without a break between them.

I gritted my teeth. "I can do this. I can do this," I said to myself. The time gone by since I'd lost Cara had trained me. I had endured years of utmost agony. The pain of labor was nothing beside those years. If I could survive those, couldn't I birth my Josephine? I grunted and cried out and bit down on my husband's kind hand as the pain took me.

I closed my eyes and slipped back into my parking lot. There it was. I looked for my weed. But it was nowhere to be seen. There, instead, a woman stood, with her back to me. I recognized her.

Cara turned to greet me. She held her hands on her hips and smiled with half of her mouth. She was radiant.

She was with me.

I walked to her and fell at her feet. She pulled me up and brushed off the bits of rock that clung to my bare knees. We stood face-to-face holding hands, my baby tucked safely in my womb between us. Cara drew her hands down to my belly and held on to Josephine. I gave in to her embrace and she rocked us both. As the wind blew, her hair whipped her face but she didn't pay it any mind. Her arms were strong and I felt their safety as my body opened.

"I need to push," I heard myself cry out. Tony looked at the midwife and at Mary who nodded that yes, it was time. The hands on a wall clock ticked loudly. It was just after four in the morning and Josephine was nearly here. I pushed as hard as I could and in the middle of my push I was swept into a contraction. I retreated to my sister.

I was no longer in the parking lot with her but she was there with me in the birthing room. She stood beside me, coaching me just as I imagine she would have had she lived. "Push," I heard her say, "push." And I did. I pushed with all of my might.

I locked eyes with Cara as the pain became too much to bear. I was lost in her gaze. For the first time since she'd died I allowed the feeling of her care to pour over me. It wasn't only about loss anymore; it was about our great love. I took a long deep breath and braced myself for another contraction. It battered me. I was a little rowboat carrying precious cargo, banging against the dock I was tied to. Cara cut the rope.

Josephine crowned.

The midwife wheeled over a giant heating lamp for the baby and a light to shine down on her so she would easily be seen.

"Put your hand down and touch your baby's head. She's on her way." Mary guided my hand to Josephine.

"She feels like a tomato." I stroked her impossibly squishy head and tried not to panic. "Is that normal?" I asked anyone in the room.

"Yes, sweetie." Mary laughed. "Her head is pliable so she can make her way."

I touched Josephine gently with the tips of my fingers as I pushed. With each push she moved forward and then retreated back inside. I was exhausted, but the sensation of my daughter's flesh propelled me. I closed my eyes and braced myself on the rails of the hospital bed. Cara was with me still. She stood at one of my shoulders and Tony at the other. Her expression, the one she always had when she was witness to beauty, eyes wide, filled with grace and the anticipation of a gift. She had this same expression whenever she looked into the sky at the shapes of passing clouds, like she owned them as much as God or the atmosphere could, just by noticing they were there.

Cara smiled at me, as if in thanks. It was her gratitude to me for having given myself this great opportunity for new life. Hers was over and mine was beginning again. I had her permission to live. I pushed again as hard as I could. I pushed until I heard the song of my tiny girl's cry.

Josephine was born at 5:22 a.m. into her father's loving hands. He set her on my chest to nurse. We gazed at each other, mother and daughter, taking the great responsibility of the other in. My baby's name suited her.

She blinked at me with simple love.

She looked identical to no one. She looked exactly like herself.

Acknowledgments

I am fortunate for you, Mom, for having the courage to stand by me through every day of the creation of this manuscript. You believed in the importance of this book from its first inkling, even when that seemed like crazy talk. Your support has been everything. This book is as much for you as it is for Cara; she would have insisted on that. Dara Wier, Noy Holland, and Sabina Murray, thank you for the consideration you showed my sister in her life and work. I believe it was your support that kept her going through the hardest years. She was always proud to say she was your student. My gratitude to Jayne Anne Phillips, my literary mother, my teacher. What an honor to have placed *Her* in your good hands. You were the woman I wrote to as I sat down each day. My thanks also to Alice Elliott Dark, who was a guiding force in the difficult work of balancing pain and humor, and honesty and compassion. I am blessed to have had such a brilliant woman in my corner. Thank you, too, Paul Lisicky and James Goodman at Rutgers; you both read early pages of my manuscript with insight and sensitivity. And then there is Barbara Jones, my editor, the angel at my shoulder. You picked this book up and breathed into it another kind of life. I only wish that Cara could have witnessed your grace and intelligence in this endeavor. She would have been astonished by how great a woman you are. We are so very lucky that you found our story.

And to all those at Henry Holt: Joanna Levine, Maggie Richards, Melanie DeNardo, my appreciation for the hours and care you put into the making of this book. Lisa Bankoff, my agent, you are fierce and wise, the hull of the *Her* ship. Thank you for your good advice and for seeing me through the completion of this book, warts and all. None of us would be here without you. And thanks, too, to Dan Kirschen at ICM for your good cheer. Linda Bates, Elaine Falzano, and Marguerite DiNovo-Gregorie, what would I have done without your careful eyes on Josephine? Your time with my girl gave me time with this book. Amanda Snellinger, my second sister, thank you for being just that. Devon White, your manila folder filled with Cara's love letters warmed my heart and helped me understand her better. Betsy Bonner, Danielle Pafunda, Julie Orringer, and Laurie Sandell, you are the best friends a woman could ask for. Finally, with admiration, thank you to my husband, Anthony Swofford. You appeared in my life when you were least expected. Thank you for building with me our home of love and words. It has been beneath our roof that the miracles of my life have occurred. You have my devotion. You have shepherded me through.